Abigail,

Hope you enjoy
the book.
Nice to meet
you

Nathan,

Praise for
The Cyber-Elephant in the Boardroom

"Mathieu has laid out a very simple methodology to ensure that board members, C-suite, and security people can communicate in the same business language about security matters. Having worked with hundreds of CSOs myself, I'm convinced that the 5 Pillars of Security Framework is a very effective, simple methodology that anyone can use to strategize cybersecurity and cyber-accountability efforts. I'd highly recommend using it as a key benchmark."

Ira Winkler, CISSP

author of You Can Stop Stupid

CISO, Skyline Technology Systems

"Cyber-accountability is everyone's responsibility from the board of directors and C-suite down to all staff. It is a collective duty to ensure that people, data, and systems are kept safe. *The Cyber-Elephant in the Boardroom* is a must-read that makes it simple for decision makers to drive accountability across the enterprise. Mathieu's insight and the 5 Pillars of Security Framework clearly show the way toward good cyber hygiene!"

Olivier Cadic

Sénateur des Français établis hors de France

French Senator

"VigiTrust immediately seduced us with its vision of safety according to 5 pillars. Our partnership focuses on the very pragmatic approach of adapted, translated, and demystified security for the hotel industry.

The PCI DSS platform started with the provision of eLearning to learn, understand, and apply the standard. Very quickly, we added the modules of the procedures, the evaluation of the risks, the payment terminal inventory . . .

The platform is now a complete tool and has been proven by our hotels around the world to prepare and renew their PCI DSS compliance.

We update its content every year and revise our procedures to bring them in line with the evolutions of our projects and the versions of the evolving standard.

Success with our users now leads us to adopt this model for GDPR personal data compliance. With the same methodology, each pillar will be studied and made accessible by the users of our entities.

I am very confident in the success of this new mission because it was accompanied by a team who listened to our needs and is invested with us."

Marie Christine Vittet

Data Compliance Manager, ACCOR

"The world of CEOs, CxOs, and boards continues to undergo revolutionary change at an unprecedented rate. Unfortunately, this rate of change is two paces behind the technology and security requirements. Worse still, it is one step behind the legal requirements. *The Cyber-Elephant in the Boardroom* will be key in closing these gaps and enabling the executive team to meet the new requirements for success!

Michael F. Angelo, CRISC, CISSP, CDPSE

Chief Security Architect

"*The Cyber-Elephant in the Boardroom* is an important addition to any CISO's and CIO's library. It provides practical and important guidance on how to address the current risk landscape. As someone who has studied and researched the security threats for organizations, Mathieu's 5 Pillars of Security Framework are key to achieving a strong cybersecurity posture."

Dr. Larry Ponemon

Chairman and Founder, Ponemon Institute

THE CYBER-ELEPHANT IN THE BOARDROOM

MATHIEU GORGE

THE CYBER
ELEPHANT IN THE
BOARDROOM

CYBER-ACCOUNTABILITY WITH THE FIVE PILLARS OF SECURITY FRAMEWORK

ForbesBooks

Published by ForbesBooks, Charleston, South Carolina.
Member of Advantage Media Group.

ForbesBooks is a registered trademark, and the ForbesBooks colophon is a trademark of Forbes Media, LLC.

Printed in the United States of America.

10 9 8 7 6 5 4 3 2 1

ISBN: 978-1-95086-341-9
LCCN: 2020920958

Cover design by David Taylor.
Layout design by Megan Elger.

This custom publication is intended to provide accurate information and the opinions of the author in regard to the subject matter covered. It is sold with the understanding that the publisher, Advantage|ForbesBooks, is not engaged in rendering legal, financial, or professional services of any kind. If legal advice or other expert assistance is required, the reader is advised to seek the services of a competent professional.

Advantage Media Group is proud to be a part of the Tree Neutral® program. Tree Neutral offsets the number of trees consumed in the production and printing of this book by taking proactive steps such as planting trees in direct proportion to the number of trees used to print books. To learn more about Tree Neutral, please visit **www.treeneutral.com**.

Since 1917, Forbes has remained steadfast in its mission to serve as the defining voice of entrepreneurial capitalism. ForbesBooks, launched in 2016 through a partnership with Advantage Media Group, furthers that aim by helping business and thought leaders bring their stories, passion, and knowledge to the forefront in custom books. Opinions expressed by ForbesBooks authors are their own. To be considered for publication, please visit **www.forbesbooks.com**.

CONTENTS

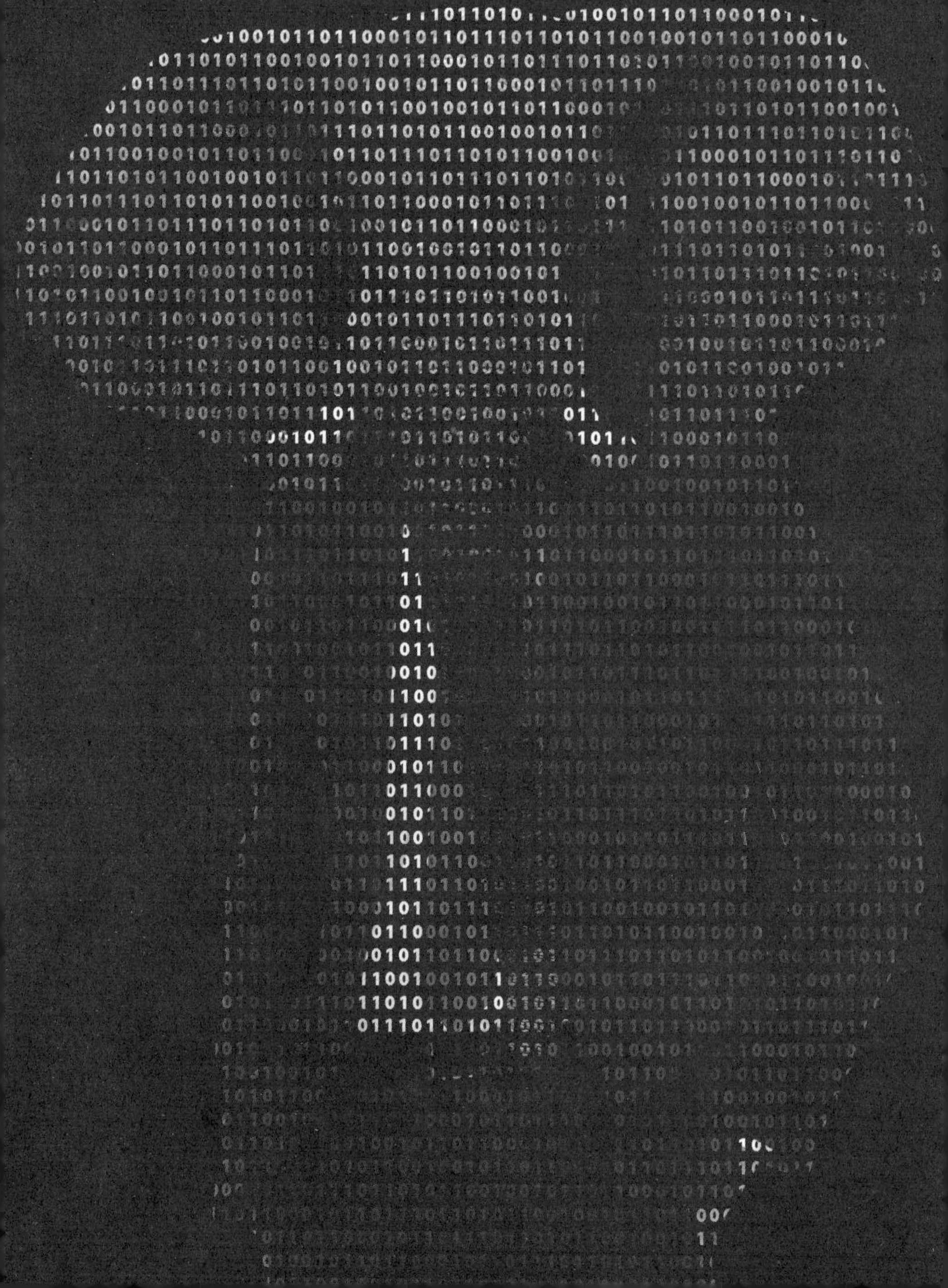

FOREWORD

by Christopher Moks

News reports describing cybersecurity breaches are frequent occurrences. Household names like Facebook, Marriott, Home Depot, Anthem, and Equifax generate headlines as large-scale attacks and breaches span all industries and sectors—financial institutions, insurance, healthcare, social networking, government, law enforcement, private sector, nonprofit, transportation, retail, and entertainment. Your business is at risk, as cyberattacks have shown that no industry, geography, sector, or scale is out of scope.

Over the past fifteen years, I have worked with many board members, CXOs, and business leaders of companies leading cyber-readiness initiatives and digital cyber-forensics investigations. In an ideal scenario, I help my clients proactively analyze, develop, and enhance their cyber-readiness and data security measures. More frequently, my clients call on me during an attack or after they have identified a fraud or data breach. The location, industry, and actors involved change, but the scenario is similar and the reaction is the same: "How did this happen?"

Businesses across all industries are facing ever-changing cyber threats and regulatory compliance challenges. With technologies playing an ever-increasing role in our corporate and personal lives, we see an increase in these cyber threats. The digital age provides us with optimizations and resources to enhance our businesses and production like never before, yet advancements of security and threat detection are offset by the increase in risks from threat actors as their techniques become more sophisticated and accessible.

In the current digital revolution, data is the new currency for businesses, with the volume of data increasing exponentially. This asset must be protected from both external and internal security threats. Businesses must also remain compliant as authorities and governing bodies around the world pass regulations and guidelines requiring greater protections for managing and protecting data. This digital transformation forces businesses and industries to adapt to emerging technologies and evolve their business processes.

Most recently, we have witnessed the effects a global pandemic can have on our business processes, especially in regard to technology. As businesses around the world moved to remote working locations, security risks increased and threat actors attacked, causing reported increases of cyberattacks.

Addressing the cyber-threat landscape requires businesses to continually review their methodologies, tools, and protocols. CXOs, business executives, board members, and business leaders need to understand at the macro level the components of a cybersecurity program and to understand the philosophies for protecting their business. Understanding these cyber risks to your enterprise, together with proven framework methodologies and procedures, will help you protect your business from an incident and understand the best response when one does occur.

The Cyber-Elephant in the Boardroom looks at these cyber and enterprise risks at the macro level, using Mathieu Gorge's 5 Pillars of Security Framework to help you, your CXOs, and your board members prepare to meet these challenges. You hold in your hands the reference you need to address and adapt your business to these challenges and to avoid being the next headline.

I met Mathieu during a panel discussion on blockchain and cryptocurrencies. We shared an interest in emerging technologies and shortly discovered our passion for the digital and cyber sector. Our discussions around cyber, IT, and digital security have forged a camaraderie, and Mathieu has become a trusted advisor. When Mathieu introduced me to his 5 Pillars of Security Framework, I immediately recognized and admired how this framework identifies the critical areas of a digital security and regulatory compliance program—and, most importantly, makes them relatable and understandable to someone of any technical level.

The 5 Pillars of Security Framework addresses key points in developing and maintaining a cyber-readiness, cyber incident response, and compliance program: physical security, people security, data security, infrastructure security, and crisis management. Each pillar plays a critical role in supporting a strong cyber defense, effective cyber investigation and response, and adherence to compliance programs. Using the 5 Pillars of Security Framework will help to identify areas of risk within your cybersecurity and compliance programs and guide you to developing strategies to mitigate these. Together, these pillars provide the flexibility to adapt to future threats, respond and investigate an incident when it occurs, and comply with regulations.

When a cyber incident occurs, the CXOs, board members, and executive team are relied on for leadership and guidance to successfully navigate the company through this time of crisis. A cyberattack can lead to financial losses, government sanctions, and penalties, along with long-term reputational loss; these ultimately impact a business's capital and valuations. To prepare for this, it is important for a company to develop and support a cyber-crisis management strategy. This strategy will guide the company in responding to the cyber incident, directing internal and external communications, investigating the breach, and remediating and implementing security enhancements to recover from the incident. *The Cyber-Elephant in the Boardroom* will be your guide in developing your cyber strategy and maintaining cyber-accountability to navigate your business through cyber incidents while lessening the impact on your company and its customer base.

As the face of a company, the CEO's response to a cyber incident can have a long-term effect on the company's public reputation and image. In 2014 we saw Frank Blake, then CEO of Home Depot, respond effectively to a cyber breach. Soon after discovering the cyber incident, Mr. Blake communicated directly to customers, delivering a clear message, apologizing to his clients, taking full responsibility, and empowering his team to resolve the problem. The following year we saw another example of effective cyber-crisis management led by Anthem Inc.'s CEO, Joseph Swedish. After identifying the cyber incident, Anthem notified federal authorities and publicly announced the incident to their customers and clients through clear and comprehensible messaging.

These examples show how a well-executed response begins with a strong fundamental understanding of the company's cybersecurity and compliance frameworks to communicate and coordinate the response. Understanding cyber-accountability is critical in shaping a company's procedures to be proactively prepared and to responsibly manage cybersecurity situations to which every company is vulnerable. Let this book be a guide to help you achieve the same when you inevitably are faced with a similar situation.

Combining Mathieu's depth of expertise in educating CXOs and board members in cyber-accountability with case studies from seven industry experts, *The Cyber-Elephant in the Boardroom* is an easy-to-implement methodology and a must-read for CXOs, board members, executives, and business leaders. It provides you with needed information and details to help you understand these concepts, including how the 5 Pillars of Security Framework will help you effectively manage your company's cybersecurity risk environment and protocols.

Christopher Moks
Director of eCrime, Digital and Cyber Forensics
Deloitte, France

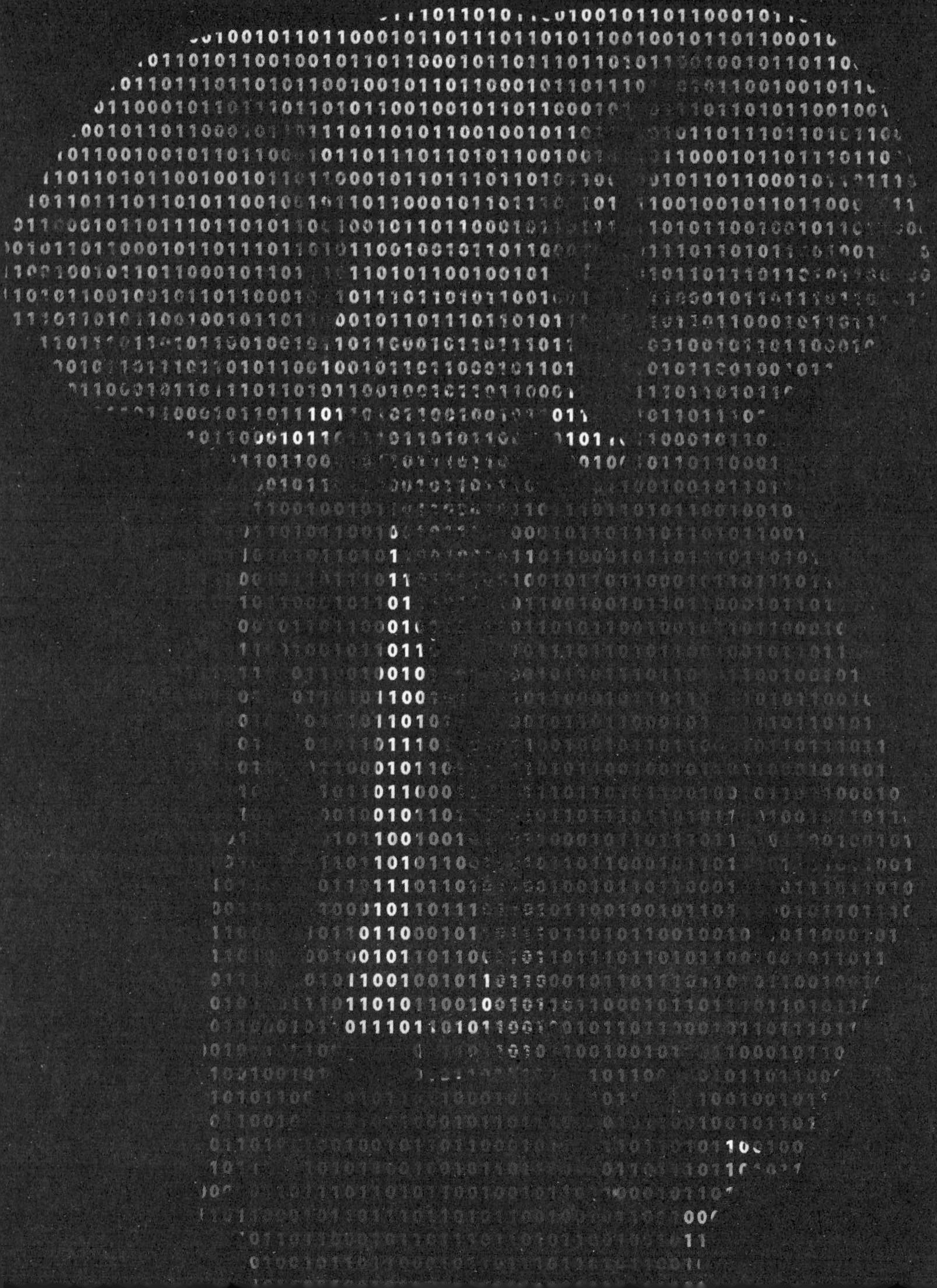

CYBER-ACCOUNTABILITY FOR CEOs, CXOs, AND BOARDS

*How to Manage Enterprise Bubbles of Risk
with the 5 Pillars of Security Framework*

When I'm asked how to describe the challenges of security professionals, I always say that security is a journey, not a destination. You can achieve compliance with key standards and regulations at pit stops along the way, but you can never really stop for long, because threats keep changing, attackers keep getting smarter, and regulations keep demanding stronger security levels.

At the human level, being responsible for enterprise security and compliance is often a thankless job: if you do your job correctly, no one knows about you, but fail once and your name is known throughout the enterprise and, oftentimes, in the whole industry. My view is that security and compliance should be a team sport and, ultimately, senior executives, CXOs (CISOs, CFOs, CLOs, COOs, and the whole C-suite), and the board will be held accountable to manage the bubbles of risk surrounding your ecosystem. So why can't—or won't—boards and CXOs take ownership of cybersecurity and embrace their cyber-accountability? There's a cyber-elephant in the boardroom, and it needs to be addressed! But how?

At the human level, being responsible for enterprise security and compliance is often a thankless job: if you do your job correctly, no one knows about you, but fail once and your name is known throughout the enterprise and, oftentimes, in the whole industry.

As I started to categorize what board members and CXOs really need to know about cyber-accountability, I looked at what I call "bubbles of risk" surrounding the enterprise. I can identify four major bubbles of risk: geo-political (impact of new governments, wars, pandemics, etc.); financial and operational; reputational and technological (IT, intellectual property, ICT-related disaster recovery and business continuity risks); and, of course, cybersecurity. The problem is that managing bubbles of risk to achieve cyber-accountability is not as sexy for boards and CXOs as growing their business. And it can be intimidating, because they're not necessarily experts at cybersecurity and may not be fully aware of enterprise risk or know how to address the cyber-accountability challenge.

Through my twenty-plus years of work as a security subject matter expert consulting with key decision makers across several industries, I realized many C-level executives and board members knew cybersecurity needed to be a regular agenda item at meetings, but they didn't really grasp the cost or impact of poor cybersecurity or their responsibility regarding data protection. They were unaware of the term *cyber-accountability*, let alone their actual legal and ethical duty to take cybersecurity seriously. Most asked me to explain the challenges in plain language and in simple business terms. I started concentrating on the education process set around key topics everyone could understand, and the result was the now multiple-award-winning 5 Pillars of Security Framework: a jargon-free, simple-to-understand, and easy-to-implement industry-agnostic methodology for C-level executives and board members to understand bubbles of risk, build enterprise cybersecurity strategies, and achieve cyber-accountability. The 5 Pillars are made up of physical security, which includes the actual premises as well as the devices on your network; people security, which includes employees and how those employees are trained; data security, which pertains to where data is stored as well as who has access to said data; infrastructure security, which includes firewalls and other third-party security applications; and crisis management, which pertains to whether you have a plan to respond to a cybersecurity breach. Each pillar is described in detail in chapter 4.

With the 5 Pillars of Security Framework, any C-level executive or board member can understand their responsibility toward cyber risk, visualize the organization's current cybersecurity and compliance posture, and know how to implement long-lasting dynamic cybersecurity strategies. I have asked some amazing industry experts to share their experience of addressing various aspects of cyber-accountability and cybersecurity-related challenges to contextualize how the 5 Pillars of Security Framework can help your organization.

The bottom line is that there is a cyber-elephant in the boardroom, and boards and CXOs need to work together, speak a common language, and implement clear plans to manage their bubbles of risk and demonstrate cyber-accountability. This book shows you the way to do that, and I hope you find it useful and enjoy it!

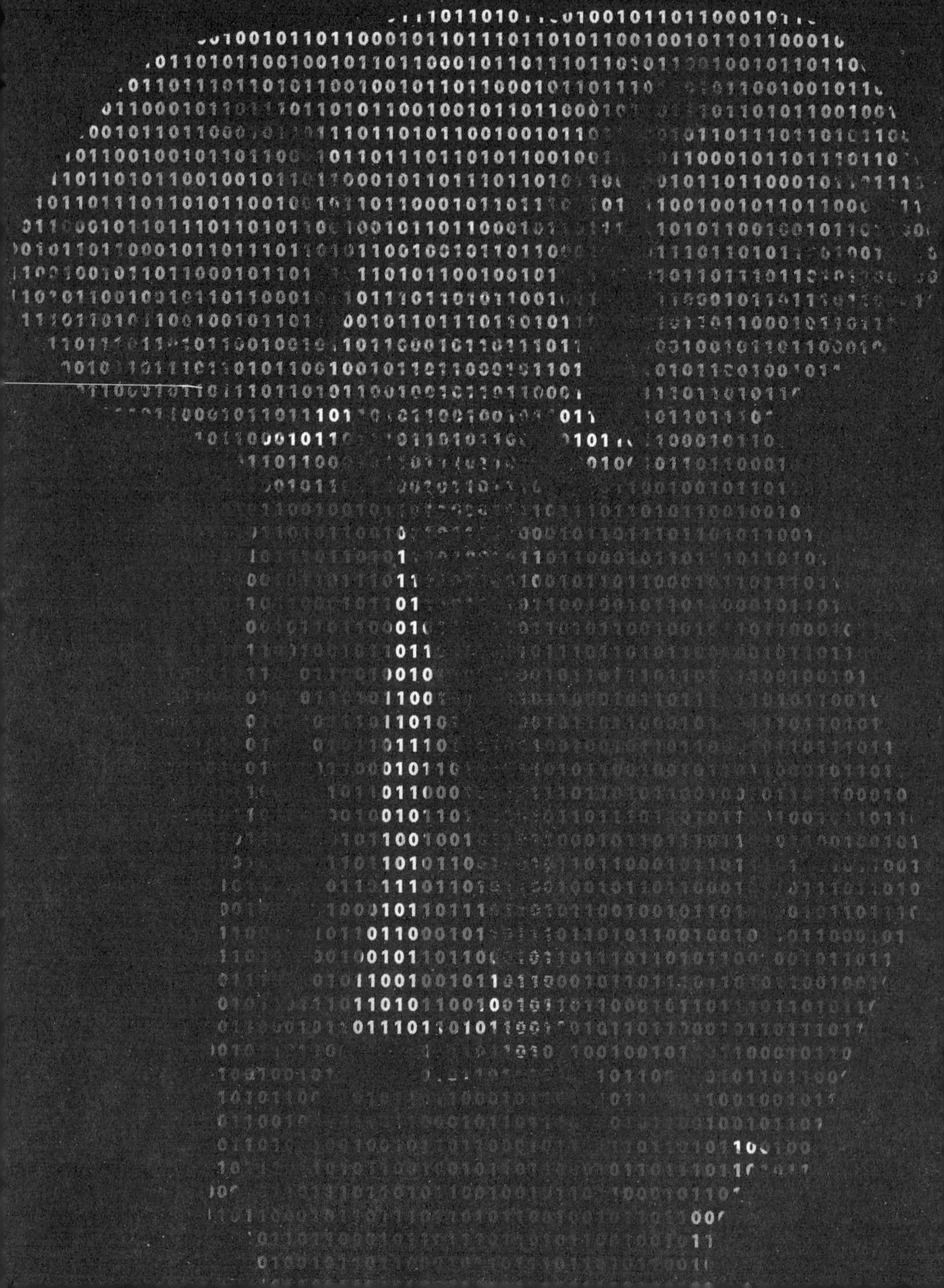

CHAPTER 1

A VETERAN'S FEEDBACK FROM THE TRENCHES

Four Simple Fails from CEOs, CXOs, and Boards

Boards of directors and C-level executives need to work in partnership with operational, legal, risk, and compliance colleagues. While cybersecurity strategies need to be sponsored by top management, they can only be successful if they filter down to more operational people who think about the organization. Oftentimes, though, board members and C-level execs struggle with understanding the overall legal and regulatory landscape that applies to their environment, so this needs to be a collaborative effort. Operational people need to manage up in terms of regulatory compliance education for the board and C-level, who, in turn, need to sponsor the overall initiative, allocate budgets and resources, and manage down to ensure the agreed cybersecurity strategy is implemented.

To do this efficiently, it is vital that key decision makers be aware of the standards, regulations, and frameworks they need to comply with or adhere to. One of the main challenges is ensuring compliance with security and trying to see mandates in every jurisdiction the firm operates in.

Some regulations are robustly enforced, whereas others are not. For instance, HIPAA has been around for a number of years, but it's only been enforced for three or four, with a number of key cases involving hefty fines. A subsidiary of Northwell Health paid a $3.9 million HIPAA fine in 2016, resolving its 2012 research data breach.[1] In a separate medical data breach case, Dallas-based Children's Medical Center agreed to pay a $3.2 million HIPAA fine for failing to comply with government regulations. The center lost a Blackberry at the Dallas-Fort Worth Airport holding "3,800 unencrypted patient files" in 2009, then lost a laptop with an additional 2,500 patient records in 2013.[2]

It's also important to recognize that large international firms operate within jurisdictions with data security regulations that might conflict and cover different aspects. Indeed, data security regulation coverage can include basic data security breach notification rules on data collection processing and transfer. It tests for age requirements, and it links to cover-related regulations in areas such as electronic marketing, online privacy, and even critical infrastructure protection in the case of critical infrastructure firms, especially in financial services, healthcare, and government.[3]

---

1   "Northwell Health's Research Branch Agrees to $3.9M HIPAA Settlement," *Becker's Health IT*, ASC Communications, accessed October 5, 2020, https://www.beckershospitalreview.com/healthcare-information-technology/northwell-health-s-research-branch-agrees-to-3-9m-hipaa-settlement.html.

2   Jermya Moody, "HIPPA [sic] Violation Lawsuit" (undergraduate paper, Brightwood College), https://www.coursehero.com/file/28346885/HIPPAdocx/.

3   "ECI Directive," enisa, accessed September 28, 2020, https://www.enisa.europa.eu/topics/threat-risk-management/risk-management/current-risk/laws-regulation/national-security/eci-directive.

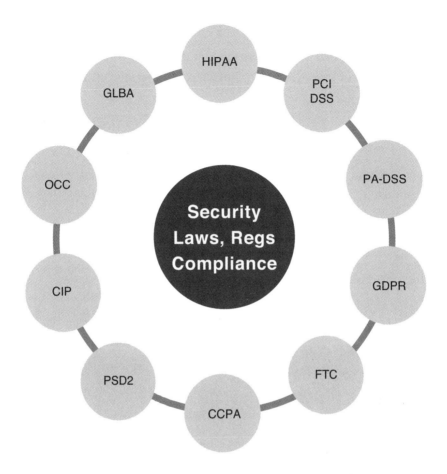

When you want to be secure, you put the right technical solutions in place, implement policies and procedures, provide security training, and document the whole process. You then achieve a higher level of security; what I call "compliance pit stops" come with that. For instance, you may be in compliance with one or a mix of standards, regulations, and frameworks, but compliance is a point-in-time status. If you are in compliance with PCI, for instance, and you fill out your self-assessment questionnaire and show compliance, you must maintain your compliance levels at all times; otherwise, you're noncompliant and most likely not secure, because attacks and threats change all the time and new vulnerabilities arise every day.

The challenge becomes, "How do you prepare to validate and maintain compliance with complex and often conflicting regulations, standards, and frameworks around data protection and information governance?"

Successful compliance and security programs are always sponsored by senior management and ideally by executive management as well as the board of directors. Indeed, company directors may be liable for not putting the right security safeguards in place to protect the organization employees' client data.

> *The challenge becomes, "How do you prepare to validate and maintain compliance with complex and often conflicting regulations, standards, and frameworks around data protection and information governance?"*

And therein lies the biggest challenge. How do you ensure that senior executives, C-level folks, and members of the board of directors understand regulations, standards, and frameworks if they are not technically savvy regarding cybersecurity or in tune with legal mandates for data protection?

The hundreds of C-level people and members of boards of directors I've worked with all bring different skills. Few of them understand their responsibilities with regard to data security and good data governance. This is not because they are not interested or don't have the skills to understand the cybersecurity and compliance requirements their firms need to comply with.

I believe it's because cybersecurity is a new item on the board's agenda, and there is indeed a learning curve of understanding the value of data, how vulnerable they might be, how to protect data, and how to demonstrate compliance.

Let's look at a couple of examples to put this into perspective. Consider a health system in the US comprising hospitals, medical practitioners, and maybe even a medical school or university. This enterprise will need to comply with state privacy regulations, HIPAA, PCI, GDPR, and potentially iso-27001 and other frameworks. The board of directors of this health system may or may not be familiar with those regulations and standards; even if they are, they probably aren't compliance or security experts.

That's not necessarily a major issue as long as members of the board of directors know how to prepare for, validate, and maintain compliance with required security levels. In order to do that, they will need to interact with their chief information security officer, chief information officer, and likely other members of the technical team, as well as physical security employees. To fulfill their duties as directors and board members, they need to speak the same language as people in security risk and operations.

VERIZON DATA BREACH INVESTIGATIONS REPORT

Let's say that you are an international bank focusing on retail wealth management and real estate. As a bank, you will be custodian of all of your clients' data including PII, credit history, home address, asset history, and probably health data. You will need to comply with all the relevant data privacy regulations in every country where the bank operates and be mindful of international data transfers and how and when to demonstrate compliance with data protection authorities and enforcement bodies. Banks are obviously scrutinized more than other firms, and they are subject to a multitude of local and international regulations and standards. With the right baseline strategy, any bank can probably comply with 70 to 80 percent of all requirements and controls. Why? Controls tend to address the same intent, and it's possible to map controls between regulations and standards from a technical perspective.

This is helpful for any firm, including banks, though from a C-level vista and a board of directors perspective, most of the requirements might appear daunting. That's because they may be written in security or compliance jargon with three-letter acronyms rather than in plain English.

The 5 Pillars of Security Framework addresses this multisector problem head-on with substance and clarity. By demystifying security and compliance, the framework empowers those at the C-level and members of the board to understand their responsibilities, get a view of the regulatory landscape and industry-specific standards, and comply with and take corrective action when required.

By demystifying security and compliance, the framework empowers those at the C-level and members of the board to understand their responsibilities, get a view of the regulatory landscape and industry-specific standards, and comply with and take corrective action when required.

Ultimately, the framework makes it possible for those in power to take control of the overall enterprise security and compliance strategy from a business perspective and use terms that all managers, employees, and stakeholders understand. That will allow them to make good, informed decisions regarding compliance and provide direction for the operational staff to implement, including the chief information security officer, the data protection officers, the information technology and security staff, the physical security staff, and the legal staff, to ensure compliance with industry frameworks and all applicable laws and codes.

The 2019 Verizon Data Breach Investigations Report (DBIR), the twelfth edition, analyzes real-world cybersecurity issues in over forty thousand security incidents and two thousand data breaches provided by more than seventy international sources, both public and private entities, from over eighty countries worldwide.[4]

I would highly recommend that any chief security officer, C-level executive, and board of directors first familiarize themselves with the executive summary of the Verizon DBIR report. One key takeaway from the 2019 DBIR is that executives were twelve times more likely to be the target of social incidents and nine times more likely to be the target of social breaches than in years past.[5]

It indicates that financial and social engineering attacks, such as spear phishing, focus on company executives and directors. These top-tier incidents rose from the single digits to the dozens in 2019, compromising executives' time, focus, and resources. Ironically, very few C-level executives and board members are aware of being major targets. One example of social engineering is professionals who create fake or embellished LinkedIn profiles, which are magically aligned with the C-level executive's career and interests, in order to open a line of communication to further leverage the target. This type of social engagement is akin to a data honeypot, striving to learn more about the individual to gain further access to a company's network and digital assets.

Reading deeper into the DBIR, we can see that nearly 70 percent of attacks were by outsiders, over 30 percent involved internal staff,

---

4 "2020 Data Breach Investigations Report," Verizon, 2020, https://enterprise. verizon.com/resources/reports/2020-data-breach-investigations-report.pdf.

5 "2020 Data Breach Investigations Report: Executive Summary," Verizon, 2020, https://enterprise.verizon.com/resources/executivebriefs/2020-dbir-executive-brief.pdf.

1 percent involved partners, and 1 percent featured multiple parties. It's also worth noting that organized crime groups were behind 55 percent of the breaches, and "actors" identified as nation states or a state's affiliates were involved in just over 10 percent. Further, the Verizon DBIR report identified some key attack vectors, with 45 percent of the breaches featured hacking.

INSURANCE AUDIT, 2005

I was asked to conduct security assessments in the west of Ireland a good few years ago. The client was an insurance company, a midsize firm that needed to demonstrate that it was in compliance with the PCI DSS. My technical manager and I drove down from Dublin early one morning. We were greeted by the security team and had a kickoff meeting.

As always, we decided to explain the requirements of the standard in terms of physical and technical security as well as policies, procedures, and training. In attendance were the security manager, some technical people, and a team member looking after logistics and physical security.

PCI DSS mandates that any firm that transmits, processes, or stores credit card holder data must have controls and safeguards in place to protect data. In this case the insurance firm took credit card payments in multiple ways, including over the phone and by mail. The firm would pile the forms up in a dedicated tray on a specific desk. Once about ten forms were in the pile, which I later learned would take up to two or three days, a team member would process the payments on a PoS device and either send a policy document to the end users if the payment had been successful or put the form in another pile for follow-up. I inquired as to how the forms were securely kept and was told that those resulting in a policy were put into a folder, which in turn was put in a storage box.

Unsuccessful payments would be tried again, and if unsuccessful more than twice, a team member would call the end user and either check the details or handwrite another card's details on the form. If successful, they'd revert to the process described above.

At that stage, and without any input from my technical colleague, who was inspecting the firm's network security solutions and uncovering his own noncompliance gems, I was satisfied that the process was not compliant. However, I also suspected, rightly, that the full extent of noncompliance remained to be uncovered.

The team kept an Excel spreadsheet with full credit card holder data for each payment as a "safeguard" in case the form got lost or if they needed to double-check what the client intended to purchase. In addition, forms were scanned to email as another "backup." The cardholder data was therefore kept on paper, Excel spreadsheets, multifunctional printer hard drives (which, of course, were not purged), on the firm's main email server, and, of course, on backups for all those systems. Altogether they had at least thirteen systems and physical processes where each client's CHD was not securely kept.

The one issue that makes this story stand out, as this is by no means a unique case, is that forms were not shredded but rather kept in storage boxes, which in turn were kept in a small windowed room on the second floor overlooking the main street. I was assured that the storage boxes were regularly sent to a secure off-site third-party facility. But when I asked how often that happened and heard, "Until the piled boxes reach the window," I couldn't help but laugh out loud. The security officer was not impressed. He told me to wait in the corridor. He came back five minutes later with the firm's security guard and told me I'd be escorted to the main door and that my colleague could stay, but I couldn't, as I "was not taking the assessment seriously and this was no laughing matter."

So, what did I learn here? Mainly three points:

1. Be more diplomatic and ready to hear that even good firms can have very poor practices they don't see as bad ones.

2. Security assessments are indeed no laughing matter, but not every stakeholder knows that, and that's a major issue for most firms.

3. Key decision makers and managers within a line of business, such as operations or sales, are not security experts, and security experts are not business or operations experts. The key is to get them to speak the same language.

Ultimately my colleague left four hours after me. We submitted a detailed assessment report with easy-to-implement corrective action plans, and a few months later the security manager called to say that the firm had followed our recommendations and that the full payment process had been redesigned and no longer involved non-compliant CHD storage. He even joked that French people should know how to be more diplomatic when breaking bad news to compliance officers.

NASDAQ-LISTED COMPANY, 2017

After delivering security awareness training for the senior executive team of a NASDAQ-quoted software firm, I was invited by their CSO to have a chat about how to make his work more prominent on the board agenda. He and I agreed that we should do a short presentation at their next meeting. The main objective was to explain the overall importance of cybersecurity for the firm, as they were in M&A mode and growing very quickly. The CSO also wanted to ensure that the board was aware of the security strategy already in place, that board members were aware of their responsibility regarding the firm's security and compliance posture, and that all security projects were acknowledged and sponsored by the board.

So I prepared a standard presentation on why cybersecurity matters, the role of the board in sponsoring good cybersecurity, their responsibility, and why they should care about security like PII and other important regulations and standards. With the approval of the CSO, I conducted a Google search on the board members, whose names were available on the firm's site.

The idea was to make them aware of what bad guys could find out on them, to see their reactions, and to ascertain where changes might be required. I knew this was a somewhat risky thing to do, but it also typically yielded good results in improving board members' awareness of their roles with regard to cybersecurity.

Looking at profiles of board members on a website is fascinating. First, you realize that the folks to whom you are going to present have deep experience in their respective industries, and most of them are on numerous boards and are famous, successful businesspeople. In this case, the firm had probably asked each of them to supply a few facts about their personal life or experience to add to their profile. For instance, profiles could read something like this: "Joe is an accomplished CFO who is currently serving as a board member within our firm, in charge of the subfinance committee and overseeing our e-commerce growth. He also sits on the boards of Company X, Company Y, and Company Z. He is also the treasurer of [school name], where his two children are currently enrolled. He loves golfing and skiing." This bio is by no means atypical, and, in fact, even security professionals provide a lot of information in their bios, and that would probably be fine if kept at a high level.

A problem arose when looking at all twenty-plus board members' bios. Some read more like the following: "Joe is an accomplished CFO who is currently serving as board member within our firm, in charge of the subfinance committee and overseeing our e-commerce growth and, as such, is in charge of PCI DSS compliance as well as secure coding for e-commerce applications, which are key to our firm and are expected to bring in 40 percent of our revenues this year. He also sits on the boards of Company X, Company Y, and Company Z. He loves golfing and is the immediate past president of [golf club name] in New Jersey and also has a passion for skiing in Italy and France, where he regularly travels to every winter, with a soft spot for Meribel."

Now, I realize that anyone with a bit of compliance knowledge would have guessed that Joe would indeed be in charge of PCI DSS compliance and secure coding if applications are homegrown and that he would therefore have access to the crown jewels in terms of payment security and network security. One could also argue that the firm's annual report could have provided the 40 percent revenue figure. However, the personal details provided too much information.

In this case, nearly all board members listed where they lived, their children's names, where and when they went skiing, or which golf club they attended every Friday afternoon during the summer. I compiled a chart showing the statistics of what I found out within an hour's work, and I was in the process of explaining what a head start that would have provided me if I were a hacker or malicious employee when one of the board members stood up and asked, "And what makes you think you have the right to invade my privacy and look into my life, find my kids' names, and check out what I do outside work? This is insane and unprofessional. You should be ashamed. We are paying you to teach real stuff, not to dig into our private lives." He then turned to the CSO and said, "Where did you get this guy? We shouldn't work with him."

I was still there in the room.

The CSO explained that their overall security strategy, which was working really well, was written by my firm and that he had cleared the exercise with me in advance of the presentation. Again, the above is not atypical; it happens to listed companies as much as it does to midsize and small firms. It also demonstrates the gap between what very senior people see as an *acceptable boundary* in the digital world and what is safe. Some of the board members tried to temper the atmosphere by asking me for advice on what to make public and what not to make public. I proceeded to go over my slides and remarks on the difference between one's business digital life and one's personal digital life.

The best way to get through to people is by using simple, familiar terms to link them to the real challenges at stake. The 5 Pillars of Security Framework does that really well. I, of course, presented it to that board, and they are now using it as a benchmark they all understand.

> *The best way to get through to people is by using simple, familiar terms to link them to the real challenges at stake.*

EUROPEAN TRANSPORTATION, 2014

I was asked to do a training session for a European transportation multinational corporation. When I arrived, I realized I wasn't dealing with one security and compliance program but with several such programs for their subsidiaries. There was no linkage between the programs, as some were based on national security frameworks, others were based on ISO, others were built in-house, and others were customized by consultants. And the group's CSO had huge trouble connecting the dots. He needed a baseline framework for each program to dial back to a common foundation.

I wanted to show the team some information pertaining to the 5 Pillars on the VigiTrust website, and they allowed me to connect my laptop to their network. Once I got access to my website, I also received full, unrestricted access to the headquarters network, including security team files. After two minutes, I had already located their sets of security policies and procedures; network diagram servers; a full list of names, titles, email addresses, and phone numbers for the security and compliance team; and a memorandum from the CISO outlining gaps in their security posture.

In a bid to make friends during the workshop, I put all of the company's information on the screen. Needless to say, I got everyone's attention. And they are still talking about the incident to this day.

To their credit, they acknowledged that they would rather have me, the "white hat," doing that than an actual "black hat" cyber thief.

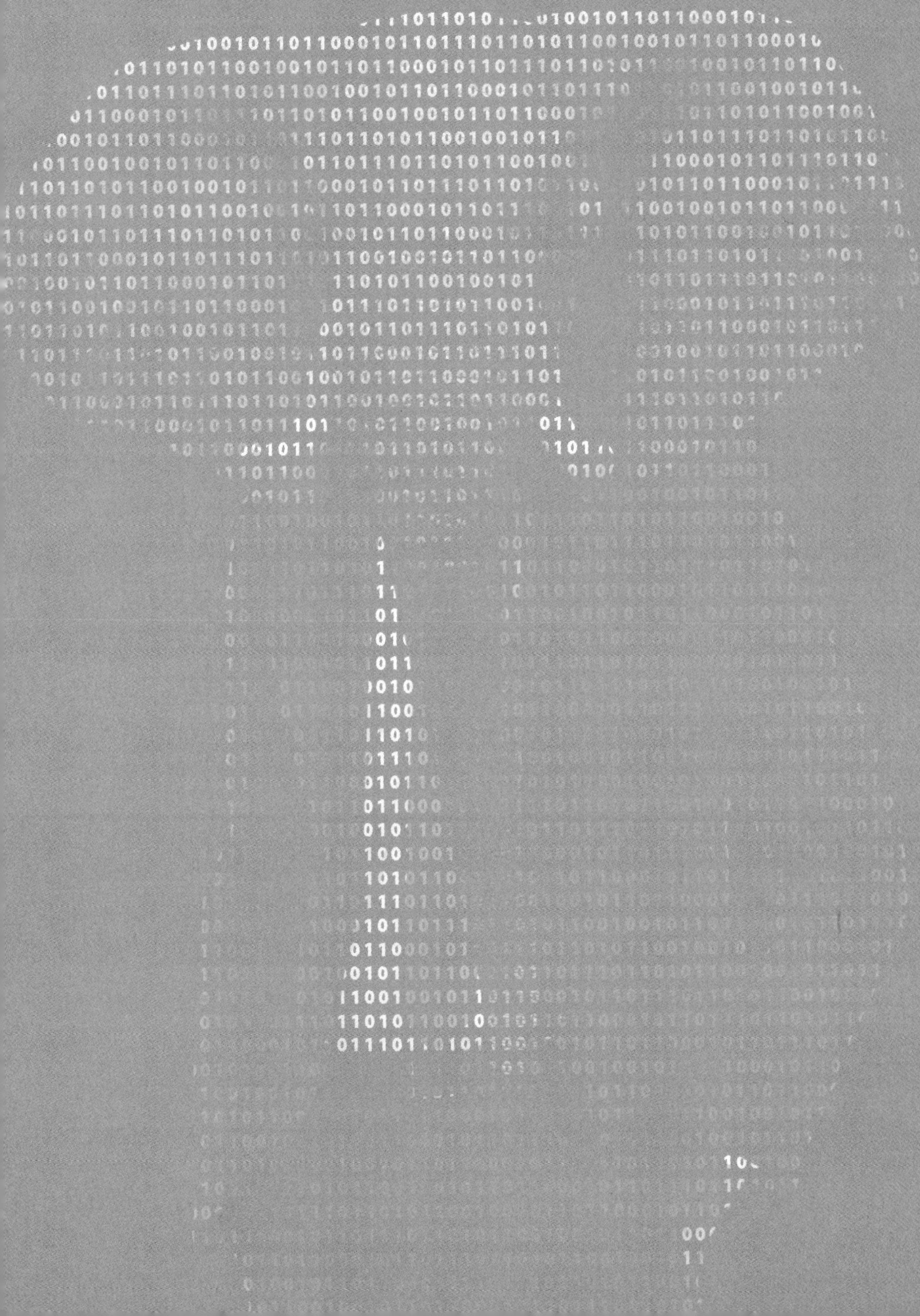

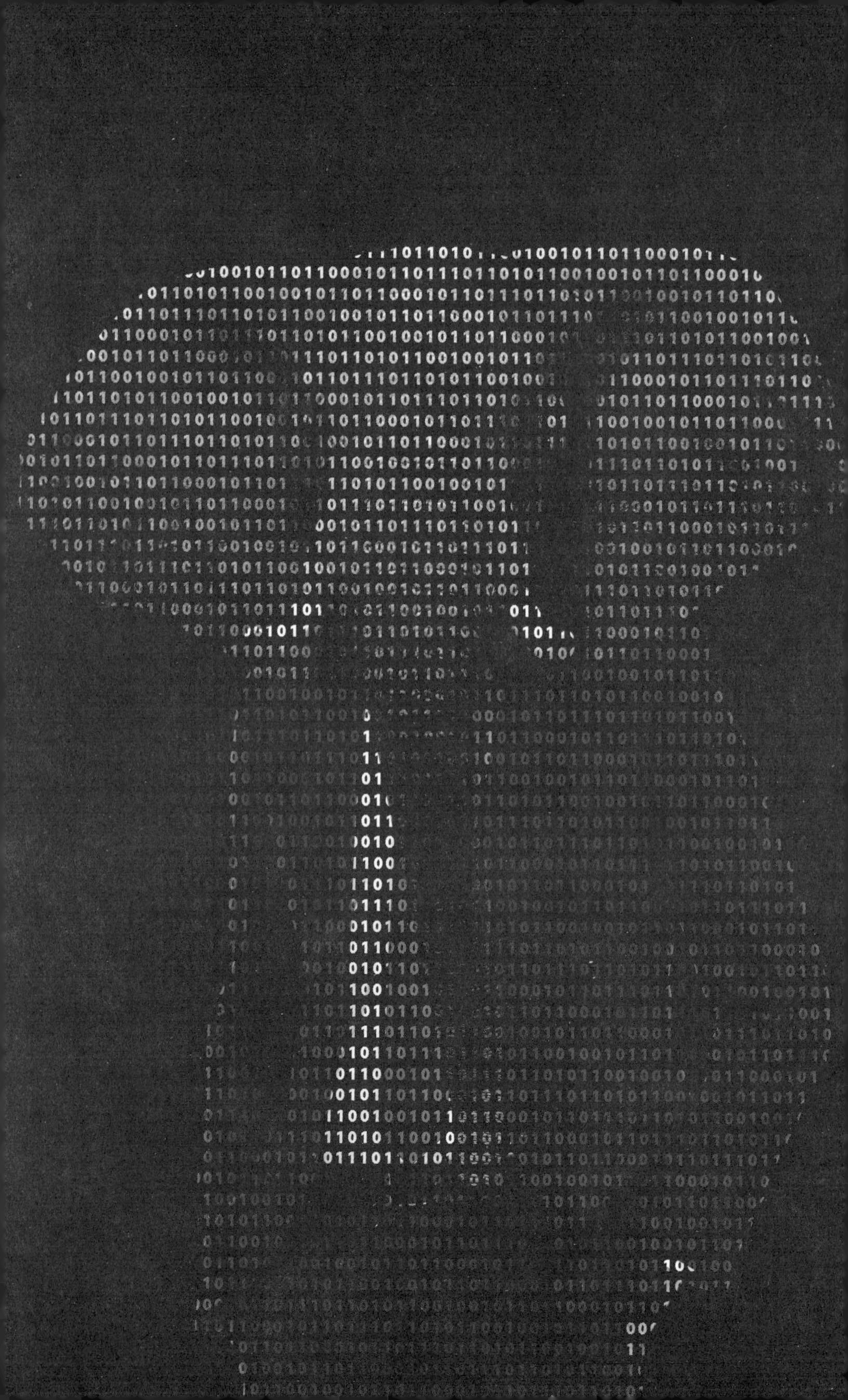

CHAPTER 2

CYBER-ACCOUNTABILITY FOR C-SUITE AND BOARDS

Why Are CEOs, CXOs, and Board Members Good Targets for Hackers and Social Engineers?

I am often asked this question: "Are hackers just not targeting systems and IT users with specific privileges?"

It's important to understand that these people are not only powerful within their own business but also potentially within a wider industry. Their knowledge of trade secrets, interaction between various lines of business, human resources and key staff, internal policies, security setups, and strategies make them good targets because that knowledge can be exploited by malicious users—internal users as well as external hackers.

In addition, the blur between digital life and real life makes it impossible for key people to fully protect their knowledge unless they are extremely disciplined. People with intimate knowledge of business processes and policies need to be fully trained as to what they can and cannot do on social media and public forums. Their digital footprint is potentially bigger and riskier than that of other team members. While the right balance needs to be struck between a CEO's public disclosures regarding travel and people met for PR and marketing purposes, the CEO also needs to take into account the potential for increasing their own and the company's risk exposure in providing unnecessary ammunition to malicious users and hackers.

People with intimate knowledge of business processes and policies need to be fully trained as to what they can and cannot do on social media and public forums.

Also, the concept of Bring Your Own Device, a.k.a. BYOD, must be taken into consideration. Very senior people expect flexibility regarding the devices they use. In fact, board members are often not issued company-owned devices because they are not full-time employees. Yet, in the course of their duties for the company, they will get access to data systems and trade secrets governed by company policies, as well as procedures relating to data security and information governance. In practice, some board members prefer to use their own email address, perhaps even a generic email from a mainstream provider like Gmail. It then becomes very difficult for the security and compliance teams to police data usage, transfer, and storage, to implement security policies and procedures, and also to provide assistance should a security issue occur.

A perfect example of this situation is a board of a large organization made up of executive and nonexecutive members; some use company email, and some use private emails. Board minutes, including details of strategic decisions, need to be circulated. The company must adapt to this challenging work environment from a compliance perspective. Very confidential strategic decision data must be fully monitored, greatly increasing risk surface and the ability to react should a security incident, data breach, or data leak occur.

While I am concentrating on the private sector, most if not all of my comments also apply to state and semistate organizations. Indeed, there have been many examples of government officials not complying with basic security measures, including, but not limited to, sending confidential government data to private email servers without authorization or the right levels of additional security put in place to facilitate the process.

CYBER-ACCOUNTABILITY IN THE BOARDROOM: FIVE STAGES OF GRIEF

Have you ever heard of the five stages of grief? They are as follows: stage one, denial; stage two, anger; stage three, bargaining; stage four, depression; stage five, acceptance. This way of looking at how people deal with difficult situations is not new. It can apply to many business and personal challenges.

As key executives and board members often refuse to accept any type of responsibility or accountability for anything to do with cybersecurity, data security, information governance, or system security within the firm, they often, eventually, go through these stages. Let's put the five stages of grief in place for cybersecurity.

Stage One: Denial

Board members and key senior executives are in complete denial regarding their responsibility toward ensuring that the organization protects its data, trade secrets, employee data, data pertaining to third parties, and any other type of confidential data. Mostly they are not even aware of the type of data the organization is either entrusted with or is creating, making it easier to deny the very existence of any legal contractual or industry requirements to put a cybersecurity program in place.

Stage Two: Anger

The board and the organization's key executives have woken up to the fact that they are responsible for designing, implementing, and maintaining a strong cybersecurity program to protect data and systems. However, they are not happy. The CFO is trying to understand the potential cost of such a program and where the budget will come from, and she is extremely frustrated because the CIO responsible for systems cannot easily quantify the amount of work required to purchase additional solutions or systems in order to comply. The chief security officer, on the other hand, is reasonably happy that cybersecurity has finally made it to the board meeting; however, he or she is facing intense questioning and scrutiny. After all, it was the chief security officer's job to build, implement, and maintain a strong cybersecurity program, wasn't it? The chief risk officer is angry: most risks applying to the organization have already been mapped many times; cyber was always one of them. The board now needs to be educated on cyber risk, exposure, impact, and, of course, countermeasures. The head of HR now faces an additional task, which is to implement a security awareness program for all staff across all business units within the organization. This will take time, and it's going to add a burden on all team members. Generally speaking, all key executives and board members realize that this is going to cost time and money and huge efforts from many business units, and their anger is made even worse by the fact that they don't fully grasp the extent of what needs to be done and how to do it. This is typically when a third-party firm is brought in to perform a gap analysis and write a report on the current security roster at the firm, identifying key risks and key exposure and providing a high-level remediating road map.

Stage Three: Bargaining

By now the board and all key executives are well aware of what needs to be done for compliance and to address immediate vulnerabilities. But they are fighting internally as to who is going to do what to get to a security posture deemed acceptable not only internally but also by regulators and enforcement bodies. So naturally they do what every firm tends to do: they start prioritizing projects within the remediation plan. They then begin to bargain internally and sometimes with regulators and enforcement bodies. For instance, they will agree to upgrade their first line of defense including firewalls, antivirus, and antispyware, but the idea of implementing a needed second line of defense will have to wait, so there's no intrusion detection system, no tokenization, no data on discovery. All of this will have to wait; the focus is on the first line of defense, and that should appease the regulator.

Stage Four: Depression

By now, cybersecurity is item number two on the agenda, after finances. Everyone knows the remediation plan nearly by heart. Some prioritization has been done, some projects have been started, and some quick wins have happened, but in the meantime the regulators and enforcement bodies are still not happy that actual corrective action has not been taken. In all fairness, the board and the key executives feel the pressure. A cybersecurity program is not easy to put in place; in fact, they wonder if it can actually be done. Is there really any point in continuing with the program? Is it really going to cost as much as the CFO is indicating? Are they really out of compliance, as the chief security officer now demonstrates at every meeting? Has the risk surface of the firm really increased that much in the last while? Why is there no silver bullet? The atmosphere is really gloomy in the boardroom.

Stage Five: Acceptance

The board and the key executives come to the inevitable conclusion that the program must go on. Yes, it is going to cost a lot of money, but if it's done properly, it can be done quite cost effectively. The chief security officer is now able to demonstrate compliance with some key regulations and standards that apply to the organization, and there's more to follow. It's a work in progress. It's traceable. It's visible. The chief risk officer is now able to show that thanks to the remediation plan, the risk surface of the organization has actually decreased. Key risks have been mitigated, and where risks have to be taken, it is done in a calculated manner, taking security and compliance into account. From HR's perspective it has actually been a win-win, because all employees across the organization are now much more security aware, able and willing to report suspicious activity as well as security incidents, therefore addressing key security mandates and improving the overall security levels within the organization. And one fine day during the board meeting, where cybersecurity is still number two on the agenda, the firm is able to give itself a good mark for cybersecu-

Until faced with an incident, and unless fully educated in their roles regarding cyber-security and compliance, most board members and CXOs will happily pay lip service to cybersecurity and turn a blind eye to their responsibility and accountability.

rity, including full accountability and responsibility from the board.

This story is extremely common. I have seen many organizations of all sizes refuse to accept their role regarding security and compliance. That was always somebody else's department. That is fine until there is a security incident, major data breach, a request from a data subject who wants to see your data, a hacker who manages to steal confidential data, or a ransomware attack. Until faced with an incident, and unless fully educated in their roles regarding cybersecurity and compliance, most board members and CXOs will happily pay lip service to cybersecurity and turn a blind eye to their responsibility and accountability.

✋	**DENIAL**	Cyber? – It doesn't apply to me, ask my managers and lines of business!
✊	**ANGER**	It isn't fair – we're trying to grow a business and create jobs here. Back off with your cyber nonsense!
⚖️	**BARGAINING**	I'll do some of it – it'll be sort of compliance "a la carte" just to fend off regulators and governing bodies. That should do the job!
☹️	**DEPRESSION**	I'll never get there – it's not just laws & standards, but also documentation, technical investment, ongoing monitoring. I just can't!
👍	**ACCEPTANCE**	It'll be okay! – it's not rocket science, we're doing a good bit already and we can now bridge the gap and stay ahead!

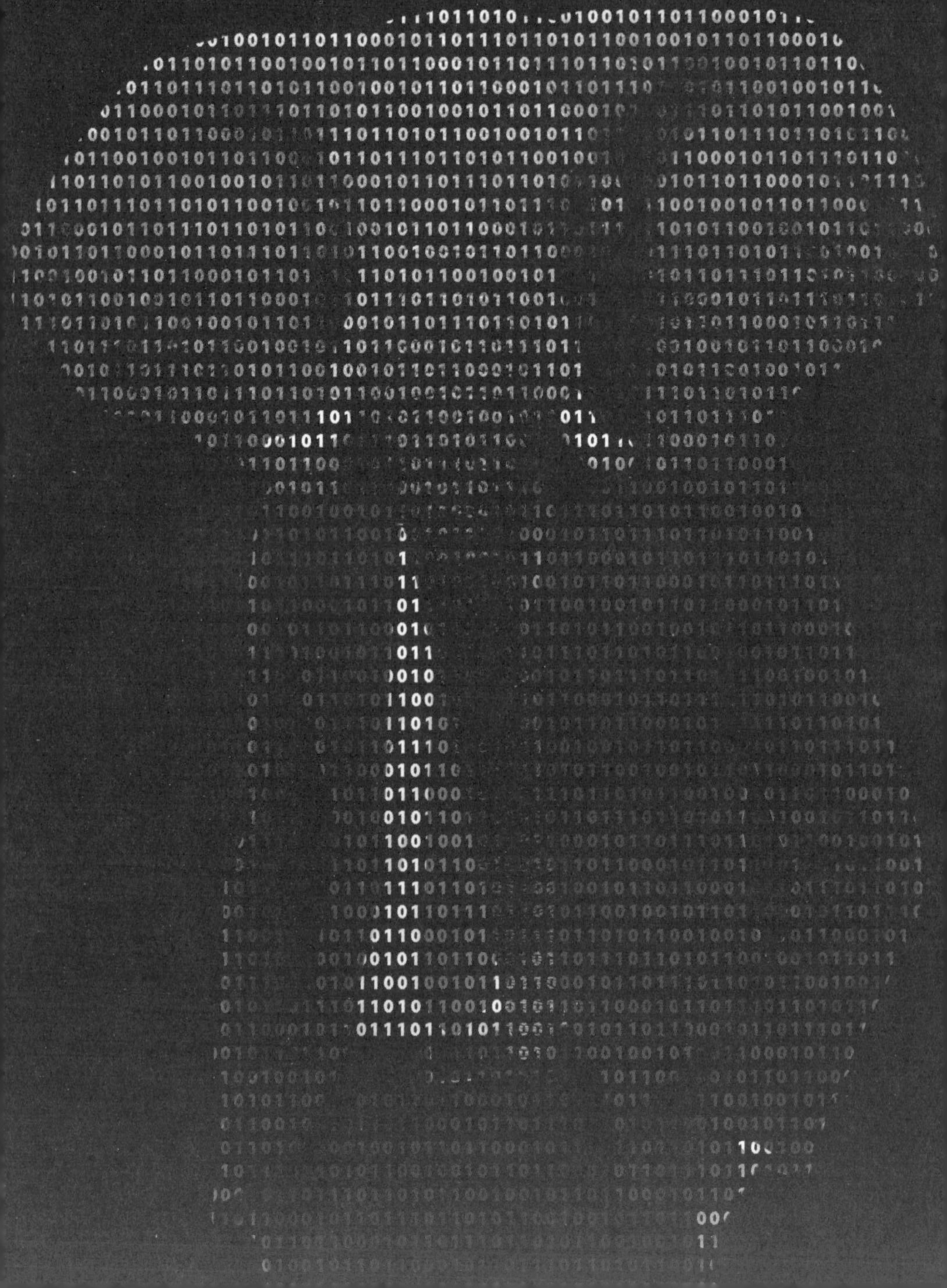

CHAPTER 3

RISK LANDSCAPE

What Every CEO, CXO, and Board Member Should Know

While I fully appreciate that not every CEO, board member, or CXO will need to be fully proficient in security and compliance jargon, technical terms, or even methodology, in my opinion there are still a few risk and risk management concepts that are prerequisites for them to understand.

In this chapter, let's look at understanding the risk landscape from a senior decision maker's perspective and understanding the concept of bubbles of risk, strategic or semistrategic/semioperational areas within the enterprise that attract high levels of risk, and how to address them. We'll look at a few models to set the scene for how to bring it all together with the 5 Pillars of Security Framework.

With the OCC (US Office of the Controller of the Currency) model as a starting point in understanding enterprise risk and associated third-party risk, key terms such as these and *due diligence* and *risk levels* should start to make sense and arrive on your security meeting's agenda. In addition, by looking at PCI DSS and HIPAA, you will be in a position to continue demystifying cybersecurity and compliance for CXOs and boards to start working on their organization's cybersecurity strategy.

UNDERSTANDING THE RISK LANDSCAPE AND HOW BOARDS, CXOS, AND LOBS NEED TO MANAGE IT

A number of excellent reports in the market can help board members and senior execs understand the compliance forces within the industry around the globe. Remember that the end goal is to better strategize on how critical and often classified data—structured and unstructured—is created, used, stored, secured, and transmitted throughout the world. Some data security and information governance legal and industry frameworks are very restrictive and heavily enforced. Some are enforced at local and regional levels, others are applied nationwide, and others even have extraterritorial jurisdiction. In other words, a regulation in Europe may apply to organizations outside of the EU. These extraterritorial mandates can have a global reach, as is the case with GDPR—which applies to all organizations dealing with data that's in the scope of this regulation, wherever they're based. Equally, some US federal and state regulations or laws apply outside of the US. This makes it even more challenging for decision makers to properly strategize around data security and governance.

Decision makers also need to understand what actions or processes are covered by applicable laws and security frameworks. Are we just talking about data breach notification (the process whereby an organization handles a security incident or a data breach)? Are we talking about the collection and processing of data? Are we talking about data transfer, especially international data transfer? Are we talking about mandatory reporting to applicable authorities or enforcement bodies?

This complex landscape means that the discussion around data security and governance needs to involve security experts, legal experts, risk experts, and financial decision makers. More importantly, it means that top senior management and board members *must* be involved. But how do you ensure that they understand the risk landscape, and how do you manage it?

I always look at risk from a super-strategic perspective first to demonstrate accountability and then from a strategic angle from which key stakeholders and decision makers can agree on a strategy to address risks and comply with applicable laws and standards. But first, at the super-strategic level, I see four types of risk that apply to enterprises and international firms. One could argue that not all of those risks apply to small- and medium-size firms; however, it really depends on the type of data they create, handle, store, or transmit.

> *This complex landscape means that the discussion around data security and governance needs to involve security experts, legal experts, risk experts, and financial decision makers. More importantly, it means that top senior management and board members* must *be involved.*

THE FOUR MAIN RISK AREAS

- Strategic geopolitical risk

- Financial, operational, rational, and contractual risk

- Reputational brand and quality risk

- ICT, data, and cyber-specific risk, which includes systems applications, disaster recovery, business continuity, intellectual property, and information governance

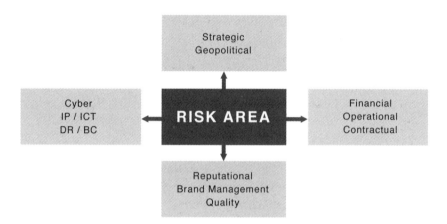

From the strategic risk perspective, key decision makers do, of course, need to know about security mandates applying to their organizations. This covers industry-specific mandates, geographical mandates, people-specific or role-specific mandates, and risk-specific mandates.

UNDERSTANDING RISK SURFACE FOR EXECUTIVES

Again, there are multiple models to understand risk surfaces. First, I'm going to use the 2017 Deloitte extended enterprise risk management model.[6] This is an extremely simple model to help executives and board members understand the concept of risk surface.

The model states that "extended enterprise risk management is

---

6   Deloitte, "Extended Enterprise Risk Management: Driving Performance through the Third-Party Ecosystem," white paper, accessed September 28, 2020, https://www2. deloitte.com/us/en/pages/risk/articles/extended-enterprise-risk-management-report. html.

the practice of anticipating and managing exposures associated with third parties across the organization's full range of operations as well as optimizing the value delivered by the third-party ecosystem." The model then asks, "What does third-party risk look like? While one often thinks of data breaches involving IT providers, the tentacles of the third-party risk extend into the farthest corners of the extended enterprise ecosystem."[7]

That model, however, doesn't just look at third-party risk. It sets the scene for boards and senior executives to understand the links between business objectives—such as growth innovation, client experience, cost reduction, improved time to markets, and finally risk and compliance management—and risk domains. The Deloitte model identifies these risk domains: financial risk, contractual risk, credit risk, business continuity risk, operations risk, reputational risk, geopolitical risk, strategic risk, quality risk, intellectual property risk, cyber risk, and, finally, compliance and legal risk.

In addition, the Extended Enterprise Management diagram maps out the core business lines of the organization—such as distribution and sales, customers, customer support, facilities, HR, marketing, insurance, technology, legal, servicing, logistics, R&D, franchisees, and joint ventures—but also maps out extensions of those first lines, specifically focusing on technology sourcing, HR, marketing, distribution, and sales. Those areas are, in the end, logistics, which inherently involve third parties, joint work or joint ventures with other firms, and external people and applications. It is clear that in an extended network and enterprise, risk surface grows with every additional area or partner involved in the business.

---

7   Deloitte, "Extended Enterprise Risk Management: Driving Performance through the Third-Party Ecosystem," accessed September 28, 2020, https://www2.deloitte.com/us/en/pages/risk/articles/extended-enterprise-risk-management-report.html.

Whether you look at internal or external stakeholders, risk exists with all of them! Anyone or any party who can access your data systems should be vetted from a risk perspective, regardless of whether they ever use that access. Indeed, they may pose a risk to your organization, to your wider network, to your third parties, and potentially to fourth or other parties as well.

THE ONLY FIVE THINGS ENTERPRISES CAN DO WITH RISK

Avoid It

You can decide not to extend your enterprise, or you can process specific data or implement specific accesses in a way that enables you to reduce the scope of your risk.

Ignore It

You are fully aware of the risks but decide not to address them. This decision is often driven by a lack of awareness of the legal, operational, reputational, and financial consequences of not dealing with risks. Unfortunately, in some cases it amounts to a gamble executives are willing to take, believing that the likelihood of having an issue is not high enough to justify looking at the risk as a strategic risk and investing time, effort, and money to address the risk.

Transfer It

You have carefully mapped, weighed, and analyzed your risks, and a decision has been made to fully or partly outsource the business process relating to the risk. An example would be outsourcing payment processing to a third party in order to reduce the scope of applicability of the payment card industry data security standards to your organization. In this case, remember that the organization may still be in scope for PCI DSS, albeit a reduced scope because it is not storing or processing credit card holder data but because it is transmitting credit card holder data. The point is that you need to be careful to map out the actual risk, liability, and accountability you are transferring. Even if you manage to fully transfer the business process to a trusted third party, the likelihood is extremely high that the liability partly or fully remains with your organization.

Mitigate It

You fully map the potential impact and likelihood of the risk being exploited and take appropriate security measures to reduce it to an acceptable residual risk level. Similar to what many laws and regulations mandate, especially with GDPR, such measures include technical security solutions, policies and procedures, staff awareness training, and continuous compliance reporting and monitoring.

Accept It

Your organization fully maps and assesses risk, manages to avoid taking unnecessary risks, successfully transfers business processes and associated risks, understands the legal ramifications of the same, and takes appropriate security measures.

Within this education process, the importance of security and compliance to your organization should become clear and transparent to top-level executives and board members. They need to be reminded of the dangers of noncompliance not only to the organization but also to their own reputation. They can include generic harm to the business, increase in costs of dealing with security breaches and incidents, inconvenience to customers and loss of customer confidence, adverse publicity for the organization such as name and shame as well as brand and reputation. There is also an additional risk of legislative interest and threat of industry regulations, bringing yet more audits and, therefore, more costs to budget for.

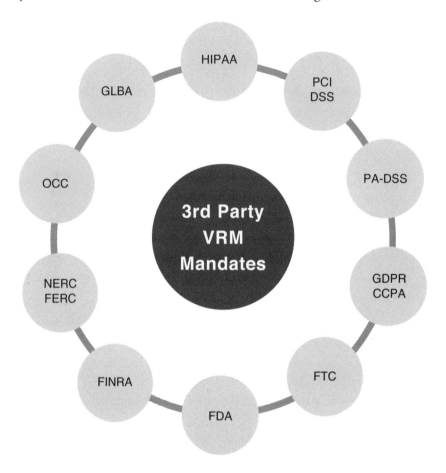

There are many mandates for vendor risk management and third-party risk checks. In my opinion, one of the most comprehensive is that of the OCC.

INTRODUCTION TO THE OCC MODEL

Another good model to educate top senior executive board members and key decision makers is the OCC model from the US. While intended for the banking and financial industry, a lot of the key points of monitoring to understand an organization's full risk surface and associated risks and compliance challenges with regard to data protection and information governance will apply to your organization.

The OCC published some guidance in 2013 in Bulletin 2013–29. It is aimed at banks, and its key objectives are to ensure that banks practice effective risk management regardless of whether the activity is internal or through a third party. That said, the bulk of the guidance revolves around dealing with third-party risk. It clearly states that banks' use of third parties does not reduce the responsibility of the board of directors and senior management to ensure that the activity is performed in a safe and sound manner and in compliance with applicable laws. This is unfortunately still lost on some people and results in lack of oversight and accountability.

The guidance is based on a number of controls; they are aimed at protecting any type of data system or process, especially those related to critical activities. The definition of a critical activity according to the OCC is actually applicable to many other industries. Similar to the general data protection regulation in Europe, the OCC guidance requires that banks adopt risk management processes commensurate with the level of risk and complexity of their third-party relationships. It also states that banks should ensure comprehensive risk management and oversight of third-party relationships involving critical activities.

THE DEFINITION OF A CRITICAL ACTIVITY IS AS FOLLOWS:

1. core function +

2. financial risks associated to the core function +

3. either reputational risks and/or systemic risks

In a 2017 supplement's frequently asked questions document, the OCC reiterated, "However a bank structures its third-party risk management process, the board is responsible for overseeing the development of an effective third-party risk management process commensurate with the level of risk and complexity of the third-party relationships. Periodic board reporting is essential to ensure that board responsibilities are fulfilled."

In my view, this model applies to any industry, and the very fact that the OCC has made board responsibility and accountability compulsory within the banking industry should be seen as a wake-up call for any industry dealing with personal data, critical data, critical processes, and any type of confidential and private information. Boards and senior executives need to take corrective action immediately if they are not in compliance already.

Indeed, all executives and board members should be extremely familiar with what constitutes a critical activity with regard to data security and information governance. After all, whether from the perspective of business, growth, an investment, or M&A activity, key stakeholders fully understand what a critical activity is. The next step is to translate that concept into the heavily regulated data compliance and information security world.

The following are key aspects of what the OCC expects in terms of significant bank functions—payments, clearing, settlements, custody—and what's known as other significant shared services, including, but not limited to, information technology or other activities that are deemed critical:

- They would cause a bank to face significant risk if the third party fails to meet expectations.

- They could have significant (bank) customer impacts.

- They require significant investment in resources to implement the third-party relationship and manage the risk.

- They could have a major impact on bank operations if the bank has to find an alternate third party or if the outsourced activity has to be rolled back in-house.

The OCC risk management life cycle is a five-step process. Step one is planning. Step two is due diligence and third-party selection. Step three is contract negotiation. Step four is ongoing monitoring. Step five is termination. In addition, any entity subject to OCC should implement the following review process and repeat it throughout the life cycle of a relationship with a third party as part of good practice for risk management.

Oversight and Accountability

Assign clear roles and responsibilities in order to manage third-party relationships, integrate the bank's third-party risk management process, and use the risk management framework to enable ongoing oversight and accountability. The main purpose is to ensure continuous oversight and ongoing accountability rather than just at the outset or when a relationship with a party is terminated.

Documentation and Reporting

Proper documentation and reporting make transparent monitoring, oversight accountability, and ongoing risk management with regard to third-party relationships easier.

Independent Reviews

Conducting periodic independent reviews of the risk management process makes it possible for management (meaning C-level execs and boards of directors) to assess whether the process still aligns with the bank's strategy and effectively manages risk posed by third-party relationships.

All of this is taken from the OCC guidance itself.

THE OCC DUE DILIGENCE PROCESS

The OCC due diligence and third-party selection is a key step of the overall accountability and oversight process for banks. Note that for this process, and generally speaking, one can substitute *bank* with any type of organization dealing with personal data in scope for some of the key regulations and standards we have been discussing so far.

The OCC mandates that the degree of due diligence should be commensurate with the level of risk and complexity of the third-party relationships. Again, this model can be applied internally, to your subsidiaries and potentially to new franchisees. Of course, more extensive due diligence is necessary if a third-party relationship involves a critical activity. This may mean a pen test, telephone audits, remote scans of specific sites or IP addresses, or full on-site assessment performed by the audit team of the organization or, ideally, by a trusted independent first party, which needs to have been vetted through the same process.

Under the OCC there are fifteen KPIs to check for:

- Regulatory compliance

- Financial condition

- Business experience and reputation

- Fee structure and incentives

- Qualifications, backgrounds, and reputations of company principals

- Risk management

- Information security

- Management of information systems

- Resilience

- Incident reporting and management programs

- Physical security

- Human resources management

- Reliance on subcontractors

- Insurance coverage

- Conflicting contractual arrangements with other third parties

All of these points are important; however, the degree to which each matters needs to be assessed based on your organization's risk appetite, existing controls, and ability to mitigate the risk to retain an acceptable residual risk level.

OCC guidance also focuses on ongoing monitoring, part of the wider concept of continuous compliance also referred to as "making security business as usual," or ongoing compliance, not a one-time pit stop. In the case of OCC, ongoing monitoring needs to take place for the duration of the third-party relationship involving critical activities. "Senior management should periodically assess existing third-party relationships to determine whether the nature of the activity performed now constitutes a critical activity."

In practical terms, this means that you should always seek to assess whether an outsourced process is still or has become a critical activity. If the criticality (level) of the activity has changed such that a new assessment needs to be performed, you need to be able to demonstrate that your firm has taken additional and appropriate security measures to address the risks and show that you are taking commensurate risk-reduction measures. OCC guidance is also very clear that management should ensure that bank employees who manage third-party relationships monitor those activities and performance. This involves training for bank employees and assumes that management fully understands the bank's risk appetite, accountability, and the risk management structure. This excellent advice from the OCC is actually reasonably industry agnostic and is applicable to internal services as well as third parties.

From an ongoing monitoring perspective, OCC guidance also offers very clear and implementable advice regarding these fourteen criteria:

- Business strategy and reputation

- Compliance with legal and regulatory requirements

- Financial condition

- Insurance coverage

- Key personnel and ability to retain essential knowledge in support of the activities

- Ability to effectively manage risk by identifying and addressing issues before they are cited in audit reports

- Process for adjusting P&Ps and controls in response to changing threats and new vulnerabilities and material breaches or serious incidents

- IT and IS systems

- Ability to respond to and recover from service disruptions and degradations and to meet business resilience expectations

- Reliance on, exposure to, or performance of subcontractors; location of subcontractors; and ongoing monitoring and control of subcontractors

- Agreements with other entities

- Ability to maintain CIA levels

- Volume/nature of customer complaints, especially with regard to risk and compliance

- Ability to appropriately remediate customer complaints

The OCC notes that "bank employees who manage third parties must be able to escalate any material issue to senior management. Controls to monitor third parties must be tested continuously, major issues escalated to the board."

Here again we see some very good, practical, easy-to-implement advice that can be used for any industry. However, it is based on the assumption that both board senior execs and generic employees are fully aware of what constitutes risks for the bank, which risks are acceptable, and what security measures are in place. The reality is often different; a worrying number of board members and senior execs I have met over the last years are not fully educated or proficient on this matter.

The OCC third-party risk management model can be used as a benchmark for assessing risk specifically for third parties and for those associated with subsidiaries and franchisees. At an operational level, the advice is extremely sound, but again, it assumes that board members and senior execs are fully aware of their duties under applicable regs and standards.

Completing the overview of the OCC guidance, the concept of *termination* covers how a bank may terminate third-party relationships with its vendors.

Reasons to terminate the third-party relationship include expiration or lack of satisfaction with the vendor, desire to seek a different third party for the same process or activity, desire to bring the activity back in-house or perhaps to discontinue the activity altogether, breach of contract, security incident, or data breach. Management should always ensure that relationships are terminated in a clear legal and operational way. In the event of a contract default or termination, for business continuity purposes the bank is required to have a plan to bring the servicing in-house if no other vendor can be identified and vetted.

For a data breach or security incident involving a third party, the compliance and security departments, as well as top management, are required to work with the third party to understand what went wrong. Even if it makes sense that the third party no longer remain a trusted partner, the organization should be fully prepared to work with them until it is appropriate to terminate the relationship. In other words, one wants to have the communication channels with that third party fully open until the data breach or security incident is not only contained but fully investigated in a manner that allows the organization to continue with its business, take appropriate legal action (if applicable), or, in some cases, resume their relationship with that third party based on a new risk assessment and updated and documented risk appetite and security measures.

MASTERING THE CONCEPT OF CRITICAL ACTIVITIES

The OCC guidance talks about what constitutes a critical activity and how one should deal with the risks associated with such activities.

There is a clear need for the organization to try to visualize the risks it has to address and mitigate. I spoke about key areas of risk from a super-strategic perspective. The OCC, being much more operationally driven, refers to items that are easy to visualize. For instance, for each of the activities, I would recommend that you check the country of origin of the service/solution, classify any information, look at the privacy implications of the activity, consider connectivity to the bank networks, and ensure business continuity.

Risk profiling and critical activities should be fully documented. This is highly dependent on your organization's risk appetite. Expanding your network, whether physically or logically, extends your risk surface and therefore potentially the legal and industry security mandates applying to it.

You may look at a few key indicators to determine whether each activity is a core function or high-risk function of the business. Such indicators include execution risk, outsourcing risk, technology risk, data sensitivity, business continuity, regulatory and compliance, concentration, financial risk, reputational impact, subcontractors, and records management. This is obviously highly subjective, and those indicators will vary based on your activities and risk appetite. In the end, the organization will make a call as to what constitutes a core function.

Senior executives and boards need to be aware of critical activities within the organization. Should business decisions be made to contract out all or part of the critical activities, then the OCC guidance model can be used to implement good security measures on an ongoing basis. The limitation of the OCC guidance remains that it is based on the assumption that senior execs and boards understand cybersecurity, data privacy, information governance, and legal and industry mandates that apply to their organization. Because this is not always the case, more business-driven super-strategic and strategic data needs to be provided to senior executives and board members in any industry dealing with sensitive or personal data and in scope for compliance with applicable mandates. This is where the 5 Pillars of Security Framework comes in: it's a simple and effective business-driven methodology addressing super-strategic and strategic needs for cybersecurity accountability for senior executives and board members, not just in the banking industry but any industry dealing with sensitive or personal data and in scope for compliance with applicable mandates.

Before we look at the 5 Pillars of Security Framework, let's look at the *foundation of a good security program*. It can be divided into four key steps:

- Mapping out the organization's ecosystem through diagrams and inventories

- Assessments to visualize risks

- Appropriate security measures supported by strong, effective, and easy-to-maintain policies and procedures

- Continuous compliance

COMPONENTS & FLOW OF A GOOD
CONTINUOUS COMPLIANCE PROGRAM

DIAGRAMS & DATA FLOWS

- Ecosystem Diagrams
- Data Flow Diagrams
- Network Diagrams
- Asset Inventory

RISK ASSESSMENT & RISK TREATMENT PLAN

- Security Assessment
- Application Security
- Vulnerability Management Policy

POLICIES & PROCEDURES FOR CONTINUOUS RISK MANAGEMENT

- Acceptable Usage Policy
- Access Control Policy
- Firewall Rules & Business Justification for Rules
- AV, Anti-Spam & Intrusion Detection-Prevention Policy
- Hardening, Log & Patch Management Policy
- Back-Up and Media Storage Policy
- Incident Response Plan
- Management of 3rd Parties

CONTINUOUS COMPLIANCE PROGRAM

An ecosystem diagram is a visual representation of the overall enterprise's environment from a business perspective. It typically covers global HQ, regional HQ, subsidiaries, franchisees, critical vendors, a "bucket" for all noncritical vendors, external consultants, internal staff, and remote staff (including part time and contract). At a glance, a good ecosystem diagram provides security and compliance professionals with a great view of the potential risk surface of the enterprise from which they can start the auditing process, zooming in quickly on high-risk areas.

ECOSYSTEM DIAGRAM EXAMPLE

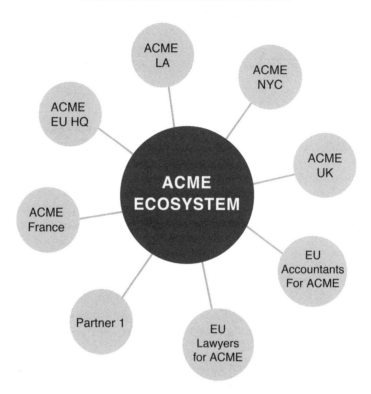

A good continuous compliance program must include education, data flow mapping, ecosystem diagrams, network diagrams, policies and procedures, regular internal and external assessments, pen testing, and ongoing vulnerability scanning as well as integrated risk management tools. It is therefore based on the accepted adage of people, process, and technology.

PCI DSS AND HIPAA

The payment card industry data security standard, also known as PCI DSS or PCI, is a good security standard. PCI DSS clearly requires senior management involvement in the risk assessment around processing transmission and storage of credit card holder data.

This standard has twelve high-level requirements grouped into six control groups aimed at building and maintaining a secure network, protecting cardholder data, maintaining a vulnerability management program, implementing strong access control measures, regularly monitoring and testing networks, and maintaining an information security policy.

Two things stand out in the high-level description of the standard. First, maintaining an information security policy, which should drive any strategic initiative to protect all data, is the last control group and the last requirement. It should be the first, in my opinion, because the policy is derived from the super-strategic aspirations of the board and senior execs and reflects the strategy for good security and compliance agreed on and sanctioned by the organization's key stakeholders, thus demonstrating their accountability toward cybersecurity and compliance. Second, this is a reasonably prescriptive standard; while providing excellent guidance on where to start, it remains very operational and fully designed around protecting credit card holder data. That said, it is easily applicable to any type of personally identifiable information or personal data.

With PCI DSS, you can use the twelve high-level requirements in the order they are provided, use a risk-based approach that is your organization's approach, or use a prioritized approach that is aimed at smaller businesses and dictates the order in which you should assess the controls. These controls can be categorized as follows: technical controls, policies and procedures, user awareness, and training. Some controls may include several control points, like a mix of technical requirements and policy requirements. Additionally, some controls require recurring tasks—daily, weekly, monthly, quarterly (e.g., mandatory quarterly ASV scans), yearly, or one-off (mandated when a major change or update on systems touching credit card holder data is implemented). This means that PCI DSS has a clear mandate for in-scope organizations to implement continuous controls and monitoring. In fact, if you are victim of a breach involving credit card holder data, you will be asked to demonstrate that you were in compliance with PCI DSS at the time of the breach, not just the last time you had to produce an attestation of compliance.

Similar to OCC, PCI DSS provides guidance on third-party security assurance. Through my work at VigiTrust, I have taken part in several task forces with the PCI SSC, and I was involved in the special interest group that produced the guidance in *2016: Information Supplement—Third-Party Security Assurance*. This document defines what third parties are from the PCI DSS perspective; how due diligence should be conducted on third-party service providers; how to engage a third-party service provider; guidance on written agreements, policies, and procedures; and how to maintain relationships with and monitor third-party service providers. The document also provides a number of appendices and checklists for high-level discussions with third-party providers as well as a sample PCI DSS responsibility matrix.

The health industry is also highly regulated. In the US, HIPAA regulates entities dealing with personal health information, also referred to as PHI. This typically includes, but is not always limited to, health systems, clinicians, and health insurance providers.

In the context of ongoing management roles and responsibilities, HIPAA defines several key roles:

- Relationship management: responsible for the management and administrative support of the VRM process within their area, including adequate staffing for the relationship manager and business coordinator roles

- Business coordinator: responsible for overseeing business as usual (BAU) execution of the VRM process in their business area

- VRM analyst: the subject matter expert who evaluates information risk controls and identifies risks during vendor risk assessments

- Corporate senior information risk officer (CSIRO or SIRO): responsible for reporting, managing, and escalating vendor risks within their business area in accordance with their associated risk appetite

- Chief information security officer (CISO): responsible for the overall security levels at your firm, ideally reporting to the CEO and working very closely with the board

- Chief legal officer (CLO): typically a senior in-house counsel responsible for ensuring legal compliance across the organization

- Chief executive officer (CEO): ultimately responsible for the overall strategy, execution, and growth of any plan for the organization, therefore ultimately in charge of third-party relationships

- BUs involved: global procurement, line of business, IT, operations, legal, management, board, etc.

This regulation also requires board accountability and senior management ongoing involvement. Just like the OCC guidance, it assumes that they understand their personal mandate and business mandates to drive good security levels in order to comply. This has clearly not always been in place, and boards and senior executives of health systems did not understand, or simply paid lip service to, putting in place the right security measures and controls on an ongoing basis, putting the health system at risk and out of compliance. This is easy to see in the data breach investigation reports from Verizon. Their analysis of breaches within the health sector highlights major gaps—strategic gaps. In a security processes event, it is subject to HIPAA.

ADDITIONAL GUIDANCE TO BE AWARE OF—LIST OF REPORTS FOR CEOS, CXOS, AND BOARDS

CEOs need to keep themselves updated at all times. There are multiple reports on cybersecurity, compliance, information security, data governance, and related topics, and the challenge is to pick the one that is relevant to your industry and business. Primarily you will want to know answers to the following:

- What new regulations or standards are affecting your industry?

- Has any firm within your industry been hacked? Any of your direct competitors?

- Is there new technology especially developed to address risks within your industry that you could benefit from?

- How can you reduce the scope of availability of compliance frameworks and laws applying to your industry?

- How can you comply with multiple regulations within your industry without having to reinvent the wheel for each of them?

- Are there any new risk assessment or management methodologies you should be aware of to make your compliance effort more cost effective and efficient?

- Are there any physical or virtual compliance conferences or associations addressing your industry you should attend/join?

I'd like to recommend a few reports just to give you a flavor of what's available in the industry:

- DBIR 2020
    - https://enterprise.verizon.com/resources/reports/2020-data-breach-investigations-report.pdf

- DBIR executive summary 2020
    - https://enterprise.verizon.com/resources/executivebriefs/2020-dbir-executive-brief.pdf

- ICIT The Healthcare Research Security Pandemic: Threats to Patient Care, National Security, and the Economy
    - Whitepaper available at: https://icitech.org/the-health-care-research-security-pandemic-threats-to-patient-care-national-security-and-the-economy

- 2020 US Cyberspace Solarium Commission Report
    - Full report at https://www.solarium.gov

- Ponemon Institute—"The Economic Value of Prevention in the Cybersecurity Lifecycle" (May 2020)
    - https://www.ponemon.org/research/ponemon-library/security/the-economic-value-of-prevention-in-the-cybersecurity-lifecycle.html

- ENISA—European Network and Information Security Agency (www.enisa.europa.eu)
    - "Cloud Security Guide for SMEs"
    - "Recommendations on shaping technology according to GDPR provisions—exploring the notion of data protection by default"

- NIST—Cybersecurity framework

    □ https://www.nist.gov/cyberframework

- "2020 Advisen Cyber Guide"

    □ https://www.advisenltd.
      com/2020-Cyber-Guide-Survey

- "2021 Tag Cyber Security Annual"

    □ https://www.tag-cyber.com/downloads/2021_
      TAG-Cyber_Annual.pdf

- Coalfire—"3rd Annual Penetration Risk Report"

    □ https://www.coalfire.com/news-and-events/press-
      releases/3rd-annual-risk-report-reveals-surprising-
      trends

I'd also highly recommend you join noncommercial peer groups like the VigiTrust Global Advisory Board—more on that later!

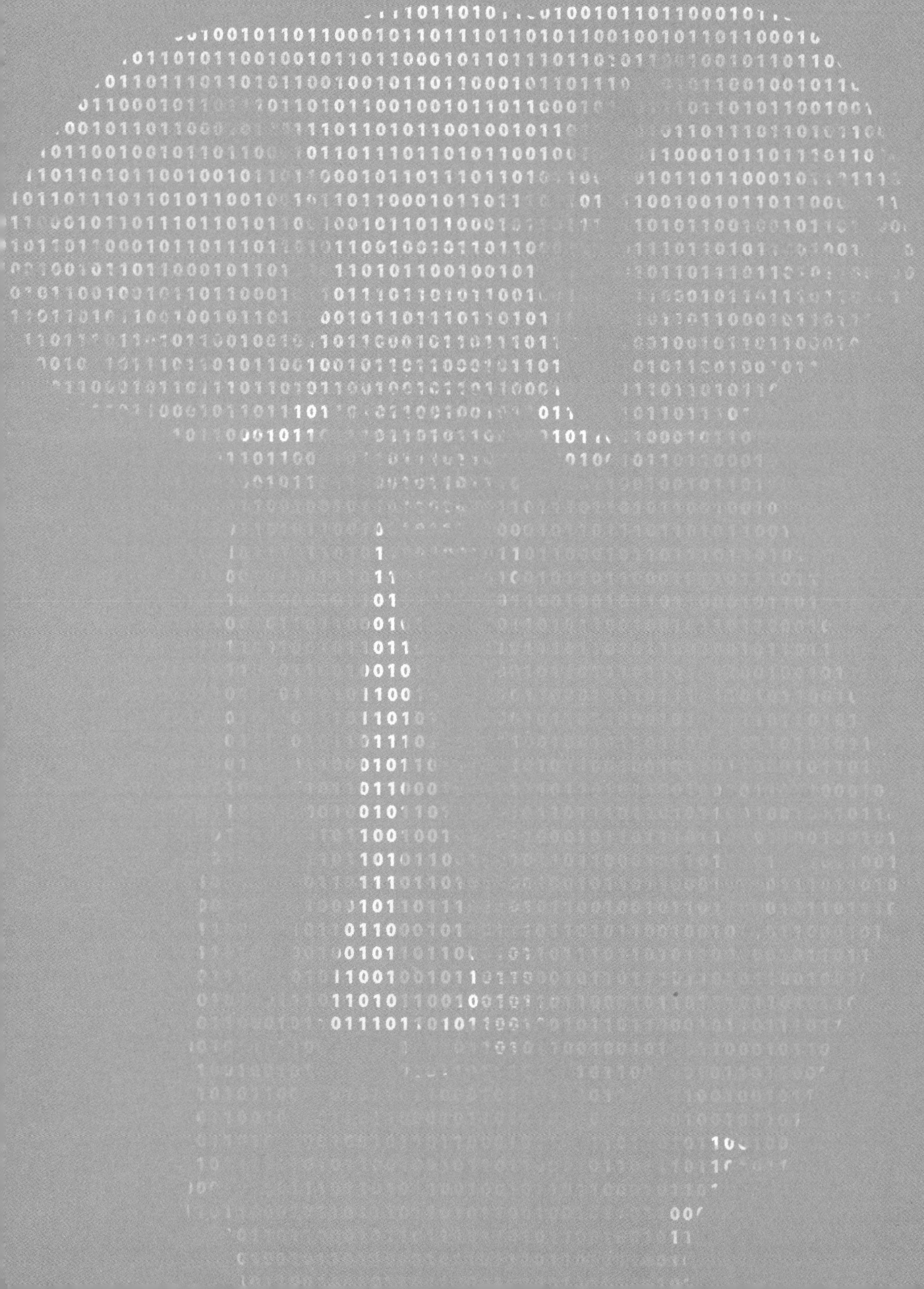

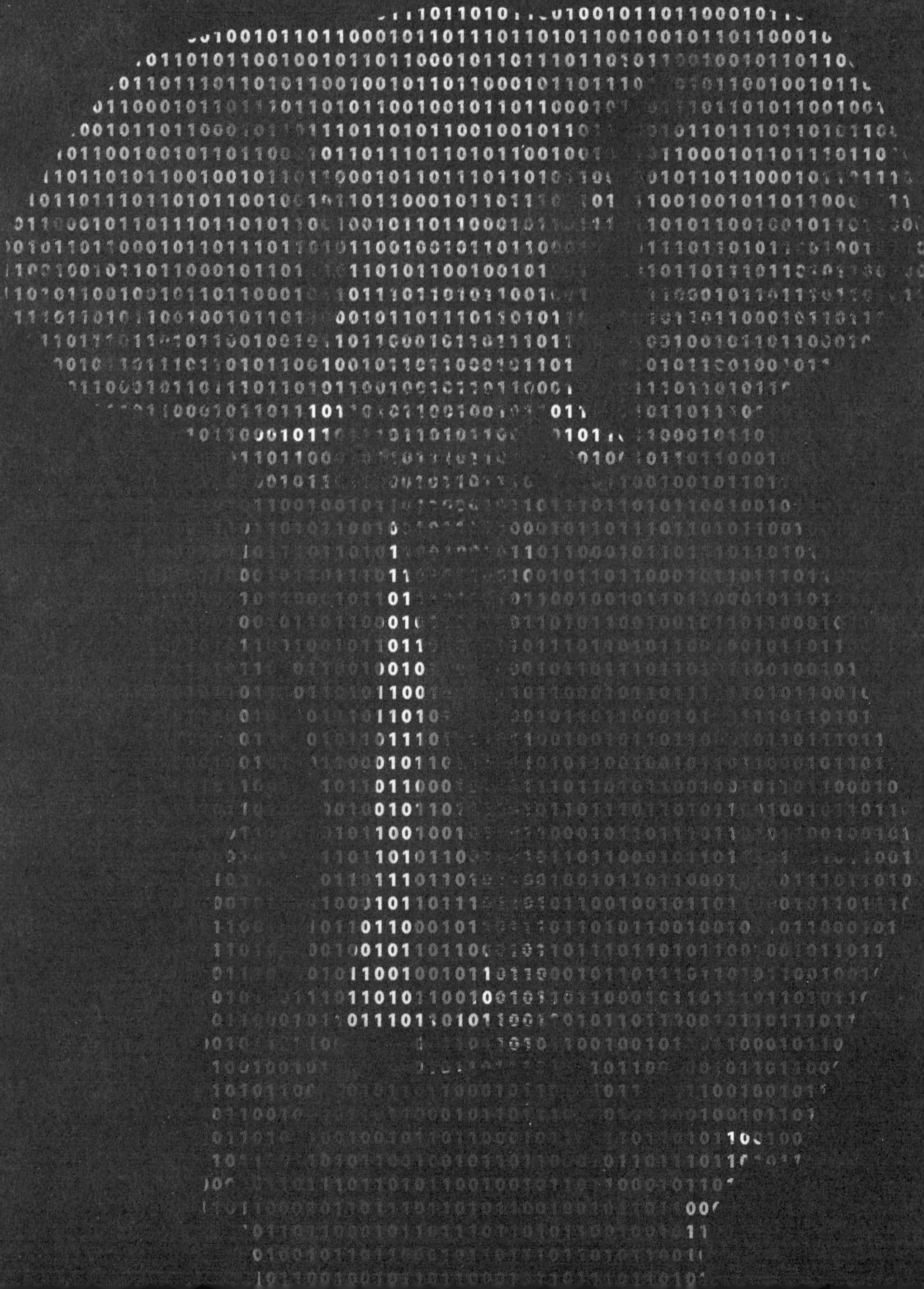

CHAPTER 4

THE 5 PILLARS OF
SECURITY FRAMEWORK

A Simple and Effective Framework for
CEOs, CXOs, and Board Members to
Demonstrate Cyber-Accountability

The 5 Pillars of Security Framework has been used by large enterprises and small- to medium-size businesses since 2008 to give CEOs, CXOs, and boards of directors cyber-accountability education so they can strategize and implement cybersecurity and compliance programs.

It is based on the concept that whatever industry your firm operates in, regardless of size, services, or solutions you provide to your target market, your firm will need to comply with myriad complex and often conflicting regulations and standards pertaining to data security, information governance, and compliance. Careful study of key standards regulations reveals five key common denominators: physical security, people security, data security, infrastructure security, and crisis management. These are the 5 Pillars of Security covered in the framework in plain, jargon-free, and easy-to-understand business language all key decision makers can understand regardless of their technology, legal, security, compliance, or information security skills.

The 5 Pillars of Security Framework not only allows key decision makers to demonstrate cyber-accountability to regulators and enforcement bodies, stakeholders, and clients, but it also shows that they are in full control of compliance and of overall organizational security levels, thus protecting company, employee, and partner data and systems.

Over the last twelve years, this award-winning methodology has helped hundreds of organizations globally to build continuous and proactive security and compliance programs. It is a timeless and industry-agnostic framework that can stay with any organization as it scales, contracts during a crisis, pivots into new sectors, or goes through digitization programs.

EACH PILLAR COVERS ONE OF THE FOLLOWING FIVE AREAS:

- Physical security
- People security
- Data security
- Infrastructure security
- Crisis management

PHYSICAL SECURITY

Simply put, if you have the best technical and network security but just about anyone can walk into your server room, all of that good security is worth nothing.

The whole concept of security started many centuries ago with physical security. Indeed, even in medieval times, kings would protect their families, jewels, and armory within the confines of a walled area. It's very easy to be reminded of physical security in Europe in particular, especially in countries such as France, Germany, England, Scotland, Wales, Spain, Italy, and Portugal, which have fortified structures in nearly every area. Castles, whether big or small, are protected by several layers of walls around ramparts that separate the heart of the activities from the outside world. Having a drawbridge between the unprotected outside and the heavily protected inside is also an old defense.

So it's a bit puzzling to understand why today's key decision makers in small, midsize, and large firms tend to forget the importance of physical security in protecting company assets, client information, and employee information.

While numerous examples of data theft don't make headlines, one should not forget that some of those data breaches were possible only because of poor physical security. Consider a malicious employee copying a confidential database onto a USB drive, taking it home, and copying the data onto a personal device without the firm's knowledge. This relates to technical (or logical) security as well as physical security. Indeed, no client should be able to copy a full database in the first place, and even if they were able to do so, there should be a mechanism to raise the alarm with the information security department that suspicious activity is taking place within the network, and it should be traceable to a specific user and system or systems. But there's also the issue of how employees can bring in or leave with USB drives. In some highly secure facilities, employees have to go through security gates similar to those in airports as a physical check that they are not coming in or leaving with unauthorized devices, which have been identified as potential platforms for exporting and importing data in and out of the enterprise networks.

Now let's talk about other examples of physical security gone wrong, such as lost or stolen laptops containing confidential information. Such devices should be encrypted, and access should only be authorized via multifactor authentication. But the real issue here is the physical security of the device itself. Had the employee been advised to exert higher levels of security when traveling? Did he get training on physical security when outside the office or traveling on business? From a firm perspective, is there a policy for remote workers who have been supplied with company devices able to access, transmit, or store confidential data?

The Northwell breach, which resulted in a fine of $3.9 million, as it was identified as a HIPAA breach, is a stark reminder that physical security breaches also result in heavy fines, damage to reputation, and costs in terms of corrective action.

PEOPLE SECURITY

There are two types of issues regarding people security.

Firstly, all staff, employees (part- and full-time), and visitors need to be in a safe environment, and therefore physical security of people is important. There are already aspects of people security within other pillars of the framework, specifically regarding physical security, which extends beyond assets and building. As such there is a potential overlap between physical and people security in terms of staff, employees, and visitors.

So within the people security pillar, you can expect to find questions about the physical security of staff and visitors as well as other questions like those concerning access control for staff and educating staff regarding how to check in and out of company buildings, a clear mix of physical and people security.

That said, some people security questions are much more detailed, and most do not relate uniquely to physical safeguards but to other aspects of security surrounding people—for instance, how people are selected for employment within the organization. They look at people's understanding of security policies and procedures with regard to privacy. They look at training around security awareness for all staff across all levels of the organization and may also relate to how staff must react to internal and external audits, how they can report suspected security incidents, and how familiar they are with security controls.

People security can also overlap with other pillars, as people interact with data, systems, and machines. This means that the human-system, human-data, and human-machine interactions increase risk surface. This, in turn, puts emphasis on people's ability and willingness to use data, systems, and machines the right way. Survey data from Egress, the leading provider of human-layer email security, announced on February 20, 2020, based on survey responses from five hundred IT leaders and five thousand employees, that insider data breaches are a major concern. According to the survey, "78% of IT leaders think employees have put data at risk accidentally in the past 12 months and 75% think employees have put data at risk intentionally."[8]

---

8   "97% of IT leaders Worried about Insider Data Breaches," Help Net Security, February 24, 2020, https://www.helpnetsecurity.com/2020/02/24/ insider-data-breaches/.

One key aspect of people security is therefore people awareness, which is also a key requirement for physical, data, and infrastructure security.

DATA SECURITY

Data security is an essential pillar of any good, effective security strategy. The interconnection between all of the 5 Pillars is clear, and most of them overlap. However, data is the new currency, and as such, it needs very high levels of attention.

Data, whether structured or unstructured, needs to be classified according to its configured security level. The integrity of data needs to be guaranteed at all times. Availability of data to the right people at the right time is also key for any organization to remain agile and able to answer any crisis. This goes back to the old CIA concept: confidentiality, integrity, and availability. One element missing in the old CIA model is the notion of accountability for data. Who created the data? Who stored the data and where? Who is responsible for the life cycle of the data? Who makes sure that data is created, or acquired, stored, transmitted, and disposed of, in accordance with applicable regulations and industry standards?

The topic of how an organization deals with a data breach or security incident related to data is one that always needs to make it to the board agenda.

Questions included under the data security pillar typically include topics such as mapping your data ecosystem, data classification, data corruption, access controls, data storage, printed data, data governance policies and procedures, and how to deal with internal or external data audits.

INFRASTRUCTURE SECURITY

Infrastructure security should include security measures around not only traditional networks behind firewalls but also subsidiaries, franchisees, third parties, applications, cloud security, and any other logical or physical assets that are part of the organization's ecosystem.

The infrastructure needs to be fully mapped out in order to allow senior executives and board members to understand the extent of the enterprise systems. This mapping informs the overall risk surface from the data on the systems perspective. Of course, it could be argued that people are also part of the ecosystem. This is an intersection area between people security, data security, and infrastructure security.

CRISIS MANAGEMENT

From the crisis management perspective, senior-level executives and board members need to ensure that the organization is able and ready to deal with a data breach, security crisis, or any crisis of information governance. As crisis management organizations, we need to know whether they have taken appropriate security measures so we can address immediate issues during the crisis, contain the crisis, investigate its roots, take corrective action, and ensure that it doesn't happen again. This will mean involving a number of stakeholders from executive management, operations, rescheduled clients, and other internal stakeholders.

External stakeholders such as consultants, specific subject matter experts, experts in crisis management, and law enforcement need to be available to deal with the crisis. The aftermath of any crisis also needs to trigger an analysis of what caused it and help eradicate any specific root cause.

PILLAR STRUCTURE

All pillars are structured as follows:

- Objective

- Scope

- Key Questions

- Value Add

- Benefits

Each pillar is attached to two types of questionnaires: a super-strategic questionnaire with five questions per pillar (twenty-five total) and a strategic questionnaire with twelve questions per pillar (sixty total).

The result of the questionnaire is the production of templated or customized reports including overall summaries, scoring, red flag questions, and action items. These can then be used to produce a detailed security and compliance road map.

5 PILLARS OF SECURITY FRAMEWORK METHODOLOGY

Now that you understand the background to the 5 Pillars of Security Framework, let's look at a simple methodology to implement it. It can be described as follows:

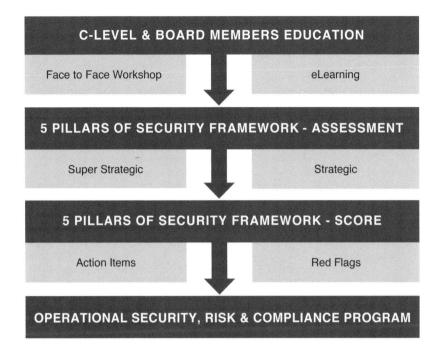

Step One—CEO, CXO, and Board Member Education

You need face time with your target audience. It's always difficult to get time with senior members of staff, but this is a key component of the 5 Pillars of Security Framework. Executive and board members must be made aware of major hacks that have affected their industry competitors and potentially their own firm. This isn't about scaremongering but rather making people aware of what they're up against. I highly recommend using examples and stats from respected industry reports that this target audience will be familiar with: Gardner, Deloitte, and Verizon, to name a few. Press clippings from the *New York Times* and *Time* magazine, and international papers such as *Le Monde, Die Welt,* and others also help, as they demonstrate the global impact of the issue at stake.

Finally, using video clips from main media outlets always helps put the challenge into perspective. You want your C-level team and board members to understand that one of those reports, press clippings, or videos could not only have your firm's name in it but their own names as well, as they might be cited in the reports.

You also need them to understand the ramifications of being the victim of a data breach or hack, regardless of how it took place.

It is important for them to understand the legal landscape they're up against. Right now, with the advance of GDPR, CCPA, HIPAA, and other regulations around privacy and the protection of personal data, a number of countries have taken to issuing fines not only against companies in breach of compliance but also against executives, data protection officers, and privacy officers. A very recent example of that is a South Korean court imposing personal liability on the privacy officer for a data breach. Travel agency Hana Tour Service was found to be in breach of compliance in failing to prevent a 2017 data breach that affected over 465,000 agency customers as well as 29,000 employees. Their privacy officer was also found guilty of negligence in failing to prevent that incident. The court imposed a penalty of ten million South Korean won against the privacy officer. This was in addition to separate fines of around US$280,000 imposed against the firm by the Ministry of Interior and Safety.[9] This is not the first instance in which South Korean prosecutors have imposed personal liability in data breach cases.

Most European countries and US states will fine organizations but stop short of issuing criminal charges against directors, execs, or board members. That said, it is not unusual for directors to be disqualified as a result of a breach and to be pressured to resign because of how the breach was dealt with.

---

9   "South Korean Court Imposes Personal Liability on Privacy Officer for Data Breach," Hunton Andrews Kurth, January 9, 2020, https://www.huntonprivacy-blog.com/2020/01/09/south-korean-court-imposes-personal-liability-on-privacy-officer-for-data-breach/.

The next step within this education process is to sell the value add of good security and compliance to your target audience. Now that they understand the risks associated with poor or nonexistent cybersecurity programs, they can be educated on the real benefits of implementing strong security measures supported by state-of-the-art security solutions, policies and procedures, and awareness training across the organization.

In an ideal world, you want this educational process to demonstrate that the investment in money, time, and effort will quickly pay for itself. The cost of implementing what the GDPR refers to as appropriate security measures to protect data covered by the regulation is, generally speaking, less than the cost of having to deal with the aftermath of a data breach or major security incident. But how do you demonstrate that to your target audience? You need data from trusted sources. The Verizon data breach security report, as well as other reports mentioned in this book, provide a cost per breached record that can be used as an indication to start running figures even on the back of an envelope. The reality is that senior executives and board members want the strategic view of the cost of dealing with an incident. At this point in the process, they're not interested in a line-by-line cost breakdown. They need high-level headings, cost centers, and one-off costs they will need to deal with. Those costs can be summarized as follows: technical solutions to be put in place as a matter of emergency; major upgrades to existing security infrastructure; consulting costs to bring in external subject matter experts to contain, investigate, and remediate the breach; and legal costs, including immediate legal work as well as mid- to long-term costs, which could include a class action. In addition to this, you may be required to provide additional training to staff, updates, and to augment your security policies and procedures. In some cases, there may be PR and communication costs associated with the breach. It is clear that some of the cost line items outlined above should be part of an ongoing cybersecurity and compliance program in the first place. These make it somewhat easy to demonstrate that taking proactive steps toward cybersecurity is in the interest of the organization, its senior executives, board members, clients, and employees.

The ultimate objective is to put cybersecurity and compliance on the profit and loss reports that the board and the organization's senior executives discuss on a regular basis.

One additional intangible benefit of promoting good cybersecurity at the board level is that it allows the chief security officer, the chief information officer, the CFO, and the CEO, as well as other senior executives and board members, to sleep better at night and concentrate on growing the business. As silly as this may sound, most chief security officers I've worked with wonder how they can get buy-in from the rest of the executive team and the board so that the right level of cybersecurity effort and funding are implemented to protect the organization.

Step Two—5 Pillars of Security Framework Assessment Methodology

So how does the 5 Pillars of Security Framework actually work?

The framework is essentially a risk assessment methodology. It is written in plain business English so CEOs, CXOs, and board members can easily understand their firm's security posture and accept accountability for cybersecurity and compliance.

SUPER-STRATEGIC ASSESSMENT

At this stage the CEO, board, and all C-level executives have made a commitment to designing, implementing, and maintaining a good cybersecurity program to protect data and achieve and maintain compliance with legal and industry standards and regulations that apply to the firm. However, they still need to figure out the top super-strategic objectives of such a program to be able to define a more detailed strategy that can be implemented by the firm's relevant lines of business. The methodology calls for five questions in the pillar to get a super-strategic view of the firm's security posture.

Ideally all senior-level executives and board members should answer the five super-strategic questions associated with each pillar. There are only twenty-five questions altogether, and the answers are extremely simple to choose from.

POSSIBLE ANSWERS TO THE
SUPER-STRATEGIC AND STRATEGIC QUESTIONNAIRES

1. Yes, absolutely

2. Yes, I think so

3. No, I don't think so

4. Absolutely not

5. I don't know

6. Not applicable to my firm

7. I am not worried about it

Each type of answer carries equal weight, unless you want to use a weighted version of the framework. In practice, however, it is clear to business owners that not all pillars carry the same weight for each organization. This is documented in step three.

The questions are super strategic and aim at raising additional awareness about the implications of having or not having good cybersecurity in place. Furthermore, each firm has the ability to flag certain questions as red flag questions. That means that internal or external cybersecurity experts may have identified those items as critical components of an appropriate cybersecurity program for the firm and assessed that despite an overall good score, one or more questions are raising serious concerns. For example, a software provider providing SaaS solutions to its clients might end up with a reasonable or even good overall score; however, if data security is not showing the highest score, that should be a red flag because of the nature of the business.

STRATEGIC ASSESSMENT

The next stage of the process is to go through the strategic questions of the 5 Pillars of Security Framework. These questions are still very strategic, but they drill down into more-detailed aspects of their comprehensive cybersecurity program. They are aimed at senior executives rather than board members, although board members may also choose to answer them.

The outcome of the sixty-question questionnaire is a much more granular view of the company's security posture. Red flag questions are also included, and the questions can be subject to a weighting system, giving some areas priority over others.

Armed with the results of the strategic questionnaire, your firm can now start designing a detailed remediation road map based on the 5 Pillars.

Indeed, a list of areas requiring immediate attention from the security and compliance perspective is identified for each of the pillars. The road map is essentially a priority list based on the sixty questions grouped into the 5 Pillars, showing the organization where to devote time, effort, and budget. This remains a strategic document, but it forms a very strong basis for the firm to implement corrective action in a structured way, putting emphasis on priority items, yet also paving the way for a midterm and long-term security strategy for the whole firm.

Step Three: 5 Pillars of Security Framework—Score

Based on your super-strategic and strategic assessments, your firm will be provided with a score relating to your answer to each question—being either of equal importance or based on weighted questions. It is anticipated that most first-time users will use the nonweighted model first, where all questions receive a score of one point, meaning that the highest overall score can be twenty-five, or five per pillar. Then they will move on to the weighted model, which is also simple and allows each firm to vary the scores of questions for the super-strategic or the strategic assessment. I refer to these as 5 Pillars of Security Framework weighted assessments.

Organizations can decide where emphasis should be and work out their own weighting system. A health system might put more weight on questions included in the infrastructure, data, and crisis management pillars, while a college might focus more on physical security, people security, and data security. In addition, within each pillar, one may decide to allocate more weight to specific questions. This is typically easier to implement if you use an integrated risk management solution—for instance, VigiOne or an equivalent—but can also be done manually.

I am working on prepackaged weighting models for specific industries such as hospitality, retail, technology/software, government, and education. A number of users have also built additional weighting models that may be made available as part of the main framework at some stage in the future.

In any event, the score will allow CEOs, CXOs, and board members to consider how to prioritize the remediation plan that follows in step four.

As a result of the strategic assessment and after answering sixty questions, the CEO, CXOs, board members, and other key decision makers are able to formulate a clear action program for operational, risk, and compliance. Actions items for each pillar can be identified under the following categories, as seen in the table: policies and procedures, technical solutions and/or implementation, and user awareness and training.

SIMPLE MODEL TO BENCHMARK YOUR ORGANIZATION'S PREPAREDNESS USING THE 5 PILLARS OF SECURITY FRAMEWORK

PILLAR	POLICIES & PROCEDURES	TECHNICAL SOLUTIONS AND/OR IMPLEMENTATION	USER AWARENESS & TRAINING
Pillar 1 Physical Security			
Pillar 2 People Security			
Pillar 3 Data Security			
Pillar 4 Infrastructure Security			
Pillar 5 Crisis Management			

Firms and their internal and external auditors can work from the same data and speak a common language to address what needs to be remediated and demonstrate their level of cyber-accountability to relevant governing bodies or authorities and how the firm is proactively addressing compliance and cybersecurity mandates.

Step Four: 5 Pillars of Security Framework Plan— Operational, Risk, and Compliance Program

As a result of the super-strategic assessment, your firm is now in a position to identify clear action items, which I highly recommend be divided into the following categories: technical solutions implementations and/or fine tuning of existing solutions or setups, policies and procedures, and training.

Once action items are listed, you can start allocating tasks based on the remediation plan in priority order. These tasks can be implemented according to a detailed project plan. At that stage, the challenge of automating the compliance process in addition to the remediation plan and tracking of all tasks becomes a logical consideration.

Any organization that can demonstrate that C-level executives, board members, and key stakeholders within the organization have been educated on cybersecurity and their accountability toward cybersecurity is in a much better position to have constructive discussions with the regulators and/or enforcement bodies. Should a breach or security incident come to the attention of the relevant authorities or enforcement bodies, being able to showcase that the organization is aware of where it is in compliance with applicable standards and regulations for data security and where it falls short but has a remediation plan is a great asset. It demonstrates that accountability for data security is recognized at the highest level within the organization and that the organization has elected to have strong cybersecurity programs, even if those programs are not fully implemented yet.

Let's talk about why you need to automate compliance and security tasks. If you look at a standard such as the payment card industry data security standard, also known as PCI DSS, you can clearly see that some tasks recur, whereas other tasks might be one-offs, only happening every few years or when a major change is implemented within the infrastructure or business processes.

With PCI DSS, there are daily, weekly, monthly, and quarterly recurring tasks. In fact, if you ask QSAs to count these tasks, they come up with 2,500 to 3,000 tasks depending on your scope of applicability for PCI DSS. Examples of daily tasks include reviewing logs, which clearly is better implemented with automated tools. Monthly tasks include updating technical solutions, reviewing policies to make sure that they are still relevant. A great example of a quarterly task is performing ASV scans. Yearly tasks may include pen testing. Regulations such as GDPR or CCPA assume that appropriate security measures including technical controls, policies and procedures, and awareness training are deployed on an ongoing basis.

It stands to reason that with hundreds or thousands of tasks to complete every year, using automated tools to reduce the burden on your staff should be considered. Within the compliance industry, such tools are referred to as governance risk compliance or integrated risk management platforms. There are three main types of such tools. First are preparedness tools, which provide templates for policies and procedures, high-level or in-depth training on compliance requirements, or high-level compliance road maps for you to derive your own compliance program from. Next are regulation- or standard-specific solutions—for instance, tools that help with one regulation or one standard. These are validation-only tools that allow you to produce official statements that attest to compliance but do not allow you to manage the process per se. Finally, more comprehensive solutions that are multistandard and regulation provide templates and actionable road maps, additional task management facilities, and also include APIs to integrate with third-party technical tools.

The 5 Pillars of Security Framework process allows your organization to prepare for the creation, implementation, and maintenance of strong cybersecurity and compliance programs that are ready to be managed using automated GRC or IRM solutions.

In the next section of this chapter we will go into more details of 5 Pillars of Security Framework road maps discussing output, best practices, business as usual, ongoing compliance, and automation checklists for organizations.

5 PILLARS OF SECURITY FRAMEWORK OUTPUT

The logical output of the 5 Pillars of Security Framework are the two analysis levels, thanks to the super-strategic and strategic questionnaire results as well as action items they help identify. Reports provide a more detailed analysis for each pillar so that each area can be looked at individually. In addition, a red flag analysis can help you focus on the impact of each flagged topic. You end up with an overall view of your firm's posture against the 5 Pillars of Security Framework.

There are some easy wins to get out of the reporting structure to get buy-in from the CXOs at an implementation level. However, I recommend making reports as visual as possible and identifying key actions and quick wins: identify the top five changes coming out of the analysis for thirty, sixty, and ninety days following the analysis.

It's important to summarize the results of the 5 Pillars of Security Framework outputs for the executive function of your organization to turn all findings into actionable projects. I recommend that executive summaries follow a simple structure. For example:

A. Visual reports (manual or GRC/IRM based)

    1. High-level summary super-strategic questionnaire output

    2. High-level summary strategic questionnaire output

B. List of outstanding items

    1. All items

    2. Focus on red flags

C. List of people within the organization who follow the 5 Pillars of Security Framework methodology

D. Time frame to implement corrective action identified through the process

E. Top five changes to implement within the next thirty/sixty/ninety days

    1. Could be one key objective per pillar for the next thirty/sixty/ninety days

    2. Could be an overall top five objectives—non–pillar specific—for the next thirty/sixty/ninety days

SUGGESTED MODEL TO CONTEXTUALIZE THE 5 PILLARS OF SECURITY FRAMEWORK

	PHYSICAL SECURITY	PEOPLE SECURITY	DATA SECURITY	INFRASTRUCTURE SECURITY	CRISIS MANAGEMENT
Objective					
Scope					
Key Questions 5 Q /Pillar					
Key Questions 5 Q/Pillar					
Value Add for the Board					
Benefits to the Organization					

THE CASE FOR CONTINUOUS COMPLIANCE AND BUSINESS AS USUAL (BAU) AND HOW TO INDUSTRIALIZE IT WITH IRM TOOLS

So you've successfully managed to educate your target audience, get them on board, and conduct your 5 Pillars for Security Framework assessments. You've also identified key actions to conduct over the next thirty/sixty/ninety days. You're now happy that you have a strong, solid compliance and security posture for your firm! You're ready for regulators and industry assessors to come in! Well done! That's a great step forward!

But wait … is it enough?

Well, actually, not really. You now need to maintain compliance with everything. Remember that threats are evolving very quickly, cybercriminals don't take a break, laws keep evolving, and standards move forward too. Cyber-accountability shouldn't rest on its laurels!

Rather, compliance should be checked and maintained on a continuous basis and be part of your firm's risk process DNA. It should be business as usual, BAU, as defined in several standards, frameworks, and laws, including PCI DSS and ISO 27001.

There are, of course, a number of checklists you can use to do that, and you can use existing project management systems to ensure this is done; however, it would make more sense to integrate this process into an integrated risk management (IRM) solution.

Industrializing Continuous Compliance with IRM Tools

There are many different definitions of IRM. It is also often interchanged with GRC (governance, risk, compliance), which really focuses on IT and data risk. My view is that IRM is wider than GRC and allows you to look into many types of risks, hearkening back to my concept of bubbles of risk that need to be managed by the board and C-suite.

An IRM solution allows you to register assets within your environment, assess risks to the environment, manage the safeguards your firm is implementing (technical, policy based, or skills transfer based) and assign one-off and continuous compliance tasks to relevant target audiences.

A good IRM solution will also enable collaboration between stakeholders—both internally within your wider teams involved in preparing for, validating, and maintaining compliance and with third parties, such as consulting firms helping you through the process—as well as, potentially, official assessors or even regulators.

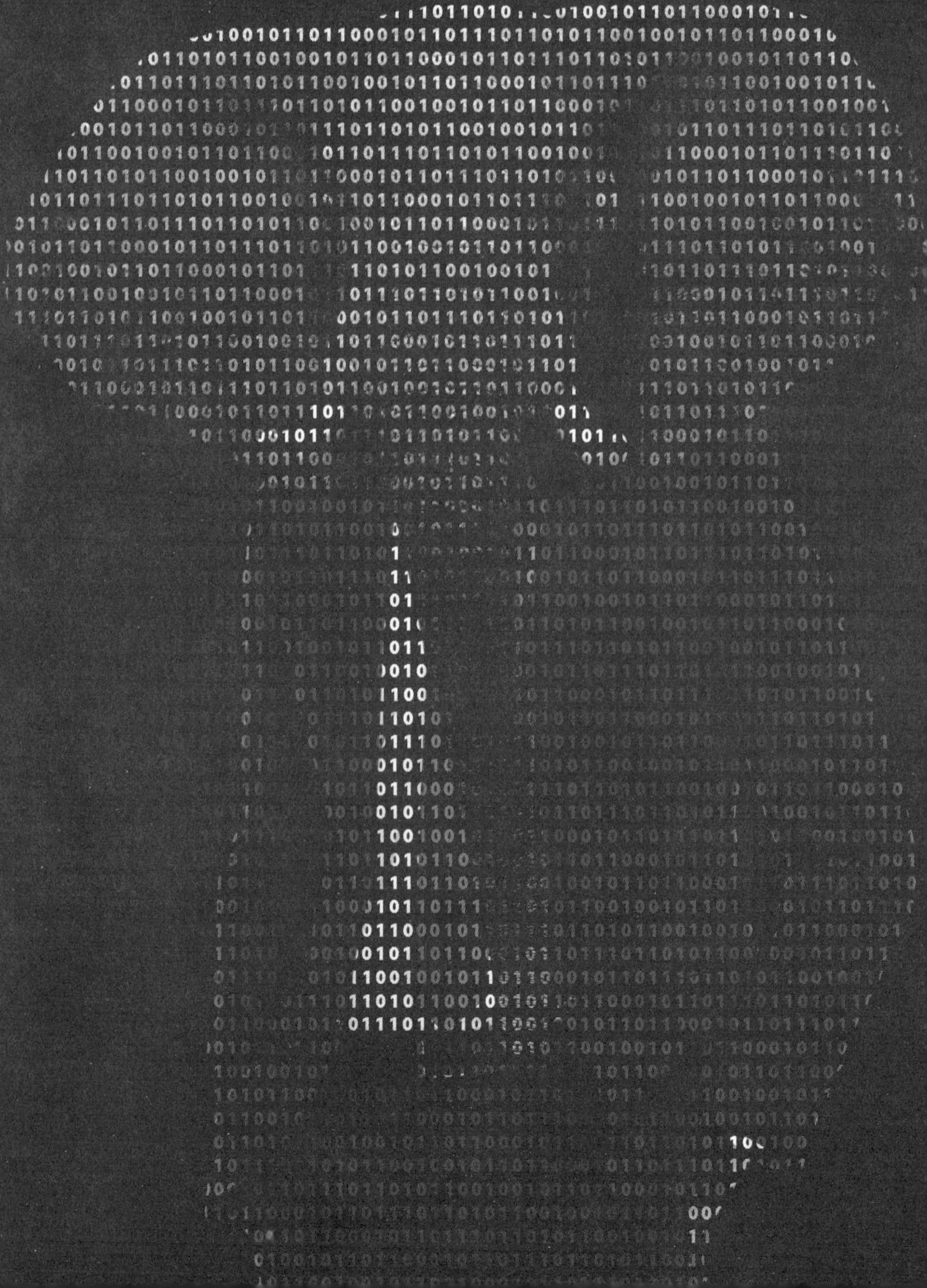

CHAPTER 5

5 PILLARS OF SECURITY FRAMEWORK DETAILED OVERVIEW

This chapter provides details of the objective, scope, key questions, value add, and benefits of each pillar.

PHYSICAL SECURITY
OPERATIONS MANAGER, SECURITY STAFF
- Access to Building
- Physical Assets
- IT Hardware
- Vehicle Fleet

PEOPLE SECURITY
HR, SECURITY STAFF
- Permanent & Contract Staff
- Partners
- 3rd Party Employees
- Visitors
- Special Events Security

DATA SECURITY
HR, IT TEAM & MANAGER
- Trade Secrets
- Employee Data
- Database
- Customer Data

INFRASTRUCTURE SECURITY
IT TEAM & MANAGER
- Networks
- Remote Sites
- Remote Users
- Application Security
- Website
- Intranet

CRISIS MANAGEMENT
OPERATIONS MANAGER, IT TEAM, HR
- Documentation & Work Procedures
- Emergency Response Plans
- Business Continuity Plans
- Disaster Recovery Plans

PILLAR 1: PHYSICAL SECURITY

1. OBJECTIVE

Ensure that appropriate levels of physical security are in place to protect the organization's physical assets and that access to such assets is provided in a secure and compliant manner to authorized people only.

2. SCOPE

Covers access to buildings, vehicles, IT assets, and any other physical assets, but also access to cloud farms (even if outsourced) as well as any external locations where employees, contractors, assets, or data might be housed. This may also include physical access to remote sites, storage sites, and subsidiaries, if and where applicable.

3. KEY QUESTIONS

PHYSICAL SECURITY
OPERATIONS MANAGER, SECURITY STAFF
- Access to Building
- Physical Assets
- IT Hardware
- Vehicle Fleet

SUPER-STRATEGIC QUESTIONNAIRE

As a CEO/C-level exec/board member, am I confident/sure/happy that:

1. Physical access to my firm is secured the right way?

2. All physical assets in my firm, including, but not limited to, buildings, vehicles, computers, servers, printers, other physical IT equipment, tablets, iPads, phones, and iPhones

are secured in a way that does not put the company's physical or data security at risk?

3. All paper-based information or other physical media is secured at all times in a way that does not put the company at risk?

4. Physical access to any area within the firm is granted on a need basis in a way that is secure and fully traceable?

5. I can lawfully and effectively track at any time physical access to the firm's critical and noncritical areas in real time and in retrospect, both for internal and remote staff as well as visitors who have been granted access to the firm?

STRATEGIC QUESTIONNAIRE

As a CEO/C-level exec/board member, am I confident/sure/happy that:

1. Access control to my building/site/facility via ID cards/near-field communications (NFC)/RFID/biometrics is secure?

2. All access points such as doors/gates/barriers are access controlled, tracked, and audited?

3. Any passwords needed for building access are changed every ninety days?

4. Any access to the building and its different sections is revoked immediately for an employee who leaves the organization?

5. The building/site/facility is comprehensively monitored by alarms and CCTV systems?

6. Sensitive areas like the server rooms are monitored and audited as stringently as these areas need to be?

7. Swipes/spot checks of the building/site/facility are conducted to look for physical hacking devices such as keyloggers and unauthorized Wi-Fi access points?

8. Paper data is secured and that access and audit procedures are in place?

9. A clean desk policy is in place and adhered to?

10. Shredders are in place and are used in accordance with policy, and content is disposed of via a suitably certified company?

11. Physical penetration testing on the building/site/facility takes place at suitable time intervals?

12. The organization has put in place policies and technical measures to efficiently and legally monitor third-party physical access to my ecosystem?

4. VALUE ADD

In today's organizations, boundaries are blurred between physical and logical assets; however, access to either may often mean a back door to the other one. Physical security needs to be maintained.

5. BENEFITS

- Ensure that access is restricted to authorized people only

- Ability to monitor and report on physical access to company areas/zones (should include a list of zones like public, restricted, highly restricted) and assets

- Compliance aspects, e.g., PCI req 9

PILLAR 2: PEOPLE SECURITY

1. OBJECTIVE

Ensure that the organization has full control over who accesses physical and logical assets in compliance with applicable regs.

2. SCOPE

Covers full-time employees, part-time employees, board members, contractors, and visitors.

3. KEY QUESTIONS

PEOPLE SECURITY
HR, SECURITY STAFF
— Permanent & Contract Staff
— Partners
— 3rd Party Employees
— Visitors
— Special Events Security

SUPER-STRATEGIC QUESTIONNAIRE

As a CEO/C-level exec/board member, am I confident/sure/happy that:

1. The security team has mapped the organization's full staff, whether full time or part time, as well as their respective access to company data?

2. The organization is able to appropriately track all staff activity within the full company ecosystem, including networks, application, and cloud systems?

3. The organization has put in place appropriate technical

security solutions and/or security measures to legally and demonstrably track staff activity?

4. If the regulator(s) or enforcement bodies perform an audit, I can demonstrate my organization's compliance (or demonstrable road map to compliance) toward protecting staff while ensuring they do not willingly or unwillingly have access to data or systems that are on a "need to" access?

5. The organization has developed and demonstrably deployed security policies and procedures to protect itself when it has third parties onsite (visitors/suppliers) either on an ongoing basis or during special events?

STRATEGIC QUESTIONNAIRE

As a CEO/C-level exec/board member, am I confident/sure/happy that:

1. All staff have been vetted properly according to applicable screening regulations?

2. All staff are trained appropriately and have an understanding of the organization's security policies and procedures and understand the different levels of privacy

3. All staff have access to the latest security policies and procedures either online or in hard copy?

4. All staff who leave the employment of the organization will have all access to the organization disabled?

5. All staff are trained and aware of social engineering techniques?

6. The organization has security policies and procedures regarding third parties on-site?

7. The organization has policies and procedures regarding visitors on-site?

8. All staff are aware of emergency procedures in the event of fire or any other dangerous happening and their responsibilities in such events?

9. All staff who use either organization or personal devices (if allowed) to access data externally are aware of the policy and procedures regarding external access?

10. All staff are audited coming in and leaving the building/site/facility?

11. All staff interactions with sensitive data are audited?

12. If the regulators or enforcement bodies perform an audit, I can demonstrate my organization's compliance regarding the staff's security awareness?

4. VALUE ADD

- Ability to demonstrate that the organization can legally monitor and report on people's activities regarding its assets and business

- Ability to provide the right level of physical and logical security for anyone involved with the organization's business

5. BENEFITS

- Map out all people involved in the organization's activities

- Ensure that people are granted the right levels of physical and logical access.

- Monitor activity in real time and for reporting

PILLAR 3: DATA SECURITY

1. OBJECTIVE

Ensure that company, employee, client, and third-party data is appropriately protected in compliance with applicable laws and standards.

2. SCOPE

- Company data

- Client data

- Third-party data

- Employee data

- Any data that has been identified as restricted, confidential, highly confidential, or otherwise critical to the organization

3. KEY QUESTIONS

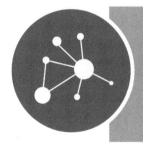

DATA SECURITY
HR, IT TEAM & MANAGER
- Trade Secrets
- Employee Data
- Database
- Customer Data

SUPER-STRATEGIC QUESTIONNAIRE

As a CEO/C-level exec/board member, am I confident/sure/happy that:

1. All data, including employee data, client data, and third-party data, is protected appropriately and in compliance with applicable laws and mandatory standards?

89

2. The organization is able to and does classify data according to its privacy level?

3. The organization has put in place appropriate technical security solutions and/or security measures to protect data we create, acquire, store, transmit, and also dispose of?

4. If the regulator(s) or enforcement bodies perform an audit I can demonstrate my organization's compliance (or demonstrable road map to compliance)?

5. The organization has developed and demonstrably deployed security policies and procedures to all staff across the organization, regardless of ranking level, location, business unit, or function?

STRATEGIC QUESTIONNAIRE

As a CEO/C-level exec/board member, am I confident/sure/happy that:

1. An up-to-date ecosystem diagram has been drawn up that shows the rest and flow of all data within the organization, including all incoming and outgoing data?

2. Data is classified according to privacy level and in accordance with applicable laws and mandatory standards?

3. All data that flows out of the organization via electronic means is encrypted appropriately?

4. Any data that is deemed sensitive is encrypted while at rest in the organization?

5. Access to the various levels of classification of data is performed on a need-to-know basis and that appropriate

audit software can log who accessed what and also alert to unauthorized access?

6. Appropriate applications are used to audit the downloading of sensitive data to devices such as USB keys and also that email and other messaging systems are monitored for the unauthorized transfer of any data?

7. The disposal of any data, be it hard copy or held on an electronic device, is dealt with appropriately or by a compliant third party?

8. Any penetration testing done on the internal network will test the security of all data held by the organization?

9. Sensitive data is not kept over any given legal limit it may come under?

10. All hard-copy sensitive data is kept locked, and access is only given to those on a need-to-know basis?

11. The organization has deployed policies and procedures to all staff on how to handle data in a secure and confidential manner?

12. If the regulator(s) or enforcement bodies perform an audit, I can demonstrate my organization's compliance?

4. VALUE ADD

- Ensures compliance with data privacy and protection frameworks and laws

- Allows the organization to protect the data while making it available to authorized people so they can securely conduct business

- Fosters a good data security culture within the organization

5. BENEFITS

- Compliance and avoidance of fines

- Good data security practices

- Good data management

PILLAR 4: INFRASTRUCTURE SECURITY

1. OBJECTIVE

Ensure that the overall organization's infrastructure is protected the right way and in compliance with applicable laws and frameworks.

2. SCOPE

- Traditional network infrastructure

- Extended networks

- Third parties connected to the network

- Cloud infrastructure

- Applications

- BYOD-based networks

- Any system connected to the network or owned or managed by the organization

- Any data asset owned or managed by the organization

3. KEY QUESTIONS

INFRASTRUCTURE SECURITY
IT TEAM & MANAGER
– Networks
– Remote Sites
– Remote Users
– Application Security
– Website
– Intranet

SUPER-STRATEGIC QUESTIONNAIRE

As a CEO/C-level exec/board member, am I confident/sure/happy that:

1. The security team has mapped the organization's full ecosystem, including, but not limited to, internal networks, websites, ecommerce sites, third-party networks linked to our system, all cloud providers, all third-party providers, subsidiary networks and, if applicable, franchisees' networks, and any system that may have company data?

2. The organization is able to appropriately protect its full eco-system's infrastructure?

3. The organization has put in place appropriate technical security solutions and/or security measures to protect systems, applications (whether built in-house or purchased), and data within its ecosystem?

4. If the regulator(s) or enforcement bodies perform an audit, I can demonstrate my organization's compliance (or demon-strable road map to compliance) toward protecting the overall company infrastructure?

5. The organization has developed and demonstrably deployed security policies and procedures to protect its infrastructure?

STRATEGIC QUESTIONNAIRE

As a CEO/C-level exec/board member, am I confident/sure/happy that:

1. The IT team has thoroughly mapped out the internal network(s), external-facing sites and applications, and connections to third parties, and that I have up-to-date schematics?

2. All public-facing IP addresses are protected by a firewall?

3. Appropriate IDS (intrusion detection systems) / IPS (intrusion protection systems) are in place to alert the IT team of any unusual activity on the internal network?

4. All workstations, servers, and laptops have antimalware software installed and that all security patches/updates are added as soon as possible?

5. All access to the internal network(s) and devices on it is securely managed via passwords or multifactor authentication?

6. Appropriate permissions are managed to ensure that people only access what they need to in order to perform their work duties?

7. Auditing of access is in place and able—either automatically or manually—to alert to any unauthorized access to the different sections and devices of the internal network?

8. External access to the internal network and its devices is by secure and encrypted channels and only to authorized parties?

9. Policies and procedures are in place to oversee the secure use of personal mobile devices on internal network(s), whether those devices are company owned or, where allowed, personal

devices?

10. WiFi connection to the internal network is secure and encrypted?

11. Penetration testing is performed on the internal network at suitable time intervals?

12. If regulator(s) or enforcement bodies perform an audit, I can demonstrate my organization's compliance toward protecting the internal network?

PILLAR 5: CRISIS MANAGEMENT

1. OBJECTIVE

Ensure that any crisis involving security and compliance can be dealt with appropriately and effectively and complies with applicable laws and frameworks.

2. SCOPE

- All incidents that constitute a crisis within the organization and may impact the other four pillars' objectives: physical, people, data, and infrastructure

- Disaster recovery

- Business continuity

- Reputational crisis

- Any other crisis about data, systems, or parties that had access to same

3. KEY QUESTIONS

CRISIS MANAGEMENT
OPERATIONS MANAGER, IT TEAM, HR
– Documentation & Work Procedures
– Emergency Response Plans
– Business Continuity Plans
– Disaster Recovery Plans

SUPER-STRATEGIC QUESTIONNAIRE

As a CEO/C-level exec/board member, am I confident/sure/happy that:

1. The organization is generally able and ready to deal with a security crisis?

2. The organization has a written crisis management/incident response plan?

3. The organization has an incident response plan that has been communicated to all relevant stakeholders?

4. Staff have been trained on their duties and how to react should a security incident happen?

5. The organization has mapped out the type of security incidents that could happen, their likelihood, and their potential impact on the business?

STRATEGIC QUESTIONNAIRE

As a CEO/C-level exec/board member, am I confident/sure/happy that:

1. The organization has a crisis management and incident response plan in place?

2. The plan has been mapped out by the crisis management

team in a fashion that truly represents the organization's infrastructure?

3. In the event of a disaster/crisis/incident there is a backup site that can sufficiently continue the organization's operations?

4. The organization's staff are trained to carry out the instructions of the plan?

5. The crisis management team is proactive in monitoring for a crisis/disaster/incident and will, as early as possible, instigate its incident response?

6. The reaction to the crisis/disaster/incident on social media, news media, and television media will be handled in a proper and truthful manner so that the organization is seen to be handling the crisis/disaster/incident swiftly and honestly?

7. All clients affected are kept aware of the crisis/disaster/incident and regularly given updates on the situation?

8. Crisis management and incident response simulations are run at appropriate intervals by the crisis management team?

9. Organization data is backed up frequently and securely enough that any loss of data will be kept to an absolute minimum in the event of a crisis/disaster/incident?

10. Auditing and logging is of a sufficient degree to allow rigorous examination of the causes of the crisis/disaster/incident?

11. The organization's crisis management team has plans to rebuild client confidence in the organization after a major crisis/disaster/incident?

12. In the event of a major crisis/disaster/incident, the organization can go back to where it was before the disaster?

4. VALUE ADD

- Ability to respond in real time to any crisis covered by the scope

- Ability to respond within timelines imposed by laws and standards applying to the organization

5. BENEFITS

- Able to deal with physical, people, data, and infrastructure security crises

- Reduce operational impact of any crisis

- Reduce financial impact of any crisis

- Opportunity to continually improve crisis management

5 PILLARS OF SECURITY FRAMEWORK MAPPING EXAMPLES

5 Pillars of Security Framework versus PCI DSS

PHYSICAL SECURITY
- Back-up and media storage policy
- Physical and logical access control guidelines
- R8: Identify and authenticate access to system components
- R9: Restrict physical access to cardholder data

PEOPLE SECURITY
- Management of 3rd parties for security purposes
- Password creation guidelines
- R12: Maintain a policy that addresses information security for all personnel

DATA SECURITY
- Anti-virus and anti-spam and intrusion detection policy
- Password creation guidelines
- R1: Install and maintain a firewall configuration to protect data
- R3: Protect stored cardholder data
- R4: Encrypt transmission of cardholder data across open, public networks
- R7: Restrict access to cardholder data by business need to know

INFRASTRUCTURE SECURITY
- Hardening, log, and patch management
- Security awareness and Acceptable use policy
- Security assessment, application security, and vulnerability management
- R2: Do not use vendor-supplied defaults for security parameters
- R5: Protect all systems against malware and regularly update anti-virus software
- R6: Develop and maintain secure systems and applications
- R10: Track and monitor all access to network resources and cardholder data
- R11: Regularly test security systems and processes

CRISIS MANAGEMENT
- Back-up and media storage policy
- Disaster recovery and business continuity policy
- Security assessment, application security, and vulnerability management
- Security incident response plan

5 Pillars of Security Framework versus GDPR

PHYSICAL SECURITY
- Limit access to personal data within the organization's premises
- Ensure that no devices or files that may contain personal data are left unattended
- Ensure physical access is tracked according to GDPR to provide appropriate security measures without affecting data subjects' rights

PEOPLE SECURITY
- Classify your users and ensure they have the appropriate access
- Make sure that only the right people have access to personal data at the right time

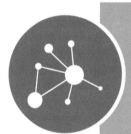

DATA SECURITY
- Personal data collection is accurate and can be erased
- Select and document a "lawful basis" for all personal data processed
- Implement a DPIA for new or changed personal data processes
- Implement a Data Subject Request procedure and ensure staff awareness
- Archive only the personal data you need
- Keep the data you collect to an absolute minimum

INFRASTRUCTURE SECURITY
- Use the latest encryption technologies
- Use secure file exchange technologies
- Only use secure cloud service providers *(look out for ISO 27001 or SOC II compliance)*
- Develop default privacy protection mechanisms and implement monitoring processes
- Implement strong data protection contracts with 3rd parties

CRISIS MANAGEMENT
- Ensure you have a data breach management plan
- Implement a disaster recovery and business continuity plan
- Make sure all relevant staff are trained on how to deal with security incidents related to personal data
- Data breaches must be reported without undue delay; if not, the company risks fines up to €20M or up to 4% of total worldwide annual turnover

VIGITRUST GLOBAL ADVISORY BOARD—WHY IT MATTERS TO CXOs AND BOARD MEMBERS

Board members and senior executives need to keep abreast of the latest cybersecurity threats as well as regulations and standards. Once a routine has been established to constantly update and maintain a cybersecurity program, demonstrate accountability for compliance with legal and industry frameworks, implement and maintain technical security solutions, and regularly train users on security matters, they can bring this process to the next level.

One way to do this is to consider cybersecurity and compliance certification and to join security associations and think tanks.

Having recognized this challenge for VG trust clients, as a CEO and founder, I started by organizing user group discussions, primarily based around the services that the company was offering at the time. Very quickly I started getting feedback from users, partners, and prospects about what would add value to their security strategies. Some ideas could be implemented by phone, others by partners (always by first parties), and others were just good to have on road maps.

One day in 2011, I was having a discussion with Alexander Abramov, who was working in risk management in JPMorgan in New York. I asked if he could introduce me to like-minded senior technology or risk people. He agreed and jokingly said, "I will bring three or four people. Pick the place, and you pick up the tab." A few days later, Alex, three risk professionals, and I got together for a drink in a busy New York bar and started discussing what was happening in the industry. The conversation was very interesting, but the format was wrong. It needed to be in a more professional setting. That group grew to about fifteen people in New York meeting every three months or so. This was the foundation for what is now the Global Advisory Board.

Today the board is a group of 150 senior risk and compliance professionals, CEOs, CXOs, chief security officers, chief risk officers, security researchers, law enforcement, regulators, academics, and distinguished invited guests.

It is made up of a number of chapters, or regional groups. They regularly meet in Dublin, London, Paris, and New York. They meet in San Francisco around the RSA Conference and again in the fall. A chapter in Sydney meets once a year.

Meetings are by invitation only and open under the Chatham House Rule. They are typically hosted by one member and last sixty to ninety minutes. Topics are agreed on in advance. The host normally welcomes the group. VigiTrust provides an update on regional and global activities. A short noncommercial presentation may set the scene for the topic discussion. This is followed by an open Q&A session, group discussions, and generally networking drinks and dinner.

Once a year, all members of the advisory board are invited to a two-day Global Advisory Board meeting in Dublin, Ireland, with keynote presentations, group discussions, short topical presentations, and panel discussions. Evening networking dinners and event hours are organized for advisory board members to connect.

The meeting typically covers several themes, including the full risk areas that members collectively try to address, like strategic geopolitical risk, financial/operational/contractual risk, reputational/brand management/QA risk, and, of course, cybersecurity and compliance risks including ICT, IP, and DR/BC. Themes are typically available in two sections: security and compliance, or future and innovation.

Security roles and compliance positions are often extremely lonely. If you do your job correctly, nobody knows about you. If there is even one issue, you unfortunately become public enemy number one. This makes it very difficult for people in most jobs to openly talk about security incidents, data security breaches, or interaction with regulators or law enforcement. The regional and global advisory boards create a safe platform for members to exchange ideas, talk about best practices, and use real cases and data to help each other.

To guarantee the integrity of the discussions, all members sign a charter that sets out rules of engagement and confidentiality. The charter also covers membership rules and a commitment to introduce me to three potential advisory board candidates every year. This is how the group has been growing over the last few years. I have the pleasure and privilege of personally meeting each member to understand their challenges and value add and how they can fit into the group.

Security roles and compliance positions are often extremely lonely. If you do your job correctly, nobody knows about you. If there is even one issue, you unfortunately become public enemy number one.

Members get access to a private advisory board portal where they can access security and compliance reports, share information with other members, and start group discussions.

The advisory board also heavily relies on the 5 Pillars of Security Framework to drive discussions. The main reason for this is that members hold extremely senior positions and need a common framework that is business driven in order to promote discussions across a pool gathering multiple skills and talents.

The value add of joining an advisory board, whether it's VigiTrust's or another, is to be able to learn from like-minded people in a trust-based environment allowing you to relate scenarios, comply with applicable regulations and standards that apply to your environment today, and prepare for future cybersecurity challenges and compliance environments.

2020 themes include the following:

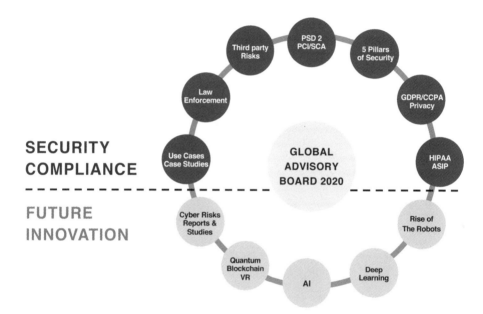

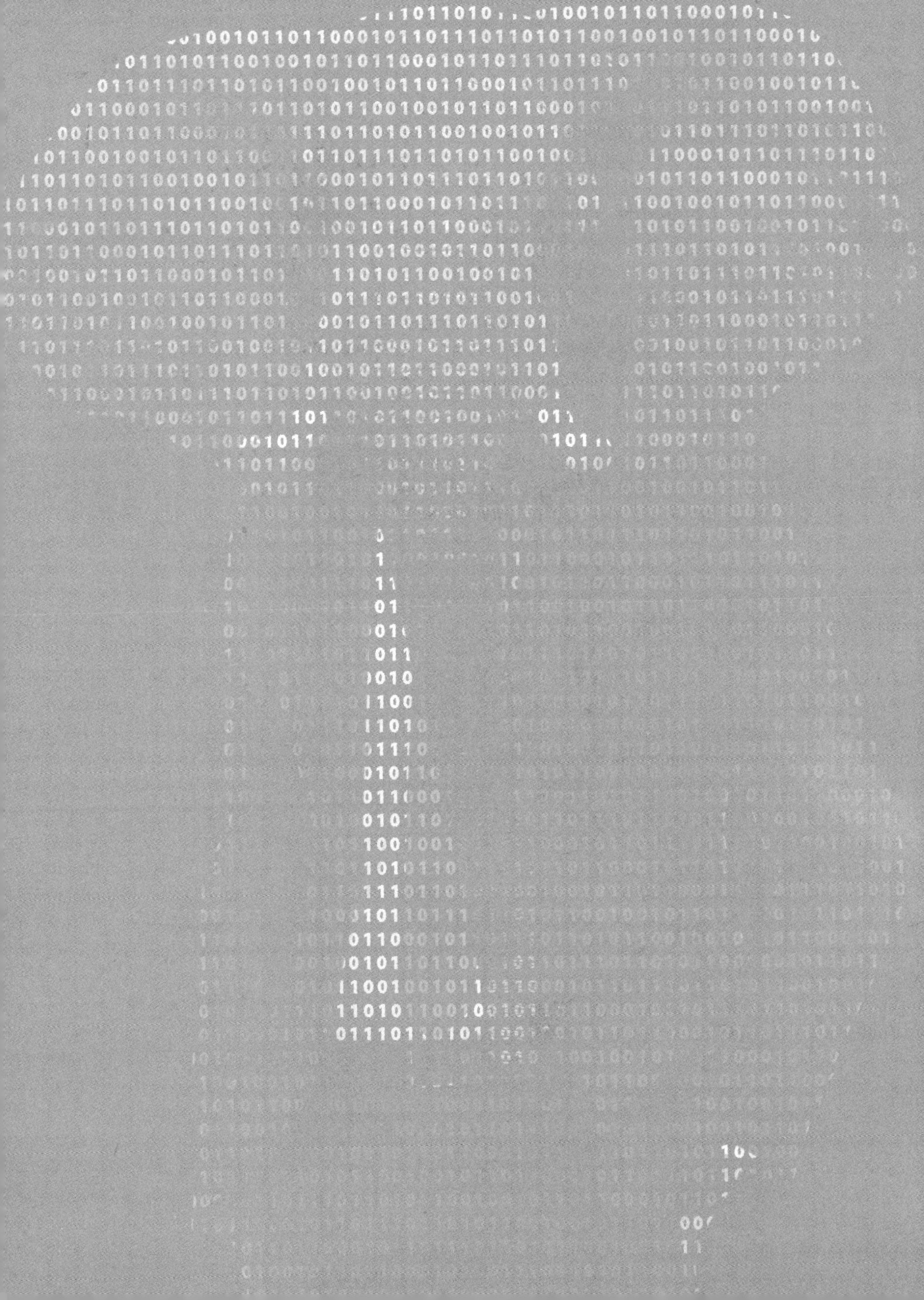

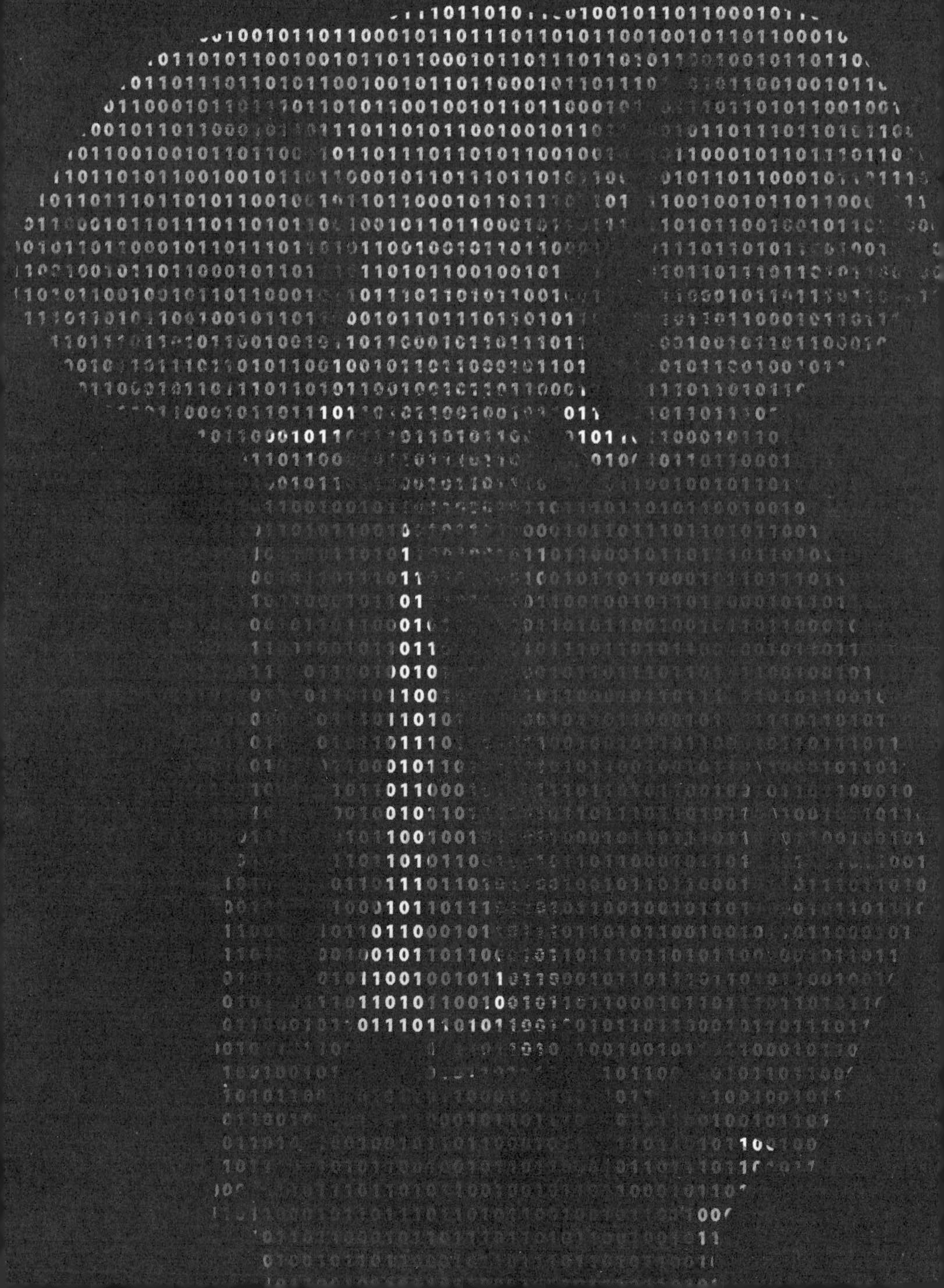

CHAPTER 6

BREACHING THE C-SUITE (CEOs, CXOs, AND BOARDS)

"Confusion of Tongues" in Tower of Security Babel

BY JAMES O. GRUNDVIG

> In order to put the 5 Pillars in context, I've asked cyber-security veteran and tech journalist James Grundvig to summarize how the industry got to where it is today.

In 1990, the business world began to evolve faster than incrementally, as it had in decades past, using a common language for production and operations that connected all business units. Within five years, searching, mining, and sharing of information moved from manual processes to email and the World Wide Web. As email spread globally and websites popped up and proliferated, businesses transformed and individual consumers soon reaped the benefits of "one-click" shopping and cloud storage, and then by 2007, mobility and mobile apps.

With the benefits and massive efficiencies of the new digital paradigm, however, emerged unseen threats. People were socially engineered and emails were phished while every data end point could turn into a potential vector for hackers to enter a device, breach a company's network, or steal identities and corporate secrets. As a result, the enterprise created new defensive and monitoring positions to support the growing IT departments. CTOs joined CEOs and CFOs in the boardroom. Yet instead of coalescing into one cohesive unit, working in unison like pistons of a sports car engine, many of the new positions that reported to the chief technology officer—CISO, CSO, CIO, cloud evangelist, and other managers—didn't speak the same language as other chief officers and the board of directors. The splintering and siloing of the various roles critical to protecting a business grew apart and receded into corner cubicles and back rooms. Instead of being on the same "digital page," they were cut off from one another.

This resulted in data fragmentation and in a company's stakeholders not speaking the same bottom-line language, focusing only on quarterly results, not seeing ahead to worst-case scenarios like becoming a victim of a well-publicized data breach.

Since 2000, this "confusion of tongues" in the C-suite and boardroom has produced new gaps, blind spots, and hacking horror stories and so created a new reason for CEOs to be fired.

As the business world races deeper into the digital age, with ever-increasing mountains of data being created, with information being shared faster than ever before across myriad devices, the risk exposure for corporations becomes clear: protect their "crown jewels" in trade secrets and intellectual property (IP) or risk losing competitive advantage and become a liability instead.

But it doesn't have to be that way.

The 5 Pillars of Security Framework offers a foundation in which to build a comprehensive cybersecurity program that is simple to follow in a common language that all employees will grasp and embrace.

WHAT DOES BREACHING THE C-SUITE MEAN?

Companies fail. Like people, they make mistakes, have blind spots, and too often are driven by bottom-line decision-making using pro forma financial statements. Sometimes those mistakes are derived from greed, such as the Enron scandal in 2001, and sometimes from hubris. Other times, they can boil down to poor leadership or conflicting personalities at the top. Still other times, failure can arise from an insider threat: employees within an enterprise harboring ill will or carrying out sabotage or an incident with an ulterior motive.

In today's world of "data being the new oil,"[10] not developing a comprehensive security program with clear policies and procedures (backed by an incident response plan when the big event occurs) can become a fatal flaw, leaving behind a digital debris field with executives fired and scorned in the wake.

Of the dozens of high-profile data breaches the past decade, several have stood out, from Target's third-party penetration of one of its mechanical vendors to Marriott International's theft of five hundred million customer records, which only surfaced after its acquisition of an already malware-infected Starwood hotel chain. In both cases, the companies failed to conduct the necessary due diligence and deep dive audits, with neither corporation being in the technology sector.

---

10   "The World's Most Valuable Resource Is No Longer Oil, but Data," *The Economist*, May 6, 2017, https://www.economist.com/leaders/2017/05/06/ the-worlds-most-valuable-resource-is-no-longer-oil-but-data.

That's what made the two Yahoo data breaches—in 2013 and 2014—so astonishing. The internet giant's hacks exposed more than one billion customer records across many large countries to two different state actors. More critically, the exposure of the breach delayed negotiations of and shaved $350 million off Yahoo's sale to Verizon.[11] Yahoo was fortunate, however; Verizon could have scuttled the deal altogether. But losing 8 percent of the final sale price and adding months of delays show the ramifications of a hack that went far beyond the loss of customer data, regulatory fines, fired executives, and reputation damage.

In the digital age, the corporate board's spreadsheet-first mindset has become a liability. Such telescoping focus on stock price, share buybacks, and growth over other crucial issues has placed blinders on the executive suite. For example, in the past few years, too many law firms and other companies have purchased Bitcoins as a means of preventive medicine: they accepted the fact that they would be hacked one day and thus prepared to pay the bounty to the ransomware attackers. That money plays into the hands of the cyber-thieves. Why didn't those law firms invest their ransom money in security tools, software, and cyber know-how? Or haven't the legal minds figured out that buying cryptocurrencies won't solve security gaps and issues; they only whet the appetites of the pirates.

To demonstrate how serious ransomware bugs have become, a new escalation in the hacker warfare revealed that, in one case, a security staffing firm chose not to pay the ransom. So the hackers released seven hundred megabytes of the firm's stolen unencrypted files to the public.[12] Competitors must have had a field day, so, too,

---

11   Dan Swinhoe, "The 15 Biggest Data Breaches of the 21st Century," CSO Online, April 17, 2020, https://www.csoonline.com/article/2130877/the-biggest-data-breaches-of-the-21st-century.html.

12   Stu Sjouwerman, "After Refusing the Maze Ransomware Payment, Their Stolen

any clients, vendors, or employees whose information had been dumped out into the open, fully exposed for all to see.

In another data breach, on July 19, 2019, Capital One bank issued a press release, stating the following:

"On July 19, 2019, we determined that an outside individual gained unauthorized access and obtained certain types of personal information about Capital One credit card customers and individuals who had applied for our credit card products."

The statement went on:

"We immediately fixed the issue and promptly began working with federal law enforcement. The outside individual who took the data was captured by the FBI. The government has stated they believe the data has been recovered and that there is no evidence the data was used for fraud or shared by this individual."[13]

The data breach exposed nearly 106 million customer records, stealing credit card applications from 2005 through 2019, which included small businesses, as well as 140,000 social security numbers and 80,000 linked bank numbers, according to an article in CNET.[14]

Full congressional and federal multiagency investigations are still to come, and there are a lot of unknown elements to the bank's attack. Were the hackers inside Capital One's network for an extended period of time? Has attribution to the hack been narrowed down to a country of origin or other party? Was the breach the result

---

Data Was Leaked," KnowBe4, accessed October 5, 2020, https://blog.knowbe4.com/heads-up.-this-is-ugly-after-refusing-the-maze-ransomware-payment-their-stolen-data-was-leaked.

13   "Information on the Capital One Cyber Incident," Capital One, updated September 23, 2019, https://www.capitalone.com/facts2019/.

14   Clifford Colby, "Capital One Data Breach: What You Can Do Now Following Bank Hack," *CNET*, August 12, 2019, https://www.cnet.com/how-to/capital-one-data-breach-what-you-can-do-now-following-bank-hack/.

of multiple points of failure, including human error? Or did the penetration occur once, in one specific area?

Clearly not enough businesses archive or destroy records older than seven years. The embarrassing and damaging Sony Pictures data breach dumped executives' emails trashing the acting and personalities of many of the stars that performed in the studio's movies.[15] Capital One's breach allowed the hackers to steal fourteen years of credit card applications. In the cybersecurity sphere, an acronym describes the failure to archive and clean out old files—ROT: Redundant, Obsolete, Trivial data.[16]

If nothing else, Capital One left too much information, too centrally located, for too long a period of time. ROT impacts five critical areas of an enterprise, with respect to cybersecurity defense. Two of them relate to impairing employees' ability to quickly access the records for compliance, discovery requests, and making quick decisions on information.

Another issue is that holding so much data for so long drives up the costs of storage on infrastructure and maintenance.

But the two biggest areas of concern for Capital One bank's ROT boiled down to the vulnerability to data breaches (by exposing a broader risk surface with more attack vectors) and to the liability, still to be determined, for holding information beyond its "legal retention period."

---

15   Joseph Steinberg, "Massive Security Breach At Sony—Here's What You Need To Know," *Forbes*, December 11, 2014, https://www.forbes.com/sites/josephsteinberg/2014/12/11/massive-security-breach-at-sony-heres-what-you-need-to-know/#51ecc2b444d8; *THR* Staff, "Angelina Jolie Speaks Out for First Time on Insults From Sony-Hack Emails," *The Hollywood Reporter*, November 5, 2015, https://www.hollywoodreporter.com/news/angelina-jolie-sony-hack-amy-pascal-837389.

16   "ROT (Redundant, Outdated, Trivial Information)," WhatIs.com, updated September 2016, https://whatis.techtarget.com/definition/ROT-redundant-outdated-trivial-information.

Since the Equifax data breach occurred more than two years ago and has been fully investigated, the focus of this chapter is on the credit rating agency's deep hack.

Before we unpack the details and the flawed corporate logic about the Equifax hack, we will examine six examples of corporate failure—not technological—across an array of issues that plague most executives and boards in 2020. The data breaches will include a "Pillar Analysis" section at the bottom of each example to see how the errors could have been prevented by a little knowledge, foresight, planning, and, of course, some means and methods.

These are the six data breaches that will be examined:

1. Facebook data breach of 267 million users

2. Exposing the Insider Threat

3. Uber and Transit Hacks

4. Healthcare Data Breaches

5. Cybersecurity Accountability in the Boardroom

6. The infamous Equifax penetration

FACEBOOK PENETRATION

When you are the biggest social media platform in the world, you become a target. Critics, competitors, regulators, and hackers all want their pound of flesh from the multibillion-dollar corporation. With all the data brokering and privacy abuses in the recent past, with Mark Zuckerberg giving congressional testimony, paying fines to France and the European Union,[17] being examined by the Federal Trade Commission to consider breaking up the monopolis-

---

17   Aria Bendix, "EU Fines Facebook $122 Million," *The Atlantic*, May 18, 2017, https://www.theatlantic.com/news/archive/2017/05/facebook-receives-122-million-fine-from-the-european-union/527325/.

tic and anticompetitor behavior of Facebook,[18] one would think the company would turn over a new leaf—maybe pull in the reins a bit, erect better internal controls, become more like Apple with a customer-first approach. But after a massive data breach, in which 267 million Facebook users had their information stolen,[19] nothing, apparently, happened at all. It was business as usual at Facebook.

In December 2019, a Ukrainian security researcher found the trove of stolen credentials sitting in criminal databases in plain text, unencrypted, including their passwords.[20] And they were searchable and available to twenty thousand Facebook employees. A "Facebook insider said access logs showed some two thousand engineers or developers made approximately nine million internal queries for data elements that contained plain text user passwords."

Facebook has had a long history of data breaches since going public in 2011, including in 2012, 2014, the Cambridge Analytica scandal in 2018 when the company notified eighty-seven million users of yet another breach,[21] and now the 2019 penetration and theft of users' data, in which Zuckerberg and the board of directors were repeatedly warned about the security flaw that led to the breach.[22]

---

18 "FTC: Break Up the Facebook Monopoly," SumofUs.com, accessed October 5, 2020, https://actions.sumofus.org/a/ftc-break-up-the-facebook-monopoly.

19 Frank Bajak, "Researcher: Data on 267 Million Facebook Users Exposed," *AP News*, December 20, 2019, https://apnews.com/article/bdf02dbe7bf266b025b6f1b0ae5860fd.

20 Paul Bischoff, "Report: 267 Million Facebook Users IDs and Phone Numbers Exposed Online," Comparitech, updated March 9, 2020, https://www.comparitech.com/blog/information-security/267-million-phone-numbers-exposed-online/.

21 Nadeem Badshah, "Facebook to Contact 87 Million Users Affected by Data Breach," *The Guardian*, April 8, 2018, https://www.theguardian.com/technology/2018/apr/08/facebook-to-contact-the-87-million-users-affected-by-data-breach.

22 Laurence Dodds, "Facebook Was Repeatedly Warned of Security Flaw

The only way to change this cavalier attitude and failure to address these security issues with resources and investment would be for government regulators and legislators to punish the executives and board members of publicly traded companies and expose them personally to lawsuits and criminal indictments. That would foster an immediate change in corporate behavior.

Pillar Analysis

Facebook failed in two key areas of the 5 Pillars Framework in people security by allowing its employees access to unencrypted users' data in a searchable database, and the social media giant also failed by not protecting users' data at all.

EXPOSING THE INSIDER THREAT

Insider threats[23] come in three different sauces. First, data exfiltration or theft where a company employee, for whatever reason, extracts corporate information and either sends it or walks out the door with it at the end of a day's work. This occurred with the Anthem breach. For a number of years, an employee had been emailing personal information of eighteen thousand employees, who were Medicare members, as discovered by an internal investigation.[24] This type of hack can be prevented with employee monitoring tools that use machine learning and artificial intelligence to track the behavior and productivity of each employee.

That Led to Biggest Data Breach in Its History," *The Telegraph*, February 9, 2020, https://www.telegraph.co.uk/technology/2020/02/09/facebook-repeatedly-warned-security-flaw-led-biggest-data-breach/.

23   Team ObserveIT, "5 Examples of Insider Threat-Caused Breaches That Illustrate the Scope of the Problem," ObserveIT.com, March 22, 2018, https://www.observeit.com/blog/5-examples-of-insider-threat-caused-breaches/.

24   Steve Ragan, "Anthem Confirms Data Breach, But Full Extent Remains Unknown," CSO Online, February 4, 2015, https://www.csoonline.com/article/2880352/anthem-confirms-data-breach-but-full-extent-remains-unknown.html.

The next insider theft comes in the form of third-party credential theft. In the case of the infamous and large data breach of the 2013 Target hack, a small mechanical contracting vendor in Pittsburgh was spear-phished. Once the hackers gained access to the small business enterprise, they breached Target's network in a backdoor theft.[25] CEOs and boards are often naïve or dismissive of their responsibility on what constitutes the data perimeter for their firm. Target is a lesson for all that the end points of a company go beyond the mobile devices in the field or travelers, remote access, and sensors. The defensive perimeter extends to their list of suppliers, subcontractors, vendors, consultants, advisors, and stakeholders as well.

The third form of insider threat comes in the way of employee as an Achilles heel vis-à-vis phishing attacks. Hackers of all kinds, including scraping bots, send emails to target employees with forged but real-looking corporate documents or fake but approximate website domains that trick the user into clicking on a link, or by social engineering the employee from that person's Twitter feed, LinkedIn profile, Facebook posts, and other online channels that allow a criminal to con an employee long enough to click on or download malware. The best way to combat this decade-old problem is through antiphishing via eLearning modules and in-house boot camps.

Pillar Analysis

The insider threat revolves around people security. It shows the complexity of protecting a company's assets along with training and monitoring employees. In the end, people security is a full-time corporate job that doesn't end at night or on weekends. In the healthcare

---

25 Kevin McCoy, "Target to Pay $18.5M for 2013 Data Breach That Affected 41 Million Consumers," *USA Today*, May 23, 2014, https://www.usatoday.com/ story/money/2017/05/23/target-pay-185m-2013-data-breach-affected-consumers/102063932/.

industry, this problem is even more pronounced, with 58 percent of the data breaches caused by insider threats.[26]

UBER AND TRANSIT HACKS

For too many years, the fast-growing, valuation-inflated startup Uber carried its "win at all costs" mantra by eschewing the rules with a pirate pride from its former CEO Travis Kalanick. The top ten reasons Kalanick was fired run the gamut from personality issues to ripping off both customers and Uber contract drivers.[27] What isn't mentioned, beyond spying on its customers after they were dropped off at their destinations, was a data breach the startup embraced at full impact in 2014. It included the theft of fifty thousand drivers' personal records in an open database, forcing the feds to launch a criminal investigation.[28] What upset the government? It took Uber five months to notify its drivers of the hack.[29] The breach also turned the spotlight on Uber's startup ride-hailing competitor Lyft. Other larger transportation sectors—from aerospace and railroad to trucking and shipping—are targeted by hackers.

---

26   Elizabeth Snell, "58% of Healthcare PHI Data Breaches Caused by Insiders," Health IT Security, March 5, 2018, https://healthitsecurity.com/news/58-of-healthcare-phi-data-breaches-caused-by-insiders.

27   Joe Kukura, "Top 10 Reasons Uber Fired CEO Travis Kalanick," *SF Weekly*, June 21, 2017, https://www.sfweekly.com/news/top-10-reasons-uber-fired-ceo-travis-kalanick/.

28   Douglass MacMillan and Danny Yadron, "Uber Breach Affecting 50,000 Drivers Went Unreported for Months," *The Wall Street Journal*, February 27, 2105, https://www.wsj.com/articles/BL-DGB-40631.

29   James Covert, "Uber Says It Got Hacked—Over Nine Months Ago," *New York Post*, February 27, 2015, https://nypost.com/2015/02/27/uber-got-hacked-almost-nine-months-ago/.

Pillar Analysis

The greatest threat to the ride-sharing and greater transportation industry comes down to information security, with a focus on locking down customers' usage data, logistics, and supply chain vulnerability.

HEALTHCARE DATA BREACHES

The target-rich environment of the healthcare industry is driven by the number of startups in mobility and blockchain, as well as large tech companies like Google, Amazon, and Microsoft entering the fold. It is also driven by the United States's push to bring more than 330 million citizens into an umbrella system under multiple health agencies and insurance and medical providers. From 1970, when healthcare was 6.9 percent of GDP, to 2019 when it reached 17.8 percent, this trend is expected to swell toward a quarter of GDP in the coming decade, according to Statista.com.[30] Hackers follow the money. Healthcare, as a result, is one of the most targeted industries as it offers opportunities in ransomware, ID theft, IP theft, social engineering of well-paid medical professionals, and access to hundreds of millions of records.

In 2018, the healthcare industry experienced five high-profile data breaches. These included a Puerto Rican insurer mailing thirty-six thousand patients information about other members, Independent Blue Cross uploading patient data onto its public website—not its private and secure database—and Baylor Medical Center having 2.65 million patient records data-jacked via its biller, AccuDoc. The other two breaches included phishing attacks on employees of Health Equity and the California Department of Developmental Disabili-

---

30   Matej Mikulic, "U.S. National Health Expenditure as Percent of GDP from 1960 to 2020," Statista, June 8, 2020, https://www.statista.com/statistics/184968/us-health-expenditure-as-percent-of-gdp-since-1960/.

ties, which had its office looted and records burned by vandals.[31]

Pillar Analysis

The attack on the state government office in California is a prime example of physical security, while the other breaches range from data and people security to information security and crisis response.

CYBERSECURITY ACCOUNTABILITY IN THE BOARDROOM

The year 2019 was another banner year for hackers, who stole billions of records from Capital One, Toyota, Facebook, First American Financial—which leaked its entire database—and several other penetrations. Boardrooms are not insulated from the fallout of penalties beyond—witness Target's shareholder derivative lawsuit or Wyndham Worldwide defending itself from a similar lawsuit. With state, federal, and European Union's crackdown on breached companies, one cybersecurity journal asks: "Can data breach liability extend to the boardroom and C-suite?"[32]

The short answer is that liability for data breaches will be coming to the C-suite and boardroom this decade, putting offenders on notice for not ensuring or performing minimum cyber-hygiene for their companies or institutions.

Pillar Analysis

The executives represent the management and knowledge side of people security, in particular, as well as the other four pillars, as

---

31   Tony Abraham, "5 Scariest Health Data Breaches of 2018," Healthcare Dive, January 4, 2019, https://www.healthcaredive.com/news/5-scariest-health-data-breaches-of-2018/544834/.

32   Ellis Rosenzweig, "Can Data Breach Liability Extend to the Boardroom and C-Suite?," Cyber GRX, accessed October 5, 2020, https://www.cybergrx.com/resources/research-and-insights/blog/can-data-breach-liability-extend-boardroom-c-suite.

ignorance will soon no longer be an excuse in which they could very likely be exposed on a personal level due to negligence.

THE EQUIFAX MEGA BREACH

In March 2017, Equifax suffered a data breach and didn't know about it for two and a half months. That allowed state actors to query forty-eight servers nine thousand times from the consumer credit reporting agency, a frequency of 128 queries per day, unimpeded, uninterrupted, and unnoticed. That led to 148 million consumers having their personal information stolen—addresses, contact information, social security numbers, dates of birth, credit scores, and a lot more. The months-long hack exposed 209,000 credit card numbers as well.

The massive breach led to the "forced retirement" of three Equifax executives in the CEO, CIO, and CISO. The Security Exchange Commission (SEC) also indicted Equifax's US Information Solutions CIO on insider trading charges, as Jun Ying dumped more than $1 million in shares before the breach was made public.[33]

One question must be asked: Was Mr. Ying involved in the data breach in any way? Clearly, he would have profited on the insider trading activities of his shares in Equifax. Was he or someone else at the firm paid by the state actors to penetrate the company's network and servers?

When Equifax belatedly made the mega breach public on September 7, 2017, nearly a half year after the hackers had gained access, members of the press and security analysts had a field day. So did Wall Street as the Equifax stock price cratered by more than 30 percent due to an avalanche of blistering criticism and ridicule for its

---

33   Ben Lane, "Former Equifax Executive Accused of Dumping Stock After Learning of Data Breach," HousingWire, March 14, 2018, https://www.housingwire.com/articles/42747-former-equifax-executive-accused-of-dumping-stock-after-learning-of-data-breach/.

mishandling of the event, as well as a loss in confidence when certain facts emerged about the people behind the company's security unit and failed leadership.

From the start, former Equifax chairman and CEO Richard F. Smith, CIO David Webb, and CISO Susan Mauldin never worked on the same page regarding the company's security program and the steps needed in the event of a breach, or an "incident response plan." This was according to the 115th Congress Majority Staff probe, hearings, and conclusion in its *The Equifax Data Breach* report in December 2018.

Furthermore, the US House of Representatives Committee on Oversight and Government Reform exposed a fractious relationship in the Equifax security business. The committee's investigation exposed that Webb and Mauldin didn't get along at the outset when the CISO joined Equifax in 2013. The friction was so bad that Smith made Mauldin report directly to the company's chief legal officer instead of the CIO, which had been the structure prior to Smith joining the firm in 2005.

That is some tough insight and painful criticism of a multibillion-dollar multinational corporation coming from the congressional committee.

The hack occurred as a result of a failure of Equifax to patch its website when Apache notified it of a security gap in its software. The Apache Software Foundation, which is open source, ran two-thirds (67 percent) of the world's web servers in 2017, due to its reliability and security. But if software isn't patched, it doesn't take much effort for hackers to take advantage of the oversight.

"Criminals exploited a US website application vulnerability to gain access to certain files. Based on the company's investigation, the unauthorized access occurred from mid-May through July 2017.

The company has found no evidence of unauthorized activity on Equifax's core consumer or commercial credit reporting databases," the company said in a statement.[34]

Right. It's easy to blame "criminals" for the company's internal security flaws on lack of policies and procedures, failed patch management, poor executive leadership, and a personality clash between its CIO and CSO that harmed Equifax to the tune of billions of dollars before, during, and after the breach. Part of the Atlanta-based company's bottom-line-first mentality became a sign of the times last decade for publicly traded enterprises on the stock market.

In 2014, Equifax Inc. was no different than Google/Alphabet, Apple, IBM, or many other multinational corporations when it "announced an additional $400 million share repurchase authorization."[35] With a focus on making then-CEO Smith and his colleagues in the C-suite and boardroom wealthier than ever before, security took a back seat to the "financial jujitsu" that benefited Equifax's executives, and protection of its customers' data took a hit, though Equifax was an information company in the digital age.

The mega breach forced Equifax to fire CEO Smith, clean house in its information solutions unit, pay steep penalties, and turn over several board seats. A review today of the company's 2020 boardroom shows there are ten board members—with only a few holdovers from prior to the 2017 hack.[36] Not one of them has a true technology or

---

34 "Equifax Announces Cybersecurity Incident Involving Consumer Information," Equifax.com, September 7, 2017, https://www.equifaxsecurity2017.com/2017/09/07/equifax-announces-cybersecurity-incident-involving-consumer-information/.

35 "Equifax Inc. Announces Additional $400 Million Share Repurchase Authorization," Equifax.com, September 11, 2014, https://investor.equifax.com/news-and-events/press-releases/2014/09-11-2014.

36 "Board of Directors," Equifax.com, accessed October 5, 2020, https://www.equifax.com/about-equifax/directors/.

security background. Represented are major brands (General Mills, Kimberly-Clarke), a "data scientist" from L. Brands, and executives from major accounting, telecom, and credit card corporations.

So where does that leave Equifax now, with more and more data and end points coming online, connected to ever-increasing numbers of servers and networks? Will Equifax suffer a Mega Breach 2.0, as Yahoo did? Or have they finally put the necessary security measures and incident response plan in place to ensure that they don't become blindsided again—like Yahoo—and leave their customers' personal information out in the open?

Equifax's media representatives chose not to respond to an email requesting an interview on what lessons they have learned since suffering the fifth-worst data breach in history.

In the first two decades of the twenty-first century, the Equifax data breach ranks fifth on the list in terms of size, damage, and penalties. It's rather shocking that an information solutions company, which does millions of transactions, credit data searches, and much more on a daily basis, was so technologically unsophisticated. Why did Equifax let the bad blood between security officers in the IT department put them in silos instead of mending the relationship? How did Equifax allow such dysfunction to govern its corporate operations and decision-making? And why did they hide the breach from the public for as long as possible, while allowing the opportunity for insider trading and other such abuses to exist?

While the US Congress found one underlying problem with Equifax's in-house reporting structure, journalists and online investigators discovered that the *Fortune 1000* company's chief security officer was a music major in college. Digging deep into Susan Mauldin's LinkedIn profile turned up a lack of cybersecurity and technology educational background, as well as a dearth of security training.[37] Was she suited for the position? It's hard to say, as that wasn't the focus of any government agency investigation. But it was enough to burn long and go viral on social media sites for a week, until her and Webb's tandem "effective immediately" retirements.

Would that explain why Equifax didn't have a real incident response plan in place when they discovered the breach? Was the apparent dysfunction in the company's C-suite and poor communication attributed to Equifax's inability to respond in an effective and timely manner? And why did it take Equifax two full days after the discovery of the breach to hire the security firm Mandiant?[38]

Why didn't CEO Richard Smith warn company executives against dumping stocks before the data breach went public, allowing yet another failure of quality assurance—insider trading stories—to leak out?

Why did it take the corporation so long to make the theft of customers' records—their credit scores being the lifeblood of the debt-driven economy—public?

Perhaps worse than the above flaws and lack of a security response plan was the reason for the breach itself.

In early February 2020, the US Department of Justice announced the indictments of four Chinese People Liberation Army (PLA) military intelligence officers who carried out the network penetration and theft of millions of records from Equifax.[39]

Such definitive attribution of state actors is a game changer in

37 A. Lee Judge, "An Embarrassing LinkedIn Profile Moment for Equifax," LinkedIn.com, September 18, 2017, https://www.linkedin.com/pulse/ embarrassing-linkedin-profile-moment-equifax-a-lee-judge/.

38 Zack Whittaker, "Security Firm Mandiant Said To Be Helping Equifax in Hack Aftermath," ZDNet, September 8, 2017, https://www.zdnet.com/article/ security-firm-mandiant-said-to-be-helping-equifax-in-hack-aftermath/.

39 Brian Barrett, "How 4 Chinese Hackers Allegedly Took Down Equifax," Wired.com, February 10, 2020, https://www.wired.com/story/equifax-hack-china/.

US-China relations and a warning to all executives and boards of directors that there are heavyweights with unlimited resources and manpower coming after them, their firms' customer records, and their corporate IP and crown jewels.

Pillar Analysis

The most egregious failure in terms of the 5 Pillars of Security Framework comes down to two simple facts. No patch management meant that no internal information security policy was in place—a clear breach of fiduciary duty. This was an auditing and oversight failure—in other words, human and not technology.

And the C-suite was not prepared for a data breach. No incident response plan. No fire drill when a breach occurs. That explains why Equifax executives reacted in a helter-skelter manner postbreach. It explains why all the key internal corporate players and external advisors and consultants could not respond in a timely, efficient manner and execute the company's response to the hack. Either they didn't have an incident response plan or didn't know how to use it.

Studying the digital debris field of the Equifax data breach, one can surmise from the government reports alone that the company broke at least two key tenets of the 5 Pillars: data security and crisis management. In both incidents, Equifax was rated an F for failure.

Of the 5 Pillars, Equifax broke (2) people security, (3) information security, and (5) crisis management. A deeper look at the detailed government reports from the US Senate, the 115th Congress, and the Government Accounting Office (GAO) would likely show that Equifax broke a few tenets of (3) data security too.

Using the 5 Pillars of Security Framework, it becomes easy to see how and why Equifax turned into a mega breach. It would also reveal to the new executives what entrenched issues—personality conflicts, lack of oversight and management, and failure of information security—existed and how to address each one of the flaws to prevent such failures from recurring.

Had the C-level executives and board members of both Capital One and Equifax used the key principles of the 5 Pillars of Security Framework, they would have, at bare minimum, reduced the severity of the data breaches and been able to manage the crises in a more proactive and effective way.

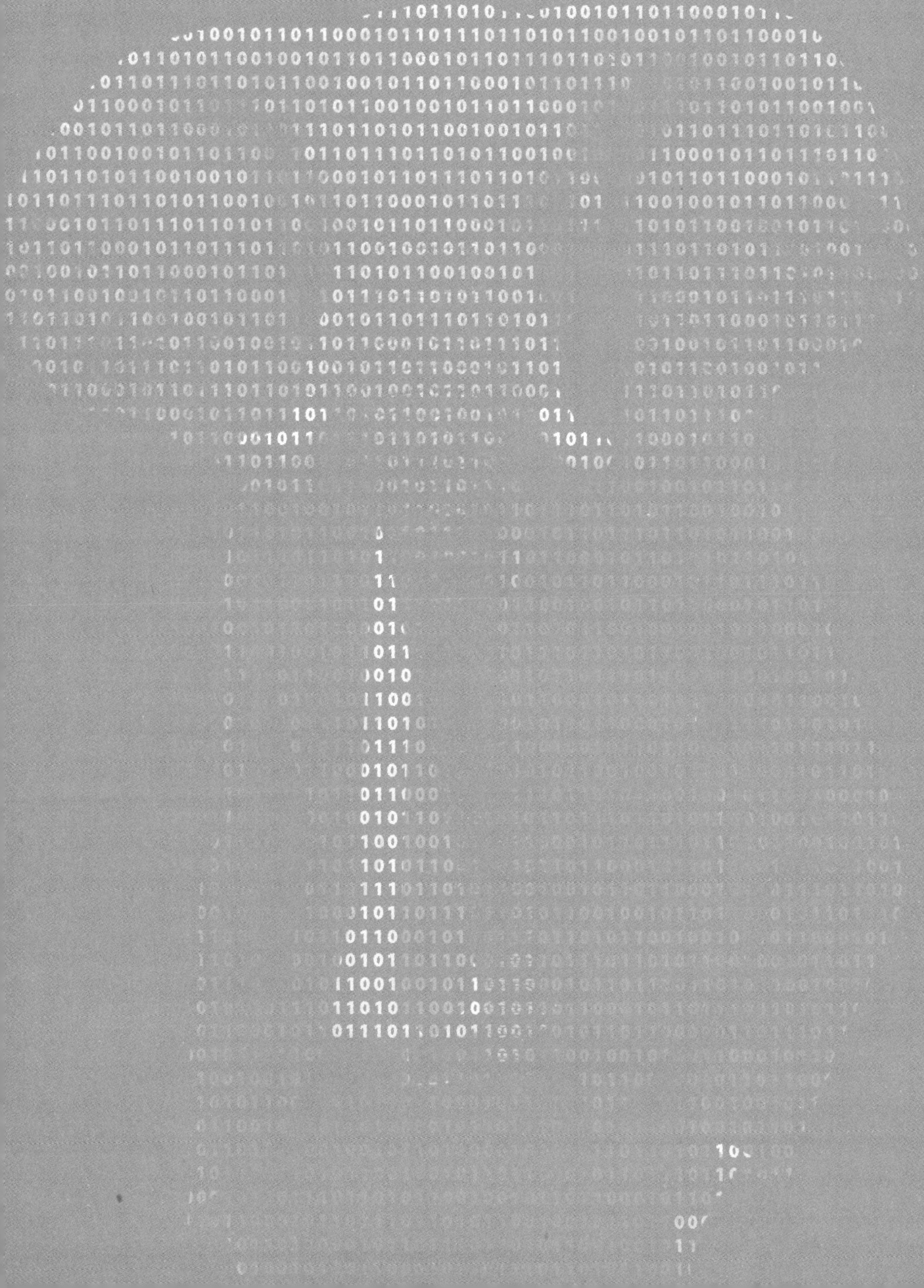

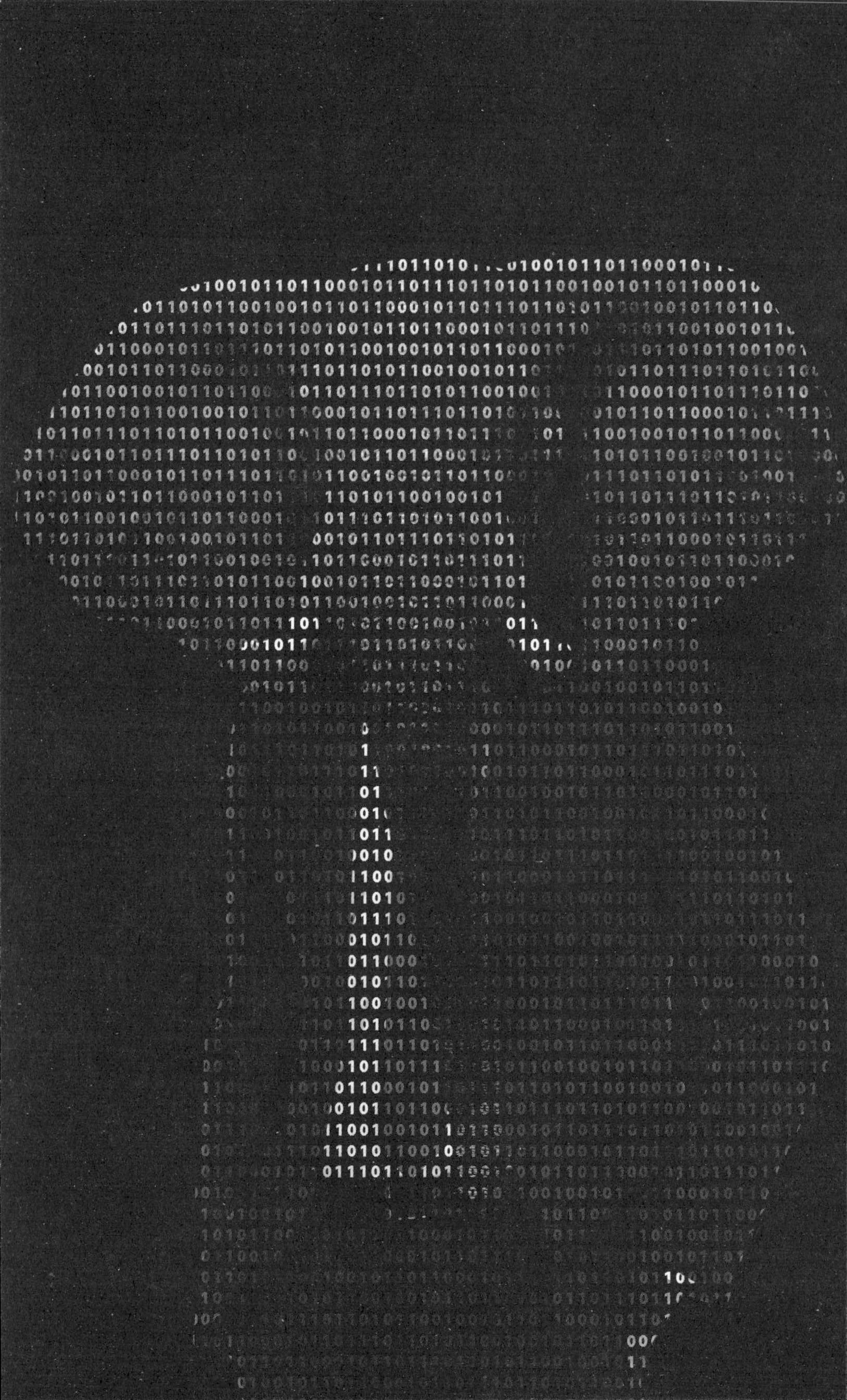

GUEST CHAPTERS
CHAPTERS 7–15

In order to increase the value add of the 5 Pillars of Security Framework, I asked some eminent cybersecurity, data protection, and information governance experts to address specific areas that CEOs, CXOs, and boards are often challenged with and that have significant impacts on the cybersecurity and compliance postures of their respective enterprises and/or industries.

The guest chapters cover the following topics:

- Protecting data as the new currency

- Cybersecurity in the context of business digitization

- Addressing cybersecurity from an investor's mindset to provide a cybersecurity handbook to decision makers

- Linking cybersecurity risk with financial metrics

- Impact of cyber risk on the board and education process

- Cybersecurity impact of software and impact on the board

- Complying with PCI DSS and keeping credit card holder data—CXO perspective

- Cybersecurity risk in Human Resources

- Educating key decision makers through security and compliance certifications

All are linked to the 5 Pillars of Security Framework and demonstrate the value of having buy-in from CEOs, CXOs, and boards for good security and continuous compliance.

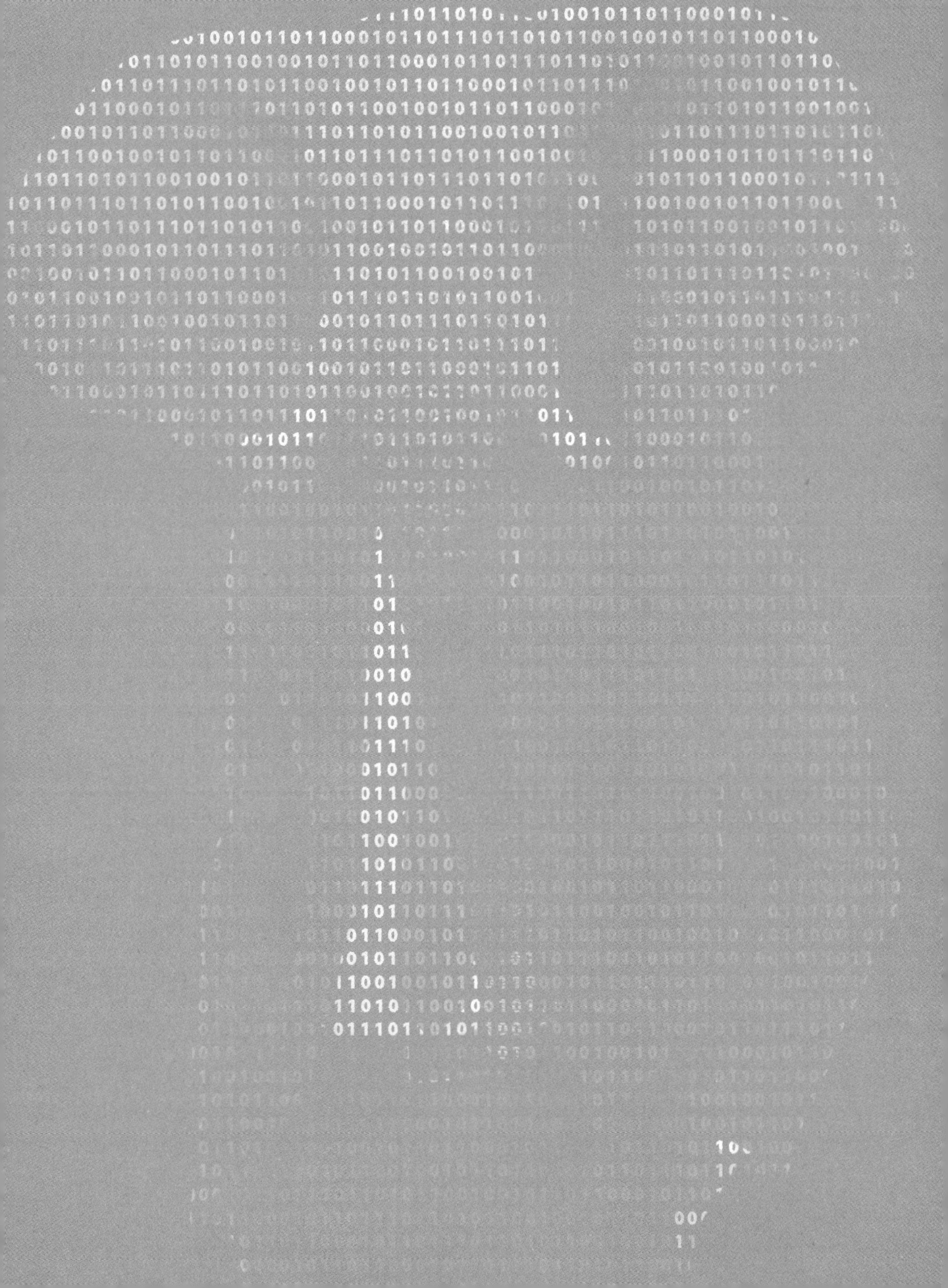

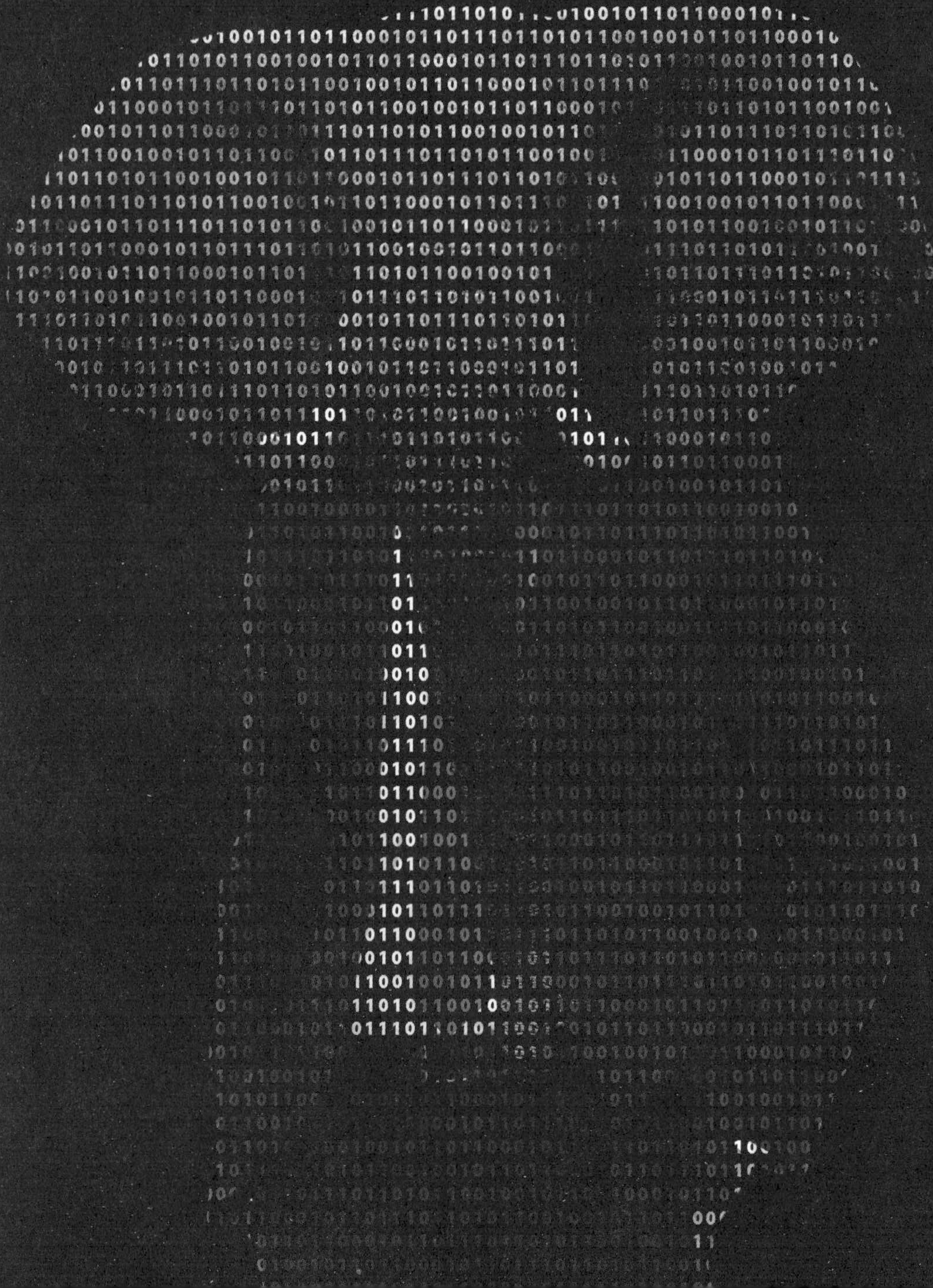

CHAPTER 7

PROTECTING DATA AS THE NEW CURRENCY

BY NINA SHULEPINA

"The threat of cybersecurity may very well be the biggest threat to the US financial system."[40]

—Jamie Dimon, in his 2019 letter to shareholders

I was introduced to Nina through the advisory board. As a regular attendee over the last few years, Nina raised cybersecurity and compliance challenges related to the banking industry, her area of expertise. She believes that in industries with a highly distributed infrastructure and workforce, hybrid teams of subject matter expertise are the key to crisis management.

---

40   Jamie Dimon, "Chairman & CEO Letter to Shareholders," JPMorgan Chase & Co., April 4, 2019, https://reports.jpmorganchase.com/investor-relations/2018/ar-ceo-letters.htm?a=1.

This concept is often discussed at the advisory board and thoroughly addressed within the 5 Pillars of Security Framework.

Nina outlines the evolution of cybersecurity in banking as well as compliance paradigms facing the industry today. A must-read road map for cybersecurity strategies in the finance sector!

The finance sector, along with insurance companies, is the most targeted industry for cyberattacks, experiencing more security incidents than energy, healthcare, and education combined.[41] JPMorgan spends nearly $600 million per year on preventing cybersecurity breaches and extends over three thousand employees to protect the bank and customer data.[42] They are not alone. In 2018, Wells Fargo prioritized operational and compliance risk and made tremendous investments in cybersecurity, infrastructure, people, and technology.[43] By 2021, cybercrime, its prevention, and its detection have captured the attention of both regulators and market participants.

Banks hold an immense amount of personal data. First, the financial assets: bank accounts and life savings, 401(k)s, mortgages and retirement accounts, college funds, investments, and stocks. Second, the personal data: social security numbers, past and present

---

41 IBM, "X-Force Threat Intelligence Index 2019," 2019, https://www.securindex.com/downloads/8b9f94c46a70c60b229b04609c07acff.pdf.

42 Dimon, "Chairman & CEO Letter to Shareholders."

43 Elizabeth A. Duke, "Letter from Chair of the Board," Wells Fargo, February 15, 2019, https://www08.wellsfargomedia.com/assets/pdf/about/investor-relations/annual-reports/2018-annual-report.pdf.

addresses, dates of birth, business affiliates, and beneficiaries. And last but not least, the spending life cycle: a credit or debit card will feature restaurants visited, vacations purchased, and the furniture decorating your home. In light of nearly real-time charges, access to a retail account is akin to placing a GPS in the boot of a car.

The sensitivity around this data is long established, but attention to cybersecurity has been an evolution, not a revolution. In the early 2000s, cybersecurity was an operational risk problem left for risk managers and IT professionals to solve. The Dodd-Frank Wall Street Reform and Consumer Protection Act (better known as "Dodd-Frank") hardly addressed cybersecurity at the time when it was signed into law in 2010. The regulation is designed to protect consumers from poor financial practices and is widely regarded as the most important piece of regulation since the Patriot Act.[44] Despite flavors of it seeping through in provisions addressing operational risk and business continuity, no prescriptive guidelines were developed specifically for cyber risk.

The 2012 presidential debates addressed Dodd-Frank endlessly, *twelve* times in the first presidential debate[45] and in increasing numbers thereafter—a priority topic in response to the 2008 recession. Cybersecurity, on the other hand, was mentioned exactly *zero* times. But fast-forward just four years to 2016, and "cybersecurity," "cyberattacks," and "cyber warfare" were mentioned eleven times at the same presidential debate[46]—receiving nearly as much spotlight as

---

44 A comprehensive redirection of financial reform, Dodd-Frank is also considered the most substantial law in finance since the Stegall Act was signed into law after the 1929 stock market crash.

45 "Transcript of the First Presidential Debate," *New York Times*, October 3, 2012, https://www.nytimes.com/2012/10/03/us/politics/transcript-of-the-first-presidential-debate-in-denver.html.

46 "Transcript of the First Presidential Debate," *New York Times*, September 27, 2016, https://www.nytimes.com/2016/09/27/us/politics/transcript-debate.html.

Dodd-Frank received in the years following the bailouts. If political campaigns are any indication of the public's interest, cybersecurity has finally earned its place front and center.

Threats of being a victim of a malicious actor on the internet have broad implications in a complex modern society. Meeting a romantic partner online surpassed any other method by 2013.[47] An average Netflix subscriber watches over 1.5 hours of online streaming *each day* compared to the five times per year a moviegoer visits the cinema.[48] Grocery shopping, therapist appointments, and even baby monitors are accessed remotely and routinely via an application on a smartphone. More often than not, these transactions require a credit card and a matching online profile.

This chapter provides an overview of banking's evolution in addressing cyber risk—in particular, the evolving landscape and industry responses in managing cyber risk across (1) people security, (2) data security, (3) physical security, (4) infrastructure security, and (5) crisis management.

References to both Dodd-Frank and cyber mentioned at both debates include mentions by the moderators, as well as the candidates.

47   Michael Rosenfeld, Reuben J. Thomas, and Sonia Hausen, "Disintermediating Your Friends: Online Dating in the United States Displaces Other Ways of Meeting," *The Proceedings of the National Academy of Sciences* 116, no. 36 (July 2019), https://web.stanford.edu/~mrosenfe/Rosenfeld_et_al_Disintermediating_Friends.pdf.

48   Victor Luckerson, "This is How Much Netflix We're All Watching Every Day," *Time*, January 19, 2016, https://time.com/4186137/netflix-hours-per-day/; Adam Rowe, "Last Year, Americans Averaged Nearly Twice As Many Trips To The Library As To The Movie Theater," *Forbes*, January 25, 2020, https://www.forbes.com/sites/adamrowe1/2020/01/25/last-year-americans-averaged-nearly-twice-as-many-trips-to-the-library-than-to-the-movie-theater/#6b95b5302a28.

PEOPLE SECURITY

According to one IBM report, more than 95 percent of investigated incidents credit "human error" as a contributing factor to a security event. That includes easy-to-guess passwords, lost devices, and phishing. IBM later reported that inadvertent activity—for example, users clicking on a link or opening a bad attachment—made up one-third of security events in 2017.[49]

Banks routinely update security awareness trainings, policies, and FAQs to educate employees and customers against common pitfalls, but hackers find new and creative ways to bait people into illegitimate links. Fake websites and email addresses are cheap, easy, and quick. A short text message or email indicating that a large sum of money was withdrawn from a popular bank may be enough to get a few clicks by customers wanting more information.

Human error is heightened across organizations employing tens of thousands of employees or serving tens of thousands of customers, like most banks. In addition to employees and consumers, security risks must account for contract staff, temporary staff, third-party vendors, and visitors. Ongoing monitoring and cross-business testing functions may help to mitigate some of the risks associated with human error.

As companies battle hackers in the race toward the newest vulnerability, people security is monumental to avoid compromising data, infrastructure, or even the physical security of an organization.

---

49 "IBM X-Force Report: Fewer Records Breached In 2017 As Cybercriminals Focused On Ransomware And Destructive Attacks," IBM, April 4, 2018, https://newsroom. ibm.com/2018-04-04-IBM-X-Force-Report-Fewer-Records-Breached-In-2017-As-Cybercriminals-Focused-On-Ransomware-And-Destructive-Attacks.

DATA SECURITY

Over the last ten years, cash has gone from king to pauper. As the amount of personal information and customer assets held online reaches new heights, so does the need for data protection. Mobile apps have supplemented (and in some cases replaced) in-person banking, allowing individuals to access bank accounts at any hour from anywhere in the world. It is typical to sit on a train next to a passenger paying her mortgage or transferring funds to a savings account. Moreover, while mobile banking affords a slew of customer protections,[50] it introduces new risks. These developments, along with cryptocurrencies, make financial data more vulnerable to attacks and more attractive to bad actors.

Data security is contingent on software that is well equipped to protect companies against attacks. Technology's rapid evolution, however, creates consistent challenges for developers. To build a defense against the unknown requires long-term visualization and hybrid approaches to still hedge against predictable vulnerabilities. IT software professionals and management must be trained in the latest malware, ready-to-use botnets, and exploitable security settings, among other developing trends. Cryptocurrencies and blockchain systems introduce additional threats to financial networks.

In addition to staying on top of technological developments, rules and regulations governing data protection lag behind the technological change. Data processing and retention practices are evolving faster than the law can adapt to them.[51] As of late 2020, there is no single uniform data protection law in the United States. The Gramm Leach

---

50   Many bank and credit card companies assume liability in fraudulent cases and recoup the customer for any losses incurred.

51   John Burn-Murdoch, "Data Protection Law is in Danger of Lagging Behind Technological Change," *The Guardian*, April 12, 2013, https://www.theguardian.com/news/datablog/2013/apr/12/data-protection-law-lagging-behind-technology.

Bliley Act governs the financial services sector's use of nonpublic personal information.[52] The Federal Trade Commission Act grants broad authority to the Federal Trade Commission (FTC) to enforce protections against unfair or deceptive practices, including federal privacy and data protection rules.[53] States have enacted their own legislation: New York, for example, adopted minimum standards for financial institutions, along with requirements for risk assessments and annual compliance certifications.[54]

The Securities Exchange Commission (SEC) incorporates cybersecurity considerations in its supervisory and disclosure programs in its critical market technology infrastructure framework and oversight of regulated entities. Cyber risk is policed under existing supervision, data protection,[55] and disclosure laws. The SEC and Commodity Futures Trading Commission (CFTC) routinely issue statements, guidelines, and interpretive notices outlining their expectations for banks.

To complicate matters further, most lawyers and IT professionals have a fundamental "lost in translation" problem that takes time, money, effort, and hybrids of professionals to decipher. In a rapidly escalating cyber incident, time is of the essence. A well-rehearsed crisis management team—made up of experts ranging from legal to tech, both internal and external—should be established long before a real-life scenario ever hits a server.

---

52   15 U.S. Code § 6802.

53   15 U.S. Code § 41.

54   23 NYCRR 500.

55   In 2016, the SEC brought an action against Morgan Stanley under Regulation S-P, which requires financial firms to adopt policies and procedures that are reasonably designed to protect customer data.

CRISIS MANAGEMENT

In 2017, the SEC announced that it fell victim to a cyberattack.[56] Edgar, the SEC's filing system used by financial institutions to make the required filings, experienced a breach. The vulnerability resulted in potential access to nonpublic information. The SEC retains company information that is not available to the public and, occasionally, even investors. By gaining access to certain filings, the hackers may trade on material nonpublic information, giving rise to a new recipe for insider trading.[57]

In a press statement, SEC chairman Jay Clayton acknowledged

I recognize that even the most diligent cybersecurity efforts will not address all cyber risks that enterprises face. That stark reality makes adequate disclosure no less important. Malicious attacks and intrusion efforts are continuous and evolving, and in certain cases, they have been successful at the most robust institutions and at the SEC itself. Cybersecurity efforts must include, in addition to assessment, prevention, and mitigation, resilience and recovery.

In this sentiment, the regulators recognize that cybersecurity compliance is less of a destination and more of a journey. The most diligent actors may be unable to design an impenetrable cybersecurity defense framework, but they can be well prepared for the aftermath of an attack.

---

56 Jay Clayton, "Statement on Cybersecurity," U.S. Securities and Exchange Commission, September 20, 2017, https://www.sec.gov/news/public-statement/statement-clayton-2017-09-20.

57 Alexandra Stevenson and Carolos Tejada, "S.E.C. Says It Was a Victim of Computer Hacking Last Year," *New York Times*, September 20, 2017, https://www.nytimes.com/2017/09/20/business/sec-hacking-attack.html.

The construction of a crisis management response will vary across industries but nearly always include a hybrid of ready experts to assess the incident and decide on appropriate disclosures to clients, customers, and counterparties. The right response may be the difference between a paper cut and an internal hemorrhage: it will contain the losses incurred and mitigate the threat of regulatory enforcement. While absolute prevention of cybercrime may be out of reach, an effective plan of crisis management allows senior executives to exercise control over the firm's security in advance of an incident.

> *The right response may be the difference between a paper cut and an internal hemorrhage: it will contain the losses incurred and mitigate the threat of regulatory enforcement.*

INFRASTRUCTURE SECURITY

Infrastructure security refers to the intangible assets of an organization, including networks, remote sites, applications, websites, and the intranet. For banks, this may include personal employee information subject to General Data Protection Regulation (GDPR), material nonpublic information stored on local shared drives, or sensitive regulatory inquiries and internal investigations. Infrastructure data may not be as appealing or vulnerable as customer data with bank accounts and credit cards, but it poses an equally threatening headline risk and enforcement action.

In 2014, JPMorgan Chase experienced one of the largest cyberattacks in banking history. Hackers successfully accessed names, emails, and postal addresses of about eighty-three million accounts—affecting customers who use the bank's web and mobile services:

Chase.com, JPMorganOnline, Chase Mobile, and JPMorgan Mobile.

The attack against JPMorgan Chase may have stemmed from an employee's stolen login credentials, most likely from a spear-phishing attack. It was widely reported that the hackers were successful in accessing customer information because one server lacked a two-factor authentication scheme for access, leaving the infrastructure vulnerable to intrusion.[58] Other banks and financial institutions were targets of similar attacks by the same group of hackers, but those organizations were either unaffected or experienced minor breaches because they did not have the same design flaw.[59]

In addressing the incident, JPMorgan Chase organized a business control group that included a dozen technology and cybersecurity executives who met regularly to assess the damage and prevent future breaches.[60] As a result, JPMorgan Chase felt confident in the hackers' limited reach—notably, there was no known access to financial or account information—and did not urge customers to change passwords or require security monitoring.

PHYSICAL SECURITY

Physical security measures at banks are older than passwords. Security guards, turnstiles, and access keys provide a layer of defense against malicious actors. On my way to work, I routinely encounter several physical barriers to access. First, the security guards in front of the building, nodding and waving hello to familiar faces. Second, a fingerprint-activated turnstile to enter the lobby of the main building. Third, an access lock activated by my personal identification card to

---

58   Matthew Goldstein et al., "Neglected Server Provided Entry for JPMorgan Hackers," *The New York Times*, December 22, 2014, https://dealbook.nytimes.com/2014/12/22/entry-point-of-jpmorgan-data-breach-is-identified/.

59   Ibid.

60   Ibid.

enter the floor. These measures generally prevent uninvited persons from gaining access, but not always.

In the twenty-first century, bank robberies are still alive and well in the United States. The FBI reported over three thousand robberies in 2018, mostly in branch offices.[61] More than two-thirds of these incidents activated alarm systems, and nearly all had surveillance cameras. Banks have evolved tremendously in protecting their assets and the safety of employees. "Bait money" is bills that are logged and tracked by serial number, and occasionally even GPS encoded. Stacks of cash with dye packs are routinely handed over to unsuspecting robbers. The packs are activated seconds after the robbery, releasing aerosol and tear gas, destroying the cash and marking the robbers with a bright stain. Video cameras and motion sensors have also improved, allowing for clear images and precise detection during or after the crime.

The average bank heist garners about $6,500.[62] The average data breach costs $3.92 million, or roughly $148 per record.[63] Luckily, the ski mask–wearing, getaway car–hopping bank robbers are not looking to infiltrate the bank's system. Bank heists simply do not pay—cybercrime does.

---

61   "Bank Crime Statistics 2018," FBI.gov, accessed October 5, 2020, https://www. fbi.gov/file-repository/bank-crime-statistics-2018.pdf/view. The FBI's report does not include cybercrimes or technology-assisted crimes like ATM skimming or identity fraud.

62   Justin Jouvenal, "A Quintessentially American Crime Declines: Robbing Banks Doesn't Pay As It Used To," *The Washington Post*, October 6, 2016, https://www. washingtonpost.com/local/public-safety/a-quintessentially-american-crime-on-the-decline--robbing-banks-doesnt-pay-as-it-used-to/2016/09/29/4f54a0a6-e7e9 -437c-b484-151a337b0e0a_story.html.

63   The numbers reported for an average data breach vary greatly. These are IBM's estimates for 2019, in its cost of a data breach report: https://www.ibm.com/ security/data-breach.

CONCLUSION

People expect banks to be safe. In order to thrive, financial companies invest a great deal into security and compliance to hold on to hard-earned customer confidence. Yet, nothing valuable can ever be completely secure. Understanding and appreciating the risks associated with cybercrimes is the first step in demystifying the landscape.

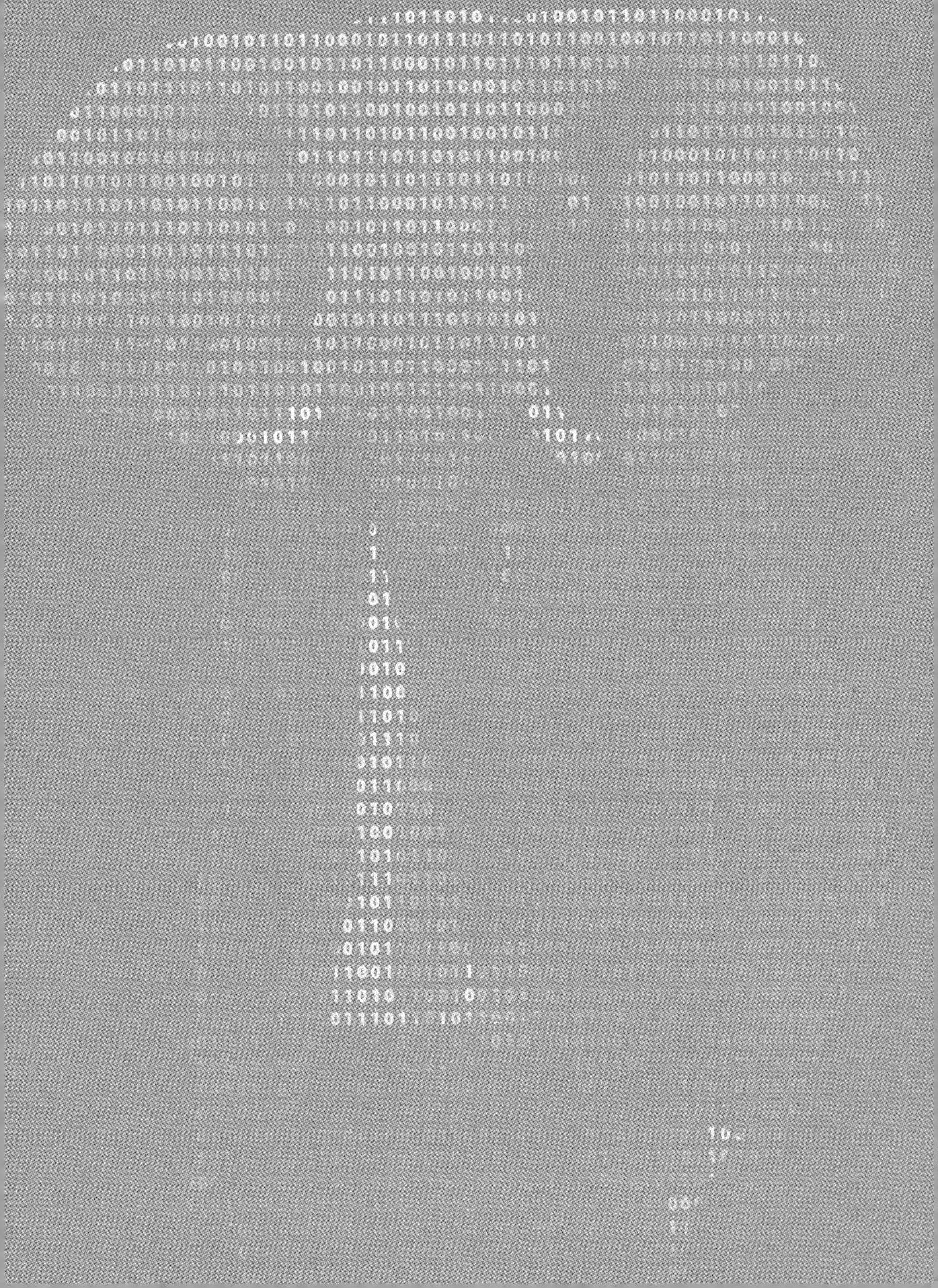

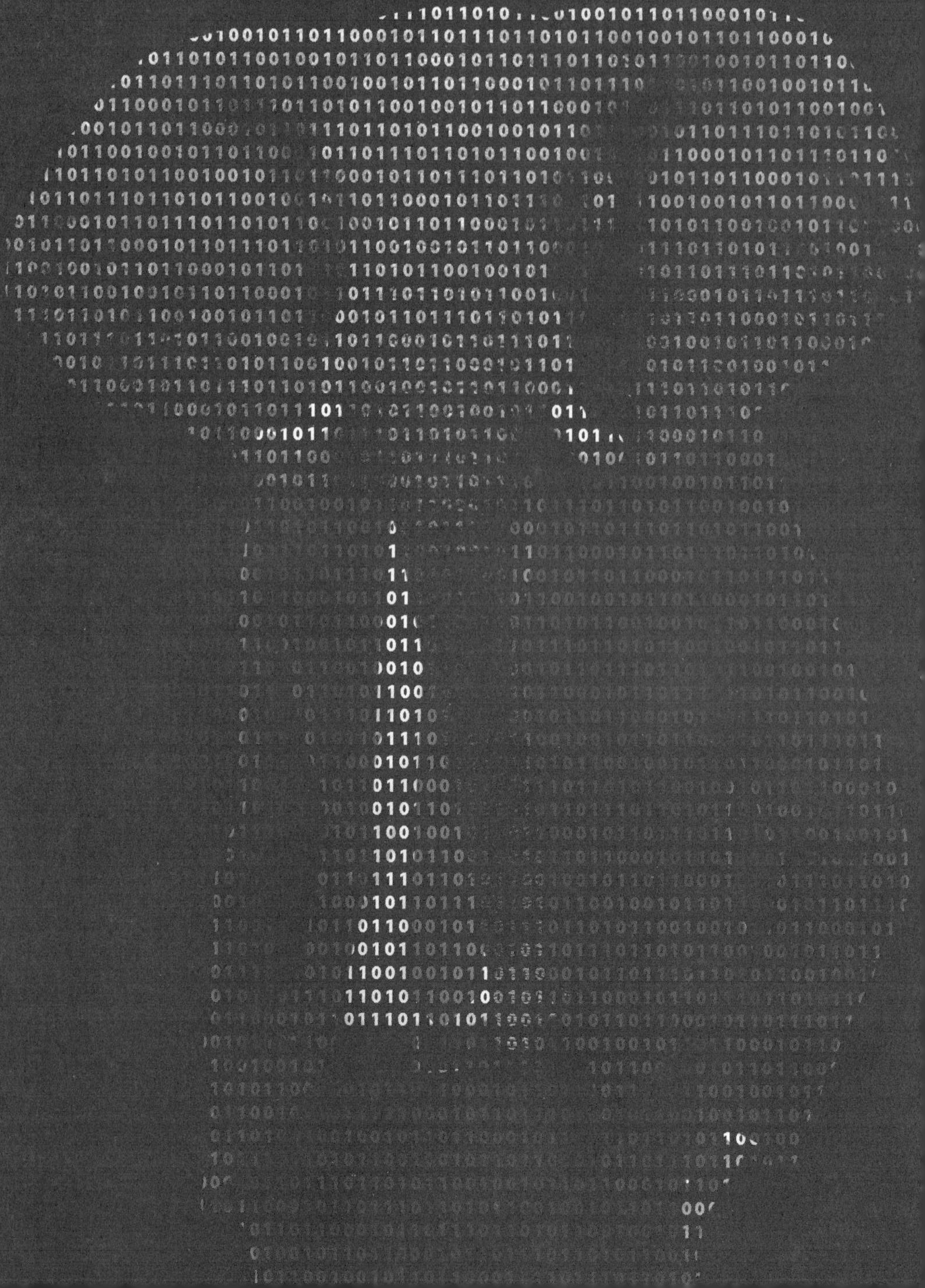

CHAPTER 8

THE INTERSECTION OF CYBERSECURITY AND BUSINESS DIGITIZATION

BY CATHY C. SMITH

Cathy Smith and I met through the VigiTrust advisory board in 2016. I was immediately taken by the way Cathy helps bring together the challenges brought by the intersection of digital transformation and cybersecurity. Her chapter covers what key decision makers need to understand about digital transformation projects and what cybersecurity risks such projects bring about. A must-read for those embarking on or in the midst of a major digitization projects ... if they want to remain cybersecure!

Cathy references all 5 Pillars of Security, focusing primarily on data security, people security, and infrastructure security.

Are you wondering how to usher your organization into the digital age? Halt your thought process for a moment. That cybersecurity is given organization-wide attention in response to a cyberattack, and not before, continues to be a pain point for businesses and corporations. Yet the Achilles' heel of protecting data marches on, as if the C-suite wore blinders without adapting to the details of new data breaches that occur each week.

> *That cybersecurity is given organization-wide attention in response to a cyberattack, and not before, continues to be a pain point for businesses and corporations.*

THE AGE-OLD PAIN OF PROTECTING INFORMATION

Outdated legacy systems on the brink of losing technical support, mounds of paper files stored in a warehouse for years incurring astronomical costs, and back-office operations with 1990s manual processes are signs of an organization ripe for new digital technologies.

All sectors are trading traditional business models for digital strategies to improve the customer experience, generate digital revenues, and diversify digital products and services at the speed of light. The rules of engagement have changed for private, nonprofit, and governmental sectors worldwide, where expectations from customers, suppliers, and partners have drastically changed. Traditional organizations can no longer afford to respond slowly, deliver mediocre products, and provide poor customer service. Amazon, Apple, Facebook, Google, and Alibaba have ramped up expectations globally on how platforms distribute products the same or next day and offer frictionless customer experiences.

Consumers can select from an array of communication preferences (i.e., chat, text, alert, social media, email, or scheduled phone call back) to engage with a firm on mobile devices, apps, or digital platforms and receive an answer in seconds, not days. Technology disruptors in the marketplace have created a gap between what organizations are capable of delivering based on their obsolete infrastructure and what digital customers expect.

Long gone are the days when organizations devoted substantial resources to compile a strategic plan over an extensive period; instead, they are developing a digital strategy to preclude disruption. Leaders are mobilizing teams to transform existing business models to generate untapped digital revenues for various timelines (i.e., one to three months, six to nine months, and one to ten years) simultaneously to see immediate results.

Global, national, and local establishments across industries should start thinking like a technology company or find themselves following in the footsteps of Borders Group (bookstore), Blockbuster, Inc. (movie rental); SYMS, Filene's Basement (clothing); Eastman Kodak, and Polaroid Corporation (photography) and going out of business. The dinosaur asteroid didn't hit these businesses; the inability of their executives and advisors to adapt to and anticipate change did. And change in the digital age continues to pick up pace.

Lagging innovation emerged as the key indicator for those struggling companies failing to keep up with customer expectations.

The good news is, sectors undergoing digital transformation are making every attempt to catch up with digitally mature companies by digitizing every aspect of an organization to stay competitive and provide value in the digital economy while identifying new revenue streams, often around data.

Building mobile capabilities, moving applications to the cloud, and outsourcing functions to technology vendors are new ways of operating for private, public, and nonprofit sectors. Going paperless and adopting robotics process automation, artificial intelligence, social media, big data, cloud computing, voice recognition, blockchain, and biometrics are keys to this digital transformation.

According to the McKinsey Global Institute May 2019 report, "Large economic potential is linked to digitization—and much of it yet to be captured."[64]

The return on investment (ROI) becomes exponential when comparing fast-moving, successful technology companies with proven digital business models, digital workforces, and digital revenues to long-established entities. This offers an incentive for all sectors to press forward even when the failure rate to manage an organization-wide digital transformation is high.

Granted, digitization is occurring in businesses, nonprofits, healthcare organizations, and governmental agencies at a rapid pace. But how many incorporate security risk management into a well-designed framework and digital strategy? The answer is very few.

It's essential to not only secure assets but also be aware of the risks that may impact an organization for several reasons. On a given day, leaders may operate a workplace filled with a blended workforce consisting of employees, consultants, contingent workers, freelancers, and offshore workers to fill the digital talent gap necessary to transition into the digital age at record speed. This diverse mixture is prone to human error, inappropriate computer usage, and making company confidential information visible. Some entities are con-

---

64   "Twenty-Five Years of Digitization: Ten Insights into How to Play It Right," McKinsey Global Institute, May 2019, https://www.mckinsey.com/~/media/mckinsey/business%20functions/mckinsey%20digital/our%20insights/twenty-five%20years%20of%20digitization%20ten%20insights%20into%20how%20to%20play%20it%20right/mgi-briefing-note-twenty-five-years-of-digitization-may-2019.ashx.

ducting mergers and acquisitions to expand market share, digital offerings, and expanded services through integration, which may pose security risks. It's challenging to ensure that an organization's most valuable digital assets are protected from cybercriminals; the same can be said of mapping the data perimeter.

Recognizing the need for digitization isn't enough; fast-moving methodologies are necessary to provide the structure of when, what, and how to manage organizational change. Teams form for short sprint engagements to execute digital transformation very quickly. Although embarking on these changes is strategic for any organization, imminent risks are associated with moving too fast. Incorporating security measures early on to mitigate the risks associated with hiring contingent digital workers using flawed methodologies or safeguarding against technology integration disasters is key to successful digitization.

> *It's challenging to ensure that an organization's most valuable digital assets are protected from cyber-criminals; the same can be said of mapping the data perimeter.*

How can leaders be sure that their organization's assets are secure during the planning stages of a digital transformation?

PREVENTION VERSUS RESPONSIVENESS

Leaders of organizations of all sizes need a defensive mindset when they embark on a digital transformation. It's crucial to include a security professional on the change initiative team at the very beginning. As technology strategies are developed to reduce costs, create efficiencies, and build digital capabilities, it's prudent to have a security risk management component while planning is underway.

A security professional can ask pertinent questions to a potential technology vendor and provide valuable input up front. Waiting to onboard a security professional after implementing a software application or outsourcing services is too late. Measures to safeguard the organization are often an afterthought and may place the company at higher risk.

Recently, a prominent government official asked why it was necessary to develop awareness about cybersecurity. This author conveyed to him that it's a risk management concern if an agency's data is handled carelessly. As a change agent, it's difficult to ask the right questions and understand the answers, but not doing so opens the door for cybercriminals to wreak havoc on an agency's network. Being clueless about the need for a security risk management strategy is "risky business."

Why is cybersecurity an essential component to a business digital transformation or change initiative?

With the prevalence of data breaches occurring in record numbers at major corporations with astronomical fines assessed by regulatory agencies, there is little debate why cybersecurity is on everyone's radar nowadays. Media coverage of the most recent data leaks and ransomware episodes will indicate how important it is to safeguard customers' personally identifiable information. A digital business transformation entails a significant change in how employees work, how data is converted from paper to digital, how legacy systems are being replaced, how applications are moving to a cloud environment, and how organizations are participating at record numbers in the digital economy.

Let's think about the digital customer who uses multiple devices (i.e., smartphones, tablets, laptops, and desktop computers) to conduct purchases online, pay bills, and communicate with governmental entities. Organizations are jumping on the digital bandwagon to stay competitive in a world of internet portals, mobile apps, voice recognition services, and subscription services.

Digital transformation activities within an organization can be risky undertakings, especially if no one is managing the risks that teams encounter in selecting and implementing new technologies. Being unable to go through the vetting process with a technology vendor properly can pose significant risk to the organization. Just imagine a company not having adequate cybersecurity insurance to safeguard its most precious asset, data.

Today's companies are requiring technology vendors to purchase cybersecurity insurance to protect data and avoid data breaches. This requirement can be a significant line item; however, without adequate coverage, an organization may be at risk for a substantial fine that can cause it to go out of business.

Preventing data breaches is top of mind for today's business leaders. Changing a business environment from traditional to digital requires layers of safety precautions. Implementing new technologies and securing vendors that use subcontractors without knowing where data is being shared, exchanged, or handled—the data perimeter—can easily set a company up for a huge data breach from which they may not be able to recover financially, in reputation, or in customer trust. Companies that go the extra mile to safeguard and protect customer data will be most likely to stay in business for the long term and use it as a competitive advantage.

Cybersecurity and data privacy are like two peas in a pod: by blending cybersecurity and data privacy into one "thing," regulators have determined that it's no longer possible to have one without the other.

My own experiences of working within the area of digitization bear this out; on most projects, no matter what technology is being developed or implemented, I have had to address the issue of security and data.

IS THE CLOUD REALLY SECURE?

With more and more software solution providers offering cloud storage as a benefit since it empowers collaboration, always-on access to data and files, and remote working, more and more data is being stored in the cloud rather than on servers. While many companies and individuals trust the cloud implicitly—that is, they don't question it from a security and privacy perspective—security experts often recommend that companies at every level hire a data security consultant to carry out independent audits and due diligence on the cloud platform in question to ensure that the data stored is 100 percent secure.

What are the key pitfalls when engaging in a digitization process? And why is cybersecurity one area of focus?

Digitization, an excellent paradigm shift, is not without risk, because with a greater digital footprint comes a greater risk surface to attack. More apps, cloud deployment, users, and data invariably increase the pressure and open exposure on cybersecurity systems, which in turn increase the risk of cracks appearing in systems tested to their max.

Another critical area to be aware of is the impact of new regulations. For example, the California Consumer Privacy Act (CCPA), which became effective in January 2020, enhances privacy rights and consumer protection for residents of California. Other US states will surely follow suit, though the regulations may differ.

The equivalent of the CCPA in Europe is the General Data

Protection Regulation (GDPR); this EU-enshrined regulation aims primarily to give back control to individuals over their data, providing a lot more power to the consumer than ever before—making businesses think differently about how they market and engage their audience.

WHAT ARE THE KEY STRATEGIES AND PRINCIPLES OF SUCCESSFUL DIGITIZATION/ DIGITAL TRANSFORMATION? DT OR DX?

1. Leadership—Who's leading the firm, band, flock, pack, troupe, herd?

As with any business transformation project or process, leadership is required to embrace a "digital first" mindset; when leaders demonstrate a commitment to the digitization process, the rest of the team welcomes the knowledge and opportunity that comes from digital technologies.

2. Change Management Model— What approach will you use?

Change management involves dealing with people, processes, and culture. It is not something that can be done by one person, but rather it is a process that requires you to encourage everyone within the organization to come on the journey. That said, change happens over time: one cannot introduce new technology and expect immediate adoption. Change may bring resistance, fear, suspicion, and even sabotage, so it needs to be implemented and managed well.

3. Capabilities—Do you have what it takes?

Every organization needs to assess its capabilities when it comes to the digitization process: while larger companies may have the resources to develop bespoke solutions in-house, others will have to partner with existing vendors and adopt third-party systems.

4. Governance—Who's minding the store?

Regardless of budget, industry type, or systems in place, every business must comply with current regulation in relation to governance; however, this is not just a box-checking exercise or developing (and living out) a policy around corporate social responsibility and contributing positively to the community and environment in which you operate. It involves oversight of tools, processes, systems, policies, procedures, governance board/body, regulations (GDPR), industry, and data privacy.

5. Security—Data protection by design

The final principle of digitization—*security*—is critical to the success of any business and refers to data, facilities, and infrastructure. Ensuring the security of physical systems, as well as confidential data, is no longer optional for any business; compromising on these can result in substantial reputational damage.

WHAT ARE THE KEY PITFALLS?

If cybersecurity and data privacy are not a priority, the fallout can be catastrophic and can result in one or all of these: cyberattacks, data breaches, data vulnerabilities, regulation fines, reputational damage, and ransomware attacks.

Here are six best practices to make sure a digitization project is implemented securely from a cyber perspective:

1. Involve certified data protection and cybersecurity professionals as early as possible in the project.

2. Evaluate vendors, subcontractors, and third-party providers within their facilities and their solutions.

3. Ensure that all cybersecurity and data privacy issues have been addressed, and subsequently educate and reassure the organization's leaders that this is the case.

4. Provide ongoing training for employees to keep them abreast of threats and potential attacks.

5. Ensure all new technologies implemented by the company are included in the existing cybersecurity and data privacy program and updated regularly.

6. Request a cybersecurity insurance policy from the tech vendor.

WHAT DOES THE FUTURE OF DIGITIZATION LOOK LIKE?

Companies that operate in a secure environment—and demonstrate a willingness to go beyond the required legal regulatory requirements—will be the winners when it comes to attracting new customers, as well as retaining existing ones.

The reason is simple: people and businesses want to know that their accounts, data, and reputation are protected at all times; any security breach that violates trust will ensure that customers move to a different provider who can give them the peace of mind they need.

The future of digitization will be an ongoing undertaking for businesses due to ever-evolving technologies. Regardless of technology advancements, security will always need to be at the forefront of change to safeguard the data of individuals.

THE INCREASING IMPACT OF WOMEN ON THIS INDUSTRY

As with all areas of the ICT and tech sector, women are highly under-represented within the cybersecurity industry. But this is a perfect moment to increase their numbers as part of the ongoing evolution of businesses.

Just as cybersecurity itself has, through education and awareness, become widely recognized and accepted as a fundamental business function, the same criteria must be applied to increase the number of women—and therefore, their overall impact—working within this industry.

There is no reason why women who already have a tech background—or are perhaps already working within the tech sector—shouldn't be looking to advance their career within the fast-growing area of cybersecurity.

Just as in politics and other areas of civic life, there is a need for dedicated awareness programs to actively drive awareness of the industry and encourage women in the field.

Can it be done? Of course it can. It won't happen overnight. But taking small steps to increase awareness will gradually encourage women to consider cybersecurity as a career option—and normalize the industry from a gender balance perspective.

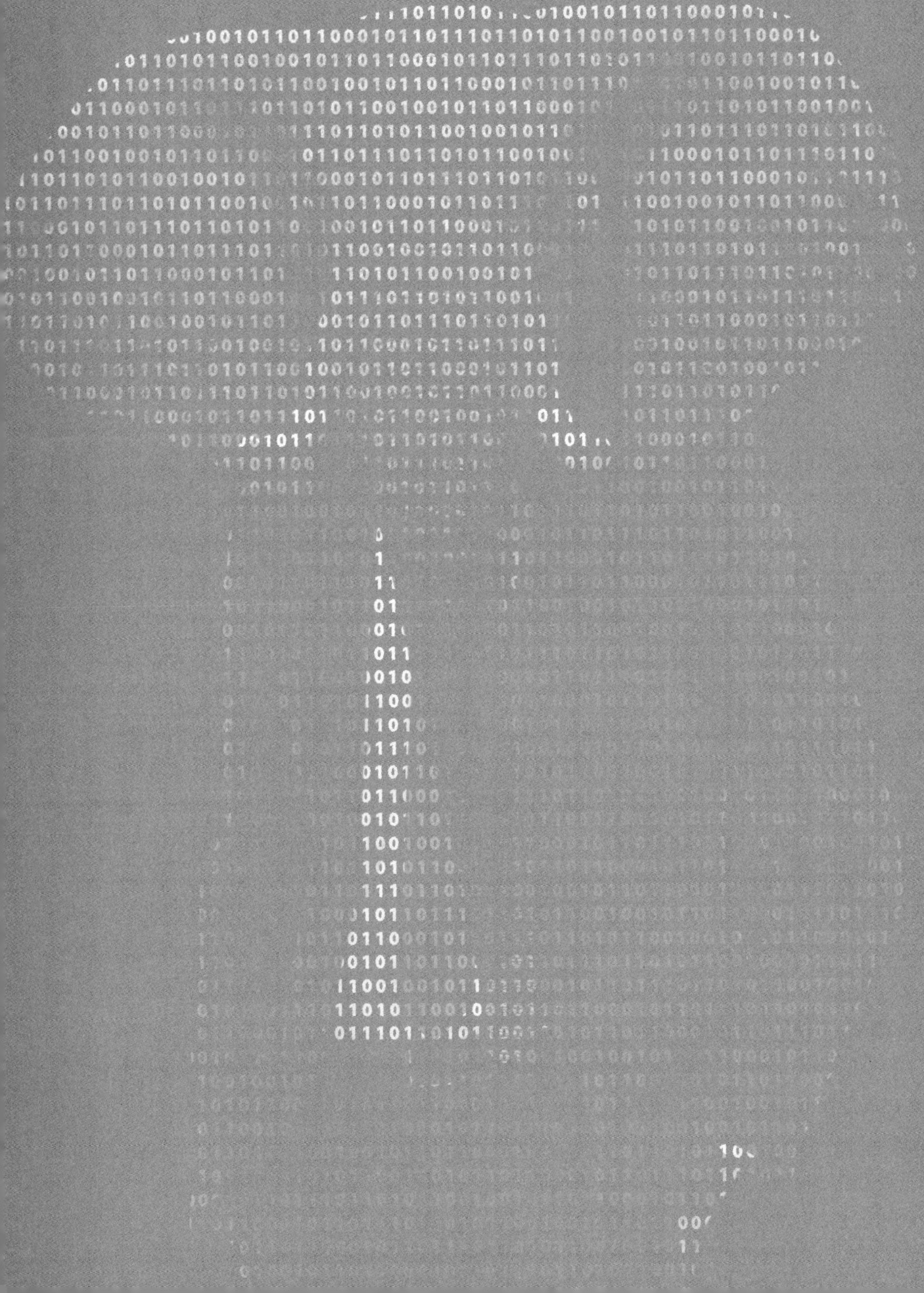

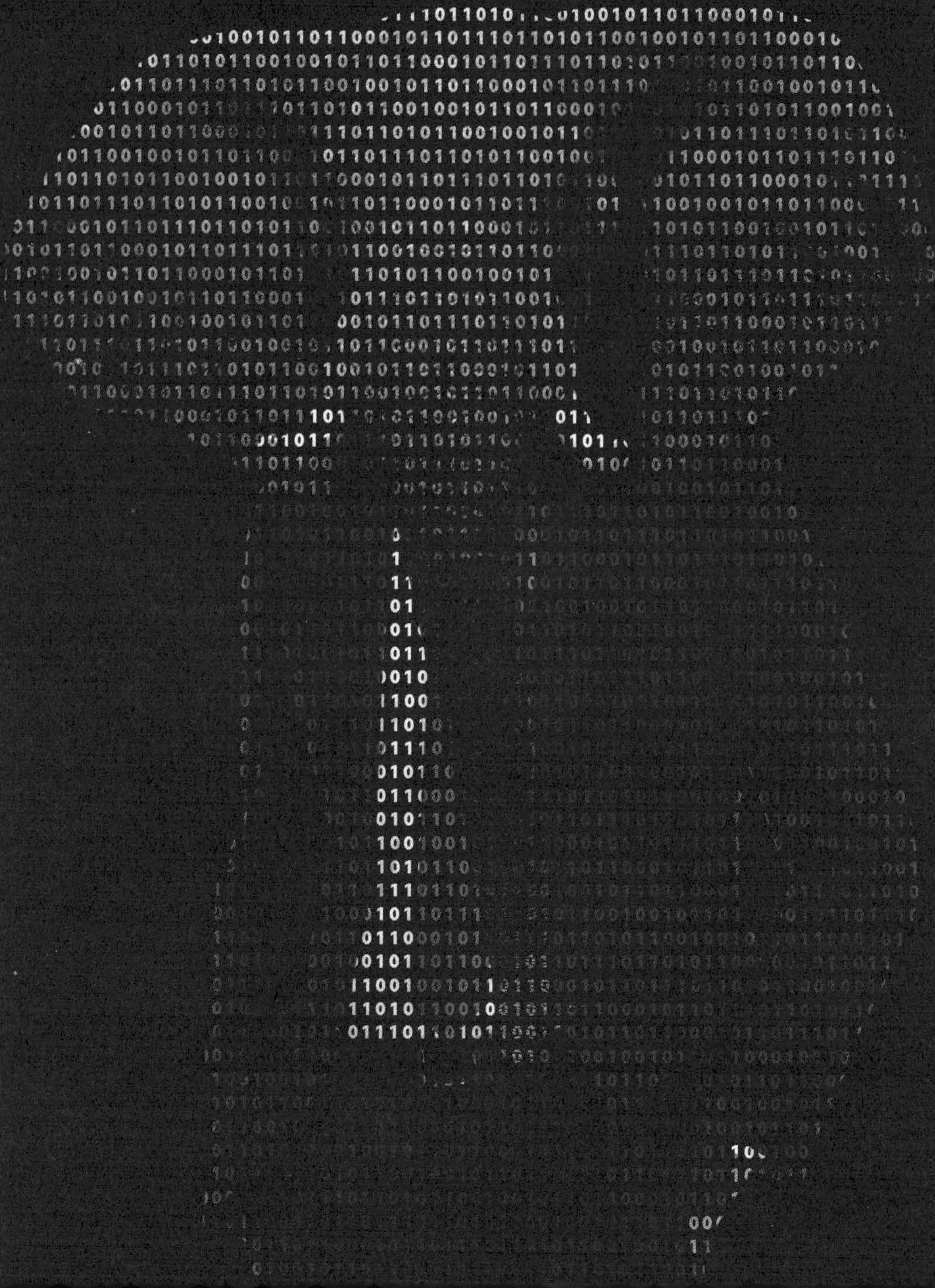

CHAPTER 9

HANDBOOK FOR C-LEVEL AND BOARD MEMBERS

BY MARCO ANTONIO SORIANO, BA, BS, MBA, CHIEF INVESTMENT OFFICER, THE SORIANO GROUP & FAMILY OFFICE

Marco is a very dynamic investor with many strings to his bows. Having met him socially through a group of very good friends in New York, I could not have imagined his depth of knowledge in the tech world, especially cyber-security, AI, and blockchain. I kept asking him what his criteria was to invest in startups and companies in those fields. His chapter explains the journey to understanding the market and making investment decisions to help build great cyber-related companies. Lots to learn here!

Marco references data security, people security, and crisis management, as well as some items related to infrastructure security.

One of the first questions global investors should ask these days, particularly in the tech sector, is this: Is cybersecurity about more than protection?

Clearly the better question would relate to all the issues that would arise from a data breach. In the real world, companies work like orchestras. Either they are in harmony, working off the same sheet of music, or they have gaps in sound and weaknesses in melody.

Like an arms race, the evolution of technology's advancement has been met by cyber risks showing up across all global business platforms. Hence, any organization that regards itself as safe from cyberattacks is likely to be in for a shock.

Business objectives have shifted in the digital age, particularly in the era of mobility and data analytics. With "data being the new oil," per *The Economist* in a 2017 article, the criteria the executive suite in most organizations need to focus on are protecting the enterprise with good cyber-hygiene and basic lines of defense. Most importantly, they need to optimize a response to an incident with more advanced tools and strategies. As digital transformation proceeds worldwide, cybersecurity must be an enabling function rather than a block to change and innovation.

> *As digital transformation proceeds worldwide, cybersecurity must be an enabling function rather than a block to change and innovation.*

In 2009, post the financial crisis and the creation of Bitcoin utilizing blockchain programming, several questions emerged. I was just finishing my MBA at New York University, where none of our professors could answer critical security questions. On the street, by chance, I met Pat Condo, the former CEO of Excalibur Technologies, which was sold to the CIA. We took the conversation to the Core Club in midtown Manhattan, and he started telling me about how he started his company.

Pat mentioned that post the Patriot Act—"Uniting and Strengthening America by Providing Appropriate Tools Required to Intercept and Obstruct Terrorism" of 2001—all information was accessible to the US government. I raised one eyebrow, and my lips formed an *o*. The idea of his company post-9/11, with its ability to predict behavior prior to anyone contemplating committing a crime long before what we call today machine learning (ML) and artificial intelligence (AI), was a game changer. I realized that we have already offered so much information to the world through social media and the digitization of communications—texts, emails, transactions— that all of this was easily and readily available.

After the initial shock, the business side of my brain started clicking. I realized the world had changed—and done so profoundly in a short span of time. Our freedoms, thoughts, and private lives and actions were gifted to the government, and such information needed protection. So began my journey to seeing the importance of securing data. I started a management consulting group that year, restructuring a family office of our private patrimonies.

We rarely stop and reflect on the ramifications of all the data we are generating on a daily basis and how the evolution of protecting our information and privacy creates a new host of issues.

PREPARING FOR ADVANCED PERSISTENT THREATS (APTS)

I started to learn from my own research so I could functionally and dynamically advise my family office's operations and its affiliated partners and corporations to our investments and other clients' monies. It was hard to know where to start. One of our core tenets is to know what you are investing in beforehand, and when 99 percent of the time traditional security solutions fail to seek out and identify advanced persistent threats (APT), choosing such a solution amounts to negligence. We quickly learned the role of malware in APTs and how to best create protection policies internally. Most executives or organizations do not grasp that they are all targets, including managers, back-office staff, and personnel in sales, marketing, and across every department and business unit. Even linking up with third-party vendors or suppliers increases the cyber risk surface. And those who invest in venture financing and scale them up for an exit become a bigger target.

> *Most executives or organizations do not grasp that they are all targets, including managers, back-office staff, and personnel in sales, marketing, and across every department and business unit.*

APTs have changed the world of enterprise security and how networks and organizations are attacked. Those threats, backed by cybercriminals, often remain hidden from traditional security but exhibit unparalleled intelligence, admirable resiliency, and long-horizon patience rarely seen in business. If corporate executives want to control these threat vectors, multiple security disciplines must work together. Hence the importance of the development of blockchain today. While no single solution will solve the problem of advance threats, next-generation security provides the visibility of, control of, and true integration of threat-prevention disciplines needed to find and stop the threats—both known and unknown.

Investments are all about budgets in place to scale them up with the use of proceeds from the capital invested from these accredited investors. Very few sophisticated investors will ask the right questions. Others will only care about the net revenue line. When investors evaluate a business but don't consider security risks and data protection in the digital economy, I deem it "dumb money."

The challenge is for organizations to progress on three fronts:

- Protect the enterprise. Focus on identifying assets and building lines of defense.

- Optimize cybersecurity. Focus on stopping low-value activities, increasing efficiency, and reinvesting the funds in emerging and innovative technologies to enhance existing protection.

- Enable growth. Focus on implementing security-by-design as a key success factor for the digital transformations most organizations are going through.

We at Soriano Group highly suggest that these three imperatives be pursued simultaneously. The frequency and scale of the security breaches around the world show that too few enterprises have implemented the most basic security.

Part of my enthusiasm for this subject mirrors my past experience as an educator within the CUNY system and most recently as an executive in residence at New York University Stern Business School. I used to teach venture finance to undergrads and grad students post-MBA. I wanted to build credibility as a business owner. Like Steve Jobs, I always thought outside the box.

I gave students plenty of research I'd done in evaluating ideas and executing them, which is what an entrepreneur does before selling the offering to investors, of course. These questions add more context year to year.

Here are a few:

- What are the most valuable information assets?

- Where are the most obvious cybersecurity weaknesses?

- What are the threats we are facing?

- Who are the potential threat actors?

- Have you already been breached or compromised?

- How do your protections compare with your competition's?

- What are your regulatory responsibilities, and do you comply with them?

Estimates identify a global shortfall of about 1.8 million security professionals within the next five years. Even in the most well-resourced sectors, organizations are struggling to recruit the expertise they need. Financial services is a great example. Top graduates do not want to work in the industry. I love this part because the entrepreneurial spirit is alive and well, especially in the US.

The industry needs to spearhead concerted efforts to fill in the shortfall, and do so properly, with women and minorities. That will make diversity an imperative in any business, as diverse teams drive better results across any organization. They tend to be more innovative, objective, and collaborative, and hence, building a diverse team becomes a critical strategic move in cybersecurity, where every day is a fight to stay ahead of the attackers.

As digital transformation agendas continue to dominate innovative ideas and investment opportunities, a bigger cybersecurity budget is necessary. Almost all companies are looking at technologies such as robotics, machine learning, artificial intelligence, blockchain, and so on. But these changes will come with additional cyber risks and necessary investments. We are already experiencing that with several of our early-stage investments such as Bellhop, Simplenight,

Airstayz, and even AI-driven systems like Hanson Robotics.

Furthermore, the most vulnerable parts of a company are, without a doubt, customer data, their financial information, and the firm's strategic plans. Board-member information and customer passwords follow those closely. See table 1 for a top-ten list of valuable information as well as cyber threats.

Executives must recognize the broad nature of the threat to our investments and that what has changed since 2018 is the growing realization that security is about maintaining the continuity of business operations—and not only about the security of data and privacy.

A really smart and forward-thinking company has two budgets: a traditional budget for what we need to do and the projects we are pursuing, and a contingency budget for unexpected eventualities, such as an emergence of a new type of threat, breach, or compromise.

The cost of cybersecurity defense is staggering. According to the CSO from IDG, the expected budget for 2021 will be $6 trillion. Yet it is not possible to create a perfect defensive barrier against everyone who might want to access computer systems or mobile devices that do not belong to them.

Today's main issue with technology innovative investment in cloud computing, networks, and connected devices is that people use them. But what if we did not have to introduce people into the equation? Here are some examples of how to recognize issues with social engineering and phishing these systems:

- Renew your subscription or membership: this preys on your underlying belief that things/routines get disrupted if you do not respond and renew ASAP.

- Government record updates: you may experience a fast heartbeat when you see an email from the IRS, Social

Security, or Homeland Security asking you to provide updated information.

- The embedded link: click this link to see your account information, to learn more, or to avoid a penalty. Clicking that link most often opens malware files that unlock access to secure systems.

- Locked and suspended accounts: these phishing emails usually appear as though they are from a financial institution. One popular phishing email appears to be from PayPal (because many use it), but with sophisticated data mining, the email may appear to be from the victim's actual bank.

- Greed based: you have got a refund. Bank error in your favor. You won two tickets. These and other financial reward emails ask you to provide banking information for direct deposit, your social security number for verification, or other types of private information to release the funds to you—which, of course, never happens.

- Delivery notifications: email that appears to be from a delivery company can prompt you for further information, such as a phone number, home address, or, once again, provide an embedded link to malware.

Such cons are inevitable unless you live off the grid in the middle of nowhere. It's extremely interesting that we are fathoming artificial intelligence as we are attempting to make machines super smart. Without our keen intelligence, we would still roam as *homo habilis* or *homo erectus*, but we are *homo sapiens* as introduced by Mr. Carl Linnaeus in 1758.

One of the important goals of AI, along with the devices that assist us, is to provide answers we would never arrive at by searching our massive archives of data. Thus, AI may prove to be the largest advance in human technology since the start of the Industrial Revolution. It was once conceived of only in science fiction books and films, but AI is finally here and impacting our lives.

Most visual pattern recognition is done using supervised learning algorithms. A significant number of training images are provided for the computer to learn and be able to recognize a pattern. We have heard of pattern recognition in text data as data mining. Another example of its use is your Gmail or LinkedIn account's auto response system that makes suggestions of email or message responses based on the content in your writing.

Most pattern recognition uses a logic where answers are close enough but not exact. Even the way AI performs math calculations allows it to arrive at answers that are "close enough." Not that your computer would say this, but if you asked an AI system to add one plus one, the answer might be, "Based on other calculations I've seen, it is close enough to the value of two."

When mining data, computers are often confronted with subjective adjectives like *young* and *old*. The machine-learning algorithm must be able to handle this sort of imprecision. Machines have become smarter and more nuanced, and this comes not only with new and better software, but also advances in machine technology. Computers run significantly faster than they did thirty years ago. Advances in sensors, cameras, and microphones have given computers an improved ability to take in their surroundings. Within the innovative tech criteria we had in-house, we discovered our AI Sophia, a humanoid robot that could maintain a logical conversation with humans. Perhaps you've seen the footage, as she has become quite the celebrity in the world. We are aiming at changing the world by educating it. Its people need information in all languages, cultural awareness, and subjects like the arts, history, geography, and math. We want our elders to have someone to converse with at all times for as long as they need, because they do get lonely, and loneliness kills. We must socialize one way or another. The idea of talking to a machine goes back to 1773, when Christian Kratzenstein built the first speaking machine.

Yes, history repeats itself. In 1954, a machine was used to translate sixty Russian sentences into English using an IBM 701 mainframe computer. This success is largely seen as the beginning of modern natural language processing (NLP). While this experiment used punch cards, the goal of NLP is to have computers understand human language as it is spoken. And this is today's AI's very heart and soul. The ability to understand NLP provides two important capabilities. The first is the ability to comprehend unstructured data, such as the 2.5 million peer-reviewed papers published every year. The second is perhaps the one that the general public is most familiar with: the ability to talk to a computer and have it understand our natural language requests.

The bottom line is that all organizations must look beyond preventive measures in their security assessments. A notable risk, based on our experience, is that many organizations have still not developed a robust cyber response plan, despite increasing risk due to the digital transformation.[65]

We want to predict the future, and protecting the internet of things (IoT) is our priority. IoT devices represent a huge expansion in the number of network end points that must be considered when

---

65   "Is cybersecurity about more than protection? EY Global Information Security Survey 2018-2019," Ernst & Young Global Limited, https://assets.ey.com/content/dam/ey-sites/ey-com/en_ca/topics/advisory/ey-global-information-security-survey-2018-19.pdf.

protecting an entire network. Anything connected to the internet that is not an actual computing device, such as your Blu-ray player and television, your security camera, and your digital assistant, is an IoT device and another end point on the network. Protecting IoT devices is a layered approach. First, the IoT operating system should be hardened. This comes with good security testing during development. Second, the network to which the IoT connects must also be hardened. The last layer is always the human layer—or the first pillar in the 5 Pillars of Security Framework.

For instance, many smart TVs now include a web browser. Malicious programs downloaded to your TV can easily spread to other devices connected to the same network. On the other hand, cognitive computing assists in the investigation of cyber threats and identifies the root cause of an attack.

China has gone one step further in its attempt to battle criminal enterprise. It has begun employing AI in the attempt to predict crimes before they happen. Li Meng, vice minister of science, announced that by using AI and facial recognition to identify people, Chinese authorities can gather information on people and their activities. Using big data, the crime-fighting AI is creating a rating system to tag highly suspicious groups of people. Not even masks will fool the facial recognition system. Trying to fool the system will only make it smarter by "re-identifying" an individual. This is unlikely to happen in a country where most places won't even allow traffic cameras to catch speeders. But it certainly points out a potential use for machines growing ever more intelligent.

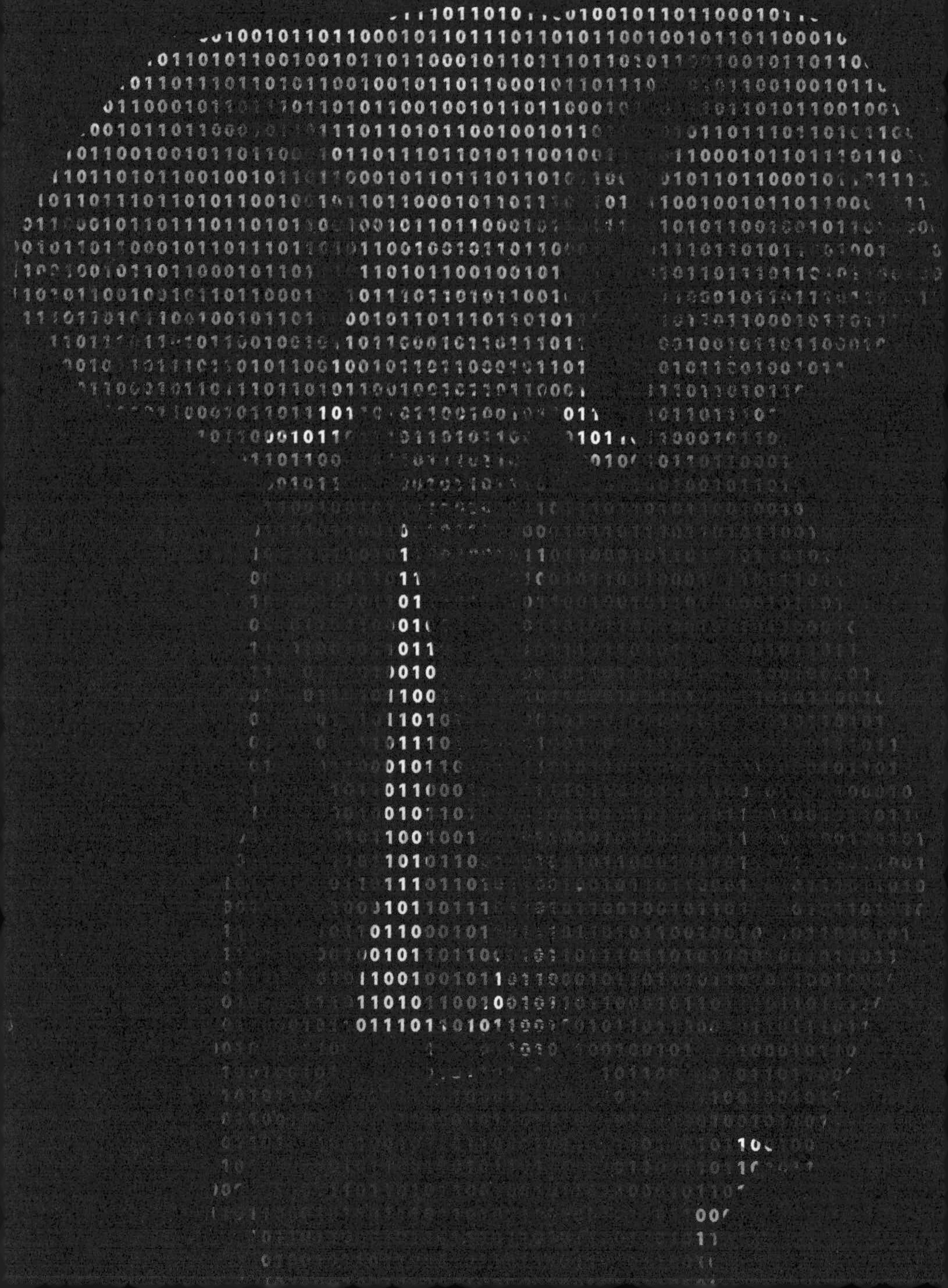

CHAPTER 10

MANAGING THE CYBER RISK IMPACT OF CAPITAL AND VALUATION

BY ROBERT K. GARDNER, PRESIDENT, NEW WORLD TECHNOLOGY PARTNERS

I have known Bob for over twelve years now. When we met, we were primarily discussing critical infrastructure protection, a topic Bob knows inside out. Little did I know that Bob was an entrepreneur and mentor. As such, his views on how to put cybersecurity on the balance sheet and as a key topic for boards always fascinated me, as this can help catapult cybersecurity into the boardroom with a proper budget and PKIs. This chapter is a must to build a strategy on how to put cyber higher on the board agenda using their financial KPIs as a tool.

Bob references people security, data security, infrastruc-

> ture security, crisis management, and, to a lesser extent, physical security.

As enterprises' cyber risk budgets approach tens and hundreds of millions of dollars annually, corporate boards need better information to justify spending such large amounts. When they cannot measure cyber risk in the same way they measure other corporate (or geopolitical) risks, they cannot integrate effective cyber risk management into their current enterprise risk management deliberations. Today's cyber assessment programs seek to measure the cost of breaches and the impact on profits, but they fall short of presenting the exposure of capital, reputation, and valuation that is vital to the interests of their shareholders. As a result, current risk assessment methods form an imprudent basis to allocate expenditures and reserves or make public disclosures required of a responsible enterprise risk management endeavor.

BEGIN BY MEASURING ENTERPRISE PARAMETERS

Public companies inform their shareholders each quarter by filing reports with the Securities Exchange Commission (SEC) known as 10-Qs and 10-Ks (supplemented by 8-Ks if and when unexpected impactful events occur). Each report contains three financial statements, a management discussion, and a summary of stock performance:

- The income statement presents the quarterly or year-to-date profit and loss picture.

- The balance sheet presents the current value of assets, liabilities, and shareholder equity.

- The cash flow statement shows the amount of cash leaving and entering the company.

Together these reports detail a company's current state of profitability, value, and ability to fund operations compared with the previous-period report. These measures are the appropriate way to present how cyber risks impact shareholder interests. However, most cyber assessments present an incomplete picture of enterprise risk.

Cybersecurity analysts often overlook important balance sheet impacts, including accounts receivable, capitalized intellectual property and software (either acquired or developed), and investments, all of which represent significant—often the most significant—elements of enterprise value. Significant financial industry regulations, such as CCAR index risk-weighted assets, from which "too big to fail" reserves must be made, may also be overlooked.

Cash risk, particularly free cash flow risk, must be included to assure solvency.

Reputation risk must be assessed for its share value/volatility and concomitant valuation impact. It may also determine workforce recruitment/retention risk and trust among partners, regulators, and the public.

Corporate boards, for this reason, must treat cybersecurity as an enterprise-wide risk management issue and direct management to present cyber-exposure information in all the financial and reputational parameters they report to their shareholders. Spe-

Corporate boards, for this reason, must treat cybersecurity as an enterprise-wide risk management issue and direct management to present cyber-exposure information in all the financial and reputational parameters they report to their shareholders.

cifically, they should report the following:

- Earnings, earning per share, or retained earnings

- Capital

- Reputation risk (separately from shareholders, clients, partners, regulators, and the public)

- Share value and volatility

- Cash flow, particularly free cash flow

QUANTIFYING THE CYBER IMPACT OF CAPITAL, VALUATION, AND REPUTATION

Unlike cyberspace in the past, where computers were used as automated filing cabinets and transaction processors, new technologies and unfettered expansion have introduced characteristics that present systemic risks and exploitable vulnerabilities, which, once triggered, cause immediate, significant, and often irreversible damage to multiple stakeholder groups and institutions.

Wireless internet access, the internet of things (IoT), and high-speed trading, among other innovations, have transformed cyberspace into a real-time system. New integrated applications have turned it into the central nervous system of the enterprise. Today's cyber-enabled critical infrastructure is a complex "system of systems" composed of thousands of interdependent nonhomogeneous components and myriad channels. Because of this, risk consequences cannot be measured by traditional cyber analysis.

A more representative model combines and concatenates analyses of adversary activity, cyber infrastructure behavior, business unit impacts, and entity consequences—a type of "enterprise risk architecture"—to determine how breaches propagate. Each stage of this comprehensive approach should measure its impact as a risk input to the next … after which remedial priorities, expenditures, and reserves may be made commensurate with enterprise exposure.

ENTERPRISE RISK ARCHITECTURE

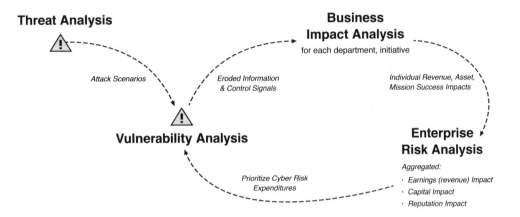

Vulnerability assessments must cover breach opportunities that erode control signals (as in IoT) and protect information assets from erosions in confidentiality, integrity, and availability (CIA).

Business units must determine their time-based cost impacts as well as their asset consequences.

An enterprise aggregation of risk-weighted income and assets for each and every individual business unit/project must be able to be analyzed in order to accurately determine income statement, balance sheet, and cash flow statement cyber risk impact, to be adjusted or footnoted as required by GAAP.

Sentiment analysis must also be performed for each major interest group (shareholders, clients, partners, regulators, and the public) in order to determine reputation as well as its impact on P/E multiples and volatility indices. From this approach, prudent disclosure policies and preparations can be determined.

INTEGRATING CYBER RISK MEASURES WITH ENTERPRISE RISK MANAGER

The COSO Framework, developed in 2004 by the Treadway Commission, is a benchmark ERM model for industry. It also underpins the federal management's own responsibility for enterprise risk management. Knowing the cyber-exposure to shareholder interests provides a yardstick from which to make COSO-based enterprise risk management decisions that determine the following:

- Risk acceptance and tolerance (often footnoted in financial statements and annual reports)

- Cyber expenditures for breach detection, protection, and incident response

- Capital reserves to protect assets and capital

- Responsible disclosures to SEC, other regulators, partners, and the press (those perpetrated upon the subject enterprise as well as one of partners or peer competitors)

ADVERSARY BEHAVIOR

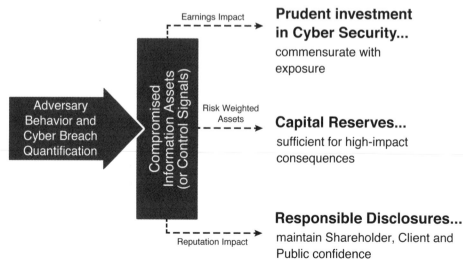

A rigorous system analysis that shows the consequence of attacks (or errors or failures) upon enterprises provides cyber risk consequence measures. These measures enable executive management to determine priorities and allocate resources commensurate with exposure—which is the calculus they apply to virtually all other enterprise risk deliberations. Combined with a program of adherence to sound regulatory and best-practice protocols, this presents the duty of care evidence required to protect the enterprise and its leaders.

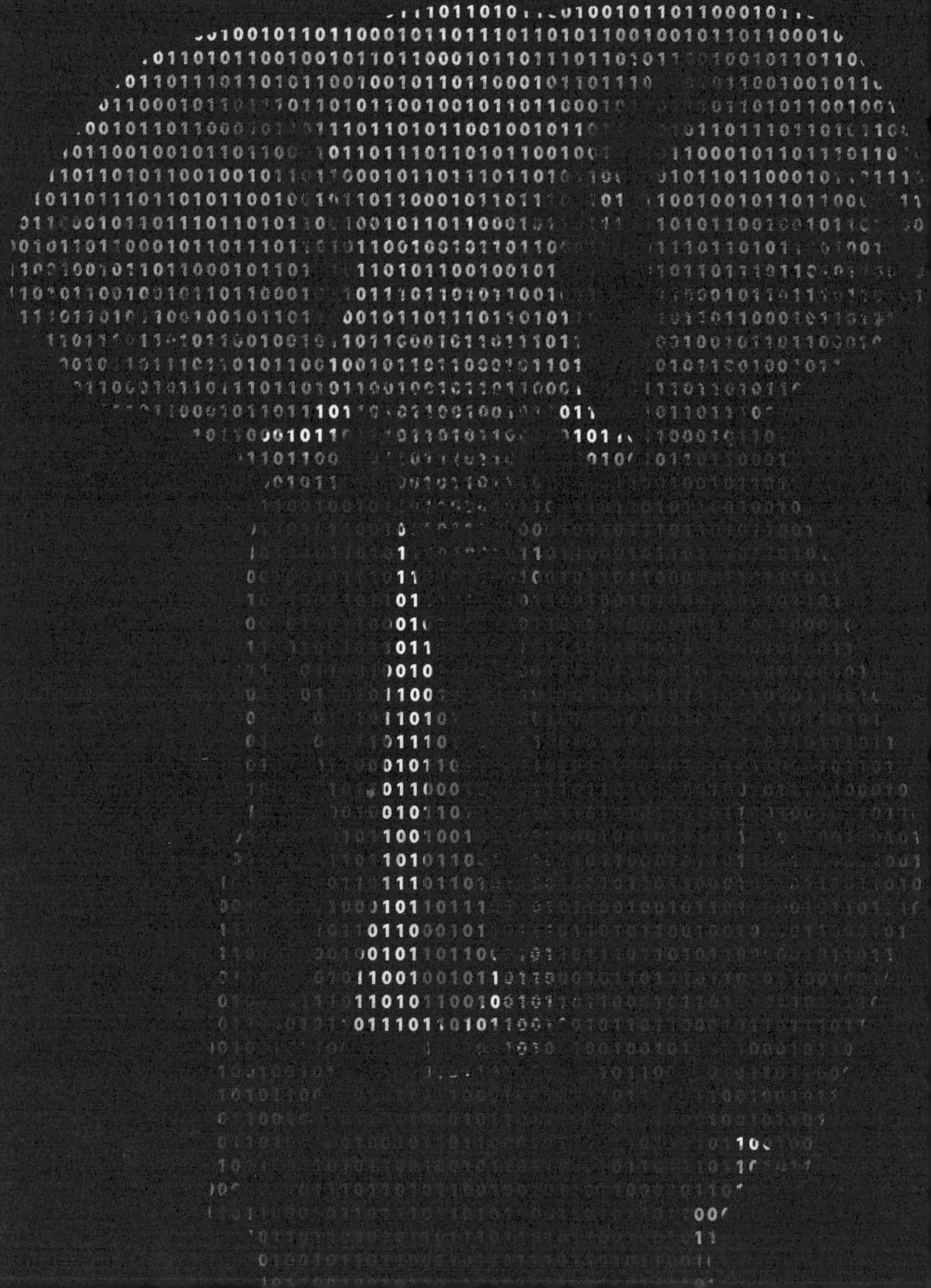

CHAPTER 11

CYBER RISK IMPACT
ON THE BOARD

BY NICK VIGIER, CXO ADVISOR, CISO, CIO AT COALFIRE

Thanks to his background as a CISO, Nick has a unique view of what happens at the board and CXO level with regard to cyber-accountability. Nick understands boards' modus operandi and priorities. He explains that very few board members have cybersecurity certifications, yet most have business degrees or MBAs. His view is that security must be a transversal enterprise function touching all business units, similar to legal and finance! By educating the board and speaking the same language as security and compliance teams can become part of the board's priorities.

Nick's chapter covers all 5 Pillars of Security and links them in plain business English to board considerations!

Security and risk management has tended, in its short history, to be an isolated discipline; at the same time, it needs visibility across the organization. This paradox usually results in security organizations that understand the business exceedingly well but have difficulty communicating their insights to the organization.

My experience indicates that the insights gained by the security team usually result in unique perspectives about the future of the company that few other teams have because a true security team has to work across the entire organization, whether that is human resources, legal, technology, or sales. Security professionals inherently combine the roles of technologist, psychologist, sociologist, and financial engineer because they have to understand the who, what, where, why, and how of the business. The breadth of visibility and the cross-functional nature of the discipline result in unique, often prophetic insights.

However, security teams often struggle to communicate those outputs effectively. Their language is usually steeped with technical jargon that is off-putting to those not well versed in such language.

> *This often deeply technical language is usually focused on negative outcomes and risks.*

This often deeply technical language is usually focused on negative outcomes and risks. Businesses would rather think about possibilities and success. The tone security teams use is often in direct juxtaposition to the goals and tone of the executive teams.

As an industry, security must identify mechanisms by which to draw in executives to the conversation and also to help them provide constructive feedback. It is essential that security leaders leverage tools and techniques that help accomplish the goals of better collaboration with executives and boards.

THE PATH PREVIOUSLY TRAVELED

Finance and legal also come to mind as being risk focused but business enabling. Remembering that others have traveled this road and ended up as strong voices within the company may help security leaders feel less isolated and unique regarding communication difficulties.

The key question is, What can we as security leaders glean from our general counsels and chief financial officers to help us achieve the same results? How have leaders in the parallel disciplines of finance and legal made their disciplines more accessible to leadership teams and their boards?

Business leaders and boards have been incentivized to learn the language of finance, as it is a common measure of business health. Everyone wants to speak the language to not only seem erudite but to have a common financial dialogue. How many on your leadership team or board have MBAs or finance backgrounds? I would guess that over half of each group have an MBA, meaning that they not only have professional experience in speaking the finance language, but they have sought out education in the area. Most security professionals do not benefit from an abundance of board and executive team members with CISSPs.

Legal leaders need to understand how to communicate true legal risk to the boards and leadership teams to make informed decisions. In the distant past, legal teams were left to clean up the messes of leaders who opted to throw caution to the wind. I would argue that in the last fifty years, legal teams have been much closer advisors to the business to find ways to enable the business while helping it find opportunities with acceptable risk profiles.

How many board members and executive teams have law degrees or legal backgrounds? Likely at least a quarter have studied some form of law. This gives them an ability to engage in that kind of thinking and have a substantive conversation around legal risk.

It is unlikely that anyone on the leadership team or board has a CISSP or security background, so security leaders need to translate the material to engage the board. And they need to make the material itself intuitive, and to frame risks in a positive light of possibilities to evoke positive emotions.

CHOOSE YOUR WORDS WISELY

One of the most important initiatives undertaken by any security leader is to learn the language of the leadership team. Different leadership teams have different core vernacular or comfort levels. The key is to find the common vocabulary and identify ways to frame information sharing in those terms.

A helpful practice in understanding the leadership team's and board's comfort levels is by listening as much as possible. Be part of meetings longer than the presentation time, or spend time with the constituents outside of meetings. Learn to understand their penchants, concerns, drivers, and so on. Use the data points gathered to contextualize the security program and risks. The more leadership and the board relate to the material, the more likely they are to engage in a meaningful fashion with the security program.

Understanding the language and vocabulary is also essential in determining an appropriate delivery mechanism for the leadership team and board. Humans are good at identifying patterns when presented in a format to which they are accustomed. Board members may be very in tune with identifying anomalies in a P&L statement to immediately start asking questions but less so for a security dashboard. Understanding the language and context may allow for better representation of important issues that help the leadership team intuitively understand the issue at hand and make rapid decisions.

TAKE THE TEMPERATURE

Now that we have context, the key is to derive meaning. Essential to any security program is an understanding of the risk appetite and perspectives of the leadership team and board. Security leaders are often trying to meet goals and objectives disconnected with the goals and concerns of the business. The best position to be in is to understand the thought process behind different leaders' risk tolerances and objectives.

A great way to obtain the insights and align through them is by asking straightforward questions that inform on the mindset of the leadership team and board. The answers will not only help determine risk tolerances but may also provide insights about where to focus educational efforts.

> *The best position to be in is to understand the thought process behind different leaders' risk tolerances and objectives.*

The 5 Pillars methodology can help. The questions are broken down by pillar and allow for a straightforward understanding of the risk tolerances and objectives of members of the leadership team. The goal of the exercise is to identify areas of concern or of no concern to the team.

Understand that there are no universally right answers to the questions. The exercise is meant to be an objective perspective about the security objectives of nonpractitioners. Fundamentally the members of the leadership team and board are the ones who will be held to account by regulators, customers, and the media. They need to express their areas of concern and areas of disinterest.

In any case, there are always situations where sentiments and approaches may be based on a lack of information or context. Using this methodology makes it possible to uncover areas of ignorance that may beget indifference. Leveraging these data points opens opportunities to target education and awareness for these individuals. Effective education can lead to the acquisition of a team champion who may understand the issues better than their peers. Such people are a key to success for any security leader.

CONCLUSION

Security needs to migrate off the desert island on which it often lives and find ways to join the leadership team on their journey. The leadership team exists because every member of it understands the business and how to drive business results. Oftentimes security leaders know the language of security but do not understand the mechanics of how a company makes money or how to positively influence business success.

By acquiring knowledge around the language of the leadership teams and boards, and understanding their intuitions and drivers, security leaders can better frame and highlight their security programs and objectives. Success and reward are more likely when goals align and a common mission is defined.

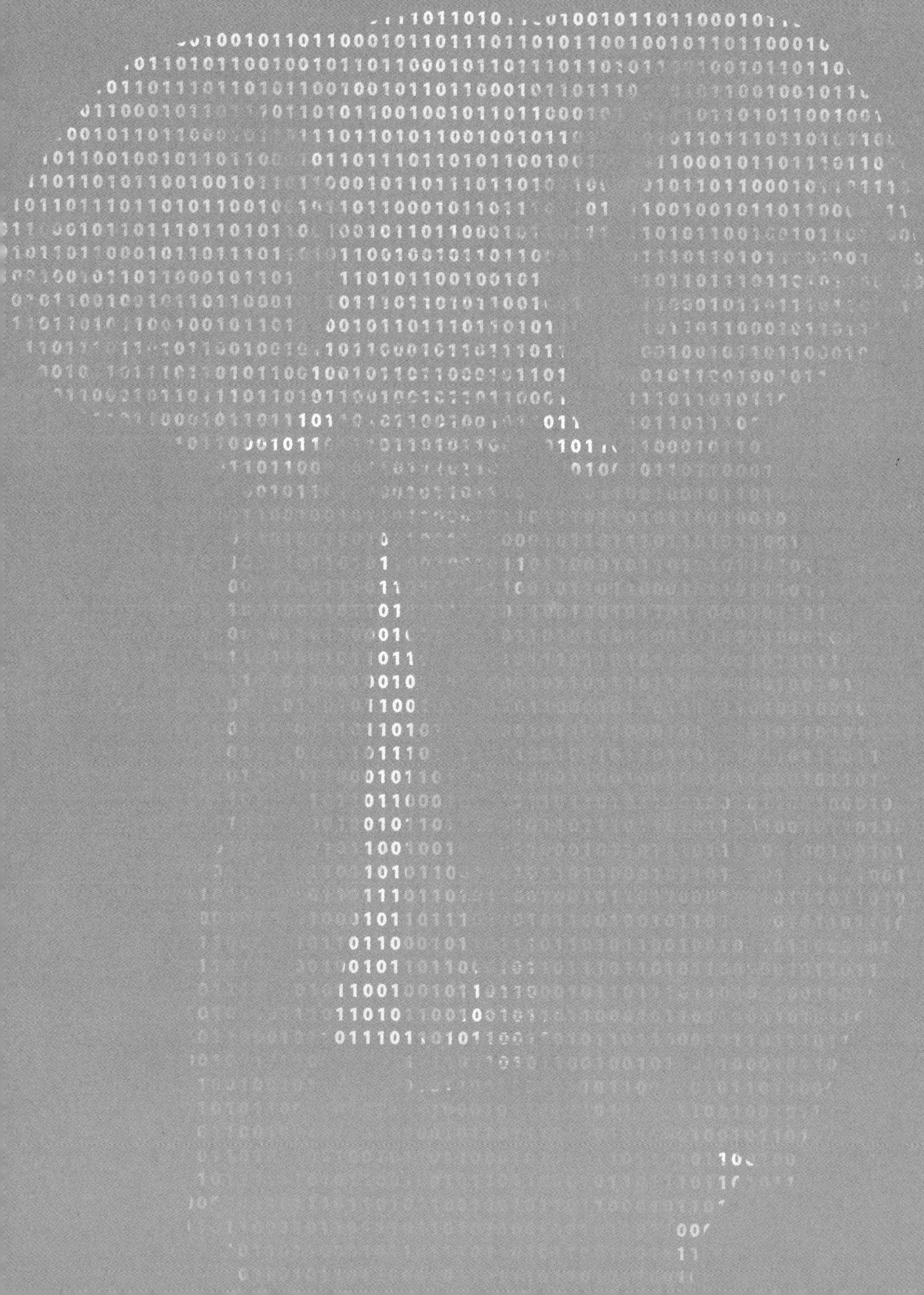

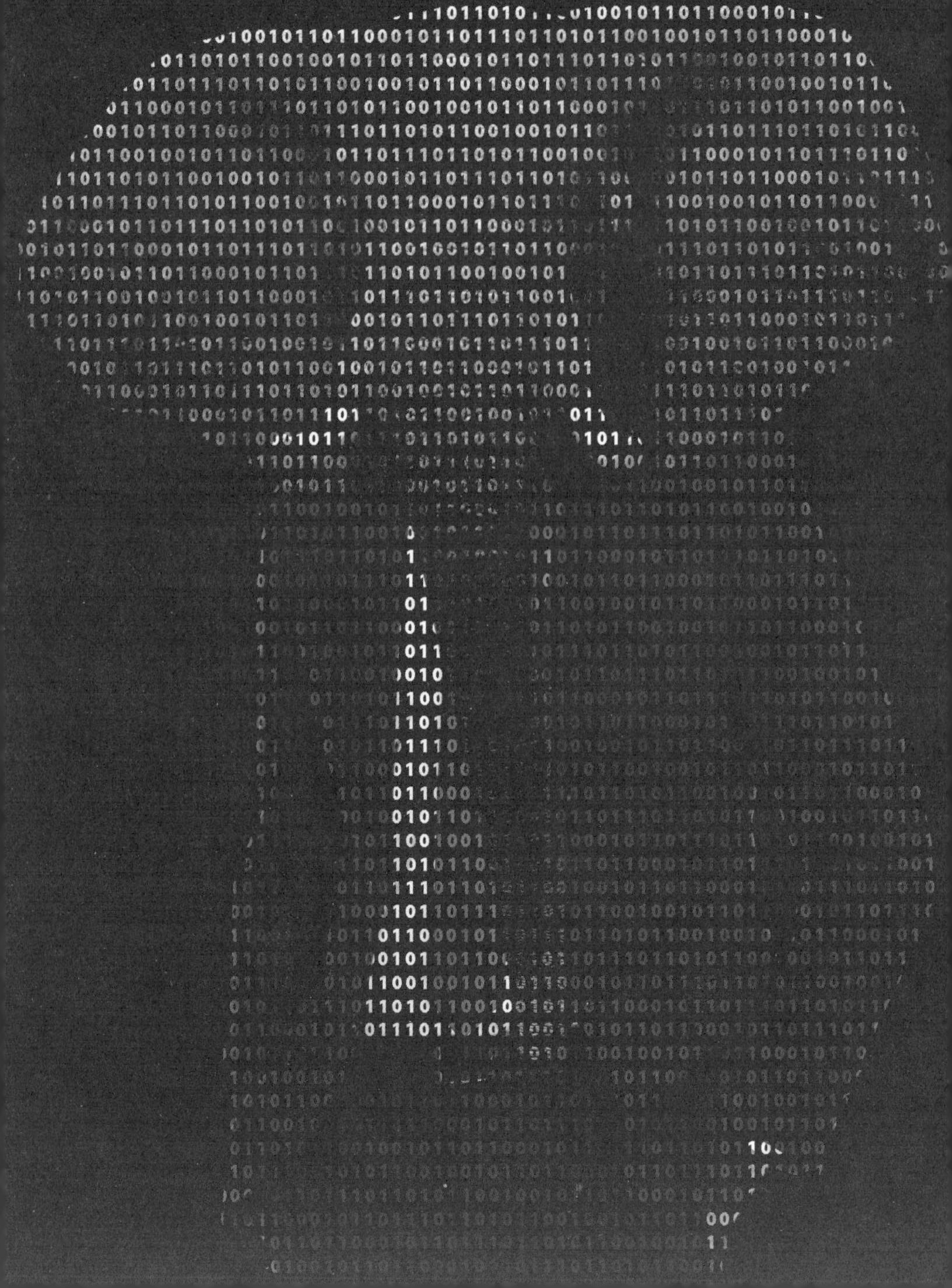

CHAPTER 12

SOFTWARE—CATALYST FOR TODAY'S DIGITAL BUSINESS

BY ED ADAMS, PRESIDENT AND CEO
OF SECURITY INNOVATION

Ed and I go back a very long way. We met at the very first PCI Community Meeting in Toronto in 2007. We immediately clicked, as we both seemed to have a similar vision on cybersecurity education, though from different viewpoints: Ed was concentrating on making enterprise software (and therefore enterprises) secure by design, while I was concentrating on making all employees at all levels up to the board more security aware. In his chapter, Ed offers a clear path toward making software design secure from the word *go* and how to keep it secure. He details a number of strategies and methodologies to make security part of any software DNA! A must-read, as it is full of industry insights.

Ed's chapter focuses on data security, people security, infrastructure security, and crisis management.

Our world is driven by software. Our phones, homes, cars, commerce, and communications all depend on it. The marvelous conveniences of our on-demand economy have also created large attack surfaces for our adversaries. An always-on, connected-everywhere world doesn't just put digital data at risk anymore; there is a lot more at stake and, therefore, a lot more to secure and protect.

The cyber/physical boundaries are quickly disappearing. If you subscribe to the theory that there is no safety without security (as I do), you'll understand why we have a dire need to get serious about software security.

By now you are familiar with the 5 Pillars of Security. How dependent is each on software today? Consider how much they interact with each other as well. You have home appliances and perhaps an alarm system. Your car has millions of lines of software code. Your office many have RFID badges for door access, digital identity management systems, and connectivity for communication devices. Your organization's infrastructure consists of many digital assets, and when something goes wrong, you communicate via email, phone, instant messages, and the like, all driven by software. Now consider how many things could go wrong if each one of those things had obvious security holes.

Leaders looking to decode cybersecurity need to understand which products, systems, and teams are putting their business at most risk so they can deploy appropriate action plans. Trying to do so without considering software risks is akin to driving a car blindfolded.

PRACTICAL RISK-BASED CYBERSECURITY

I read a lot about risk-based cybersecurity, but I don't see much practical advice on how to apply it. This chapter will endeavor to provide such practical advice with a focus on software-based system assessment and action plans.

Business requirements and concerns come in many forms, all of which need to be considered: regulatory and compliance mandates, customer and legal obligations, third-party services, supply chain dependencies, intellectual property protection, critical systems where safety may depend upon cyber/software security, and so on.

High-risk software systems require more security controls and more rigor—and organizations struggle with this calibration. The approach I recommend will assist in identifying and prioritizing the highest-risk applications through risk analysis and threat modeling. This approach enables accurate assessment of software risks and leads to the development of a customized remediation road map that will help manage the business more effectively (security engineering activities, policies and procedures, tools, training, etc.). I call the approach SToRM, for Software Total Risk Management.

SToRM

Conventional approaches to software security are not risk based, typically encompassing no more than vulnerability scanning. They frequently fail to address each application's unique vulnerabilities, whether at the level of code, system, business logic, or workflow. More importantly, they provide little practical guidance on prioritizing threat remediation or creating a road map to guide software security posture improvements.

SToRM represents a new approach—one that enables enterprises to more accurately assess software risks, prioritize them correctly, and develop a customized remediation road map that will help manage the business more effectively. The value of understanding security risks is only realized when you can decide whether to dive deeper into specific problems and where to take risk mitigation actions.

ASSET RATING AND SDLC GAP ANALYSIS

Begin with a discovery phase wherein you document critical assets—consider this a portfolio analysis, if you will. Prioritize business applications and rate them on a scale that makes sense to you (1 to 10, A to F, whatever—so long as there is a relative scale). These ratings are likely to change after the next step, but this gives you a fine starting point.

For those systems built internally, an SLDC gap analysis is a must. This can be as simple as a questionnaire whose results are compared against an acceptable standard—for example, PCI SSF and the associated Secure Software Life Cycle (Secure SLC) Requirements published at https://www.pcisecuritystandards.org/.

SDLC GAP ANALYSIS

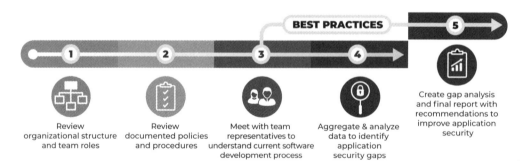

BEST PRACTICES

1. Review organizational structure and team roles

2. Review documented policies and procedures

3. Meet with team representatives to understand current software development process

4. Aggregate & analyze data to identify application security gaps

5. Create gap analysis and final report with recommendations to improve application security

This will help you quickly gather a sampling of your development team practices and determine where your biggest gaps are, benchmarking discrepancies in the development process based on product line, technology, locality, and so on. The result should be both the gap report and creation of a secure development policy.

Merely documenting a policy is not a guarantee that the policy is being followed, of course. The questionnaire should be reissued at regular intervals and validated to ensure that progress is being made toward policy adherence. Keep your change requests simply organized into those affecting people (training needs), technology (tool changes), and process (activity adjustments).

A similar questionnaire should be developed for your third-party IT system providers. This analysis, combined with your risk-ranked asset documentation, is the baseline you need to get started with SToRM.

RISK DISCOVERY AND ASSESSMENT

Risk discovery entails the review of application or systems-level technical specifications in order to understand exactly how the system in question has been designed and deployed. To ensure that the risk implications of each application are correctly assessed, start by constructing a unified view of threats and risks at both business workflow and technical system levels. Different modeling techniques can be used to ensure a 360-degree view. I prefer STRIDE, created and adopted by Microsoft in the early 2000s; however, you may find others like PASTA more to your liking. Carnegie Mellon University's Software Engineering Institute lists twelve different methods.[66]

Assessment activities should include the review and/or development of the following:

- Asset and data classification schemas

- Security classification schema for applications, which specifies classification criterion (e.g., type of data processed, internal versus external)

- Tabletop exercises to discuss additional threat vectors

---

66 Nataliya Shevchenko, "Threat Modeling: 12 Available Methods," Carnegie Mellon University, December 3, 2018, https://insights.sei.cmu.edu/sei_blog/2018/12/threat-modeling-12-available-methods.html.

- Current secure software development/SDLC security practices and controls

- Existing software application portfolio risk-rating framework considering the following:

    □ Business impacts

    □ Security threats

    □ Compliance and regulation mandates

    □ Customer requirements

    □ Operational safety and cybersecurity risk

SToRM RISK ACTIVITY MATRIX

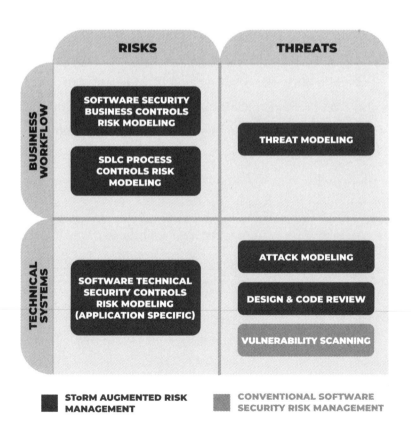

Look at each business application *and its environment* to generate a business-level threat model and as many deep threat vectors as possible:

- Identification and prioritization of high-risk applications based on business impact, security threats, compliance mandates, and operational risk.

- Recommended security assessment activities based on application and data security risk. Recommendations may range from a deep manual inspection driven by a threat model to a rapid, fully automated test.

- Risk-rating framework that will enable you to allocate security budget and resources to match the level of effort to the criticality of each application.

- Threat modeling of the application workflow, coupled with attack modeling and design/code review of the application, traces how application end users and administrators might accidentally or intentionally exploit faulty application control logic or coding errors.

- Risk modeling, incorporating Secure Software Development Life Cycle (SSDLC) and other best practices drawn from such internationally accepted standards as the NIST Cybersecurity Framework (CSF), ISO 2700x series, and PCI SSF, helps ensure that application vulnerabilities are viewed in the broader risk context of business asset valuation, regulatory compliance, and operational efficiency.

The insight gained from threat modeling may be used to determine the next steps for your application's life cycle, including deeper testing, rebuilding, replacing with another application, accepting the risks, deploying different/additional mitigation controls, or taking it out of service completely. Regardless of the outcome, you will have better insight into the following:

- Digital assets most at risk and requiring protection

- Most likely threats to those at-risk assets

- Specific malicious attacks that could be used to realize those threats

- Design and deployment conditions under which attacks would be successful

- Mitigations or additional testing that must be conducted to reduce the identified threats or prove/disprove their existence

APPLICATION REORDERING AND SECURITY TEST CALIBRATION

When threat modeling is completed, reassess the risk ranking of your applications. I find it simplest to create three tiers of application: critical, high, and medium-to-low risk. Place each application in its appropriate tier. I provide an example in the following diagram, but this exercise is highly contextual to each organization. Most likely, you're going to end up with many medium-to-low risk applications and only a handful of critical ones. The objective here is to apply your limited staff and budget appropriately.

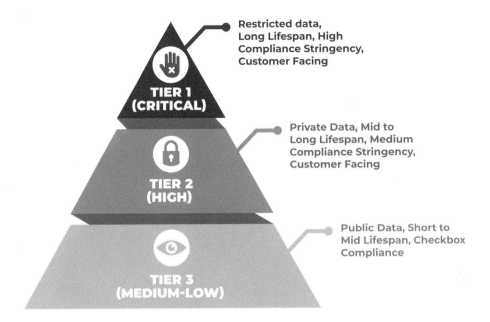

To help group applications, I've used a simple scoring system in the past and found it effective. Again, choose whatever scale makes most sense to you. In this example, I use 0 to 3, with 0 representing a low degree of risk and 3 representing the highest. I use four basic categories and assign a 0, 1, 2, or 3 based on risk. These are the categories in this example:

- Data sensitivity. Does the application store, process, or transmit sensitive information, such as intellectual property, financial records, privacy information, and so on?

- Life span. How long is the application expected to live? The longer the life, the more likely it is to be attacked and compromised, statistically speaking.

- Compliance. What legal, regulatory, or other compliance mandates is this business application expected to meet? More importantly, what is the implication should it be out of compliance?

- Customer/internet facing. This is a binary 0 or 1. I don't subscribe to the theory that internet-facing applications are riskier that internal ones, but many do.

For each application, I simply add the four numbers together to get a total. The resulting table looks something like this:

APPLICATION NAME	DATA SENSITIVITY	LIFE SPAN	COMPLIANCE	CUSTOMER/ INTERNET FACING	RISK SCORE	RISK TIER
Application 1	1	3	0	1	5	2
Application 2	3	2	2	0	7	1
Application 3	2	3	1	0	6	2
Application 4	1	1	1	0	3	3
Application 5	1	1	1	1	4	2
Application 6	2	2	1	0	5	2
Application 7	3	3	2	1	9	1
Application 8	2	3	1	0	6	2
Application 9	1	1	0	1	3	3

Let's walk through a couple of examples.

EXAMPLE 1

Application 1 helps the customer collect names and email addresses for newsletters. Data is stored in a shared database within the data center. This application was built by a third party; however, the customer owns all source code, maintenance, and rights to the application.

Data Sensitivity (1)—Full names, email addresses

Life Span (3)—No EOL set

Compliance (0)—No compliance requirements

Customer or Internet Facing (True)—Hosted on the shared virtual server within the DMZ. It accesses a shared database in the data center.

Risk Rank 5

EXAMPLE 2

Application 4 is an internal support help desk application for customer ticketing on a specific product. Customer records are stored in a central database within the data center; however, it contains only customer names and email addresses. This application was built in-house, and the product it supports will be end-of-life within the next nine to twelve months.

Data Sensitivity (1)—Full names, email addresses

Life Span (1)—EOL less than months

Compliance (1)—Minimal internal compliance requirements

Customer or Internet Facing (False)—Hosted on an internal server; is not accessible externally.

Risk Rank 3

EXAMPLE 3

Application 7 is an operational e-commerce application. It was built by a third party to sell the customer's products. Once the data has been collected, it is stored in an encrypted database. Data collected is sensitive and must be treated as such.

Data Sensitivity (3)—Full names, addresses, account numbers, credit card information

Life Span (3)—No EOL set

Compliance (2)—PCI, PII

Customer or Internet Facing (True)—Hosted on a dedicated virtual server within the DMZ; is internet facing; accesses a database in a colocated data center.

Risk Rank 9

From this, you can construct an application security testing framework. For each application, you've considered the combination of criticality of data stored, transmitted, or processed, plus the attack-exposure-to-risk rank in your portfolio. Data classification reflects the level of impact to your organization if the data is compromised, and it includes factors such as compliance mandates, federal laws, and internal standards. Application attack exposure is an important factor in the relative attack risk each application carries. Some applications have very little exposure, while others are exposed to large numbers of users over the internet. Some are connected to other enterprise systems, databases, or web services; others are more isolated and harder to access. The combination of data criticality and attack exposure allows you to produce the risk-ranked grouping of your applications.

There is no standard formula for this, as risk tolerance and data mapping are contextual to each organization, but again, the objective is for each application risk tier to have a specific recommended testing frequency and depth so you can apply resources intelligently. In the example below, I once again use three tiers for simplicity.

THREAT RATING	STATIC ANALYSIS (SOURCE CODE)		DYNAMIC ANALYSIS (WEB APP SCANNING)		MANUAL (PENETRATION TESTING)		THREAT MODELING	
	Complete	Frequency	Complete	Frequency	Complete	Frequency	Complete	Frequency
TIER 1 (Critical)	Required	Major Code Changes	Required	Major Code Changes	Required	Per Milestone	Required	Per Release
TIER 2 (High)	Suggested	Monthly	Required	Quarterly	Required	Per Release	Suggested	Per Release
TIER 3 (Low)	Optional	Quarterly	Required	Annually	Optional	As needed	Optional	As needed

BENEFITS AND PERSISTENT ASSETS

The by-product associated with the SToRM activities above will ensure that product and security teams are equipped with the necessary framework to implement repeatable software security and develop best practices. The application portfolio risk assessment and classification can be leveraged to provide visibility into the state of development practices and application security across an organization's business lines. Combined with asset and application classification, you can now identify and prioritize high-risk applications based on business impact, security threats, compliance mandates, and operational risk. The result is a risk-rating framework that will allow for better resource allocation and identification of high-risk areas.

SDLC RECOMMENDATIONS

The outcome of this gap analysis should contain a specific remediation road map, as mentioned above. However, the sequencing of new activities and tools needs to be considered carefully. Too often, organizations try to do too much too quickly, and efficiencies can grind to a halt. Consider training a critical success factor. Introduction of new tools without training on the objective, activity, and benefit is going to be significantly less effective. When rolling out training, consider each person's job function and the technology stack for which they need training. One size definitely does not fit all when it comes to software security education. A java developer needs very different training than a .NET developer, even though they both may be building web applications.

Business-Level Threat Model

The threat models you generate during that activity will be living, persistent assets that can be revisited in the future. Considering a significant new feature? Recently read of a new attack technique? Return to your threat model and make the necessary tweaks to view potential impact.

Software Development and Procurement Policy

Almost every organization has some combination of homegrown applications, COTS (commercial off-the-shelf) applications, and outsourced/bespoke applications. Each one poses similar types of risks and should have cybersecurity acceptance testing criteria based on your SDLC policy. Documentation of security standards and checklists for product development teams (regardless of where they reside organizationally) is a by-product of this exercise as well. Be sure to enforce them and review them regularly. These formal procedures

and steps should be used to evaluate new and existing software applications against your customer, regulatory, and security standards.

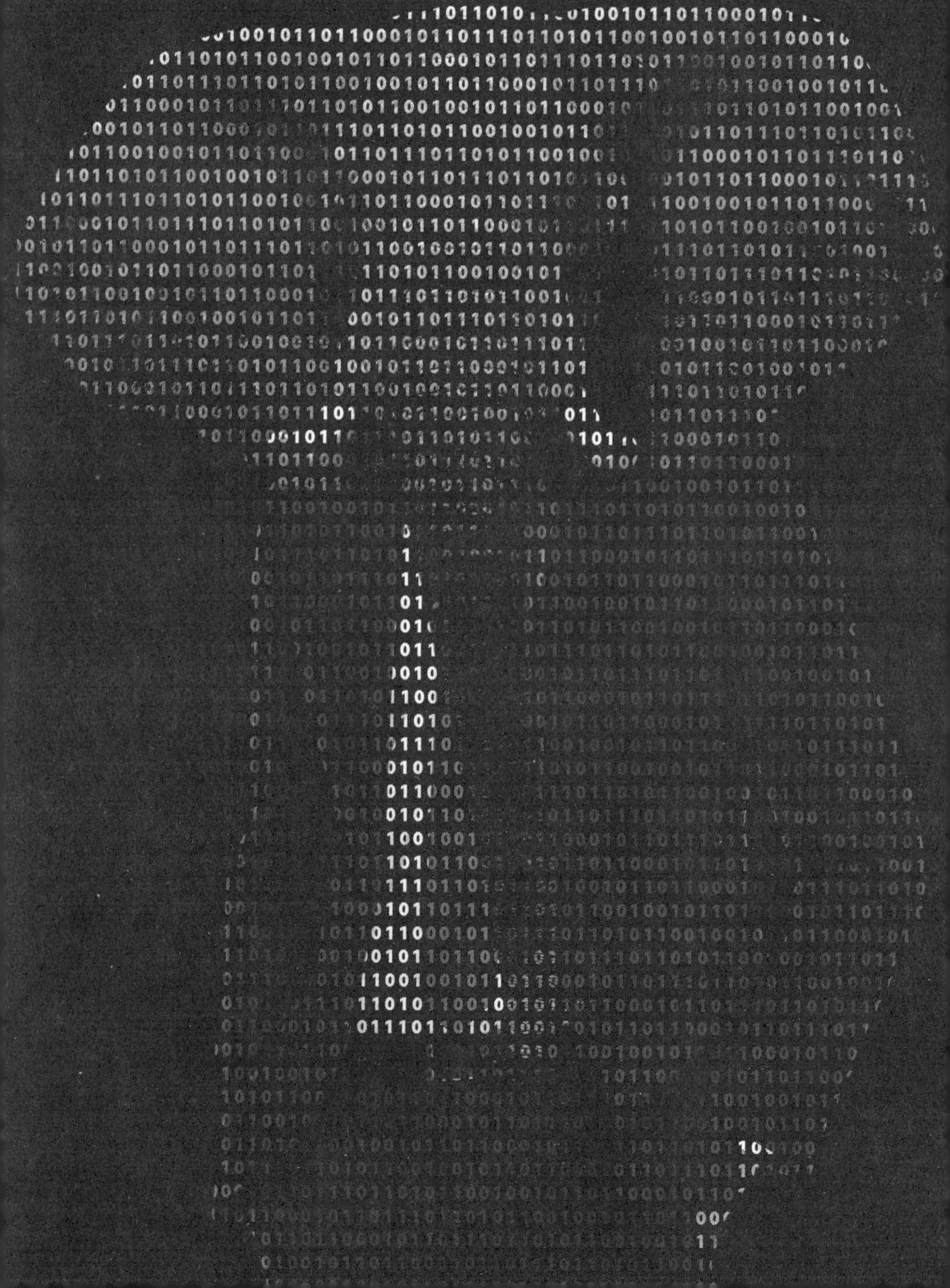

CHAPTER 13

TO COMPLY WITH PCI DSS—AND KEEP CARDHOLDER DATA SECURE

BY MARIE-CHRISTINE VITTET, DATA
COMPLIANCE MANAGER, ACCOR

Marie-Christine and I met at a VigiTrust event in Paris in 2011, the European PCI DSS Roadshow. This was a platform I had created to promote adoption of the standard and, of course, of the services VigiTrust offered in that space. It became clear very quickly that Marie-Christine was a thought leader in payment data security, and she was soon elected to the board of advisors of PCI. Throughout the years, she and I worked on white papers and articles and copresented at many events. She embraced the value add of the 5 Pillars of Security Framework to secure payment data on an ongoing basis and has been a fantastic advocate, not just for VigiTrust and myself, but also for the overall payment security industry. Her insight on how to continually improve compliance programs is a must-know!

Marie-Christine's chapter covers all 5 Pillars of Security with a strong focus on data security, people security, and physical security.

ACCOR GROUP TRAINS ITS EMPLOYEES ON DATA-HANDLING BEST PRACTICES

PCI DSS requirement 12.6 covers in-scope staff security training: "Implement a formal security awareness program to make all personnel aware of the importance of cardholder data security."

It has two subrequirements: 12.6.1—"Educate personnel upon hire and at least annually. Methods can vary depending on the role of the personnel and their level of access to the cardholder data"; and 12.6.2—"Require personnel to acknowledge at least annually that they have read and understood the security policy and procedures." This applies to all staff members who have physical or logical access to credit card holder data (CHD) regardless of whether they use that privilege.

We understand from this list of PCI requirements that any person working on computer systems that contain credit card holder data must be trained, even if he or she never accesses payment application software. Any person working as a cashier or in a call center environment where cardholder data may be provided by customers is in scope for such training. And, by extension, all technical staff managing call-recording systems, which may contain credit card information (even if encrypted according to the rules of PCI DSS), are also in scope for such training.

PCI DSS requirement 6.5.a also includes secure coding requirements for developers of in-house noncommercially sold payment applications: "Obtain and review software development processes.

Verify that processes require training in secure coding techniques for developers, based on industry best practices and guidance." Further references to training on specific procedures or technical training are spread throughout the standard. For instance, control 12.9.4 mandates that entities "provide appropriate training to staff with security breach response responsibilities."

The commitment to comply with the standard must come from top management and filter down to all staff. Therefore, program managers, their teams, and C-level team members must receive appropriate best practice security training covering physical security, personnel security, data security, IT security, and crisis management.

PCI DSS training should clearly explain the information that's on credit cards, which information is sensitive, and how it can be handled according to PCI DSS, especially requirement 3.4.

Staff needs to understand the life cycle of a credit card transaction, from the point-of-sale device or virtual terminal to the payment gateway to banks and back. All actors within the payment's ecosystem have to be in compliance, and credit card holder data must be safe at all stages of the transaction.

PCI DSS includes requirements for policies and procedures, technical settings and solutions, and requirements for awareness training.

All controls are aimed at protecting cardholder data and ensuring that all transactions, and all activity within the cardholder environment, are traceable.

Staff should not communicate credit card holder data for any other purpose than the payment it is being shared for.

Paper-based payments, including credit card holder data, are also protected under PCI DSS: data needs to be protected, stored securely, and disposed of securely.

PCI DSS is meant to be proactive to allow staff to take corrective action should anything go wrong—for example, implementing an incident response plan that helps employees identify potential incidents and to understand the steps to follow in the event of potential credit card holder data breaches.

All of the above information helps in-scope employees mitigate the most common physical, logical, and social-engineering-based attacks on CHD.

Ideally, developers should learn about the software development life cycle best practice software security. The ultimate aim is to ensure that payment application security becomes part of the DNA of your organization to protect customers' CHD.

If your entity is validating compliance using a self-assessment questionnaire (SAQ), ensure that you can demonstrate compliance with all requirements, including 12.6, 6.5.a, and 12.9.4. If assessed by a PCI audit (QSA), note that staff may be interviewed and training attendance sheets signed by staff may be requested. Training materials should be made available to assessors for both standard and secure coding training.

The best, most cost-effective way to provide training is via eLearning. Since eLearning is typically cloud based, it requires almost no maintenance from the organization. This allows PCI program managers to easily disseminate security information, forces staff to read and acknowledge security policies and procedures, and tests that staff understands CHD security best practices. Furthermore, staff can take the training on their own time, in several chunks. Given that training is required annually, eLearning also allows organizations to continually train and retrain users in a verifiable way accepted by QSAs.

Since 2014, VigiTrust has supported the ACCOR group in these awareness campaigns on PCI DSS by offering eLearning dedicated to the hotel industry and customized for the ACCOR group. More than sixty thousand employees are certified every year. The training is a KPI followed since the implementation of the PCI program at ACCOR, and periodic reviews renew the training of each employee every twelve months.

As a takeaway, find below my five tips to implement a good security awareness training:

1. MAKE SURE YOU HAVE POLICIES AND PROCEDURES IN PLACE

Data security begins (and ends) with documentation. The more time and detail you put into your documentation, the better foundation your security culture will have. You will use your policies and procedures as evidence of compliance, for employee training, and to support day-to-day operations. Give your employees easy access to reliable and updated security information.

Your policies and procedures should include things like firewall rules, system-hardening standards, data-retention policies, and, of course, password policies.

You should also combine the data security compliance mandates you may be required to follow by the GDPR.

Be sure that once you create the policies and procedures, you don't just set them on the shelf and forget about them. Make sure these documents are read, understood, and applied by the teams. Feature your policies and procedures in your trainings, and schedule time to update them regularly. Good data security is all about proper process. Documentation is key in that process.

2. LEARN ABOUT AND TRAIN EMPLOYEES ON HOW TO PROPERLY MANAGE SENSITIVE DATA

Managing sensitive data from day to day involves many people, processes, and technologies.

Some of the controls and areas you'll need to work with include risk assessment and risk management plans, data encryption, data destruction, wireless networks (Wi-Fi), and secure remote access. Not surprisingly, managing your company's sensitive data includes a significant documentation component and should begin with a risk assessment. Risk assessments include data mapping to identify your scope, listing vulnerabilities and threats, analyzing risk, creating a risk management plan, and testing your environment.[67]

3. UNDERSTAND WHICH SECURITY TOOLS YOU ACTUALLY NEED

The correct security tools are critical to protecting data at your company. Data breaches are prevalent due to a lack of appropriate tools—plus, they aren't always used or configured correctly.

Yours will likely include some or all of the following:

- Firewalls: filter potentially harmful internet traffic to protect valuable sensitive data.

- Antivirus software: offers an additional layer of protection to any system within a network.

- File integrity monitoring (FIM): will generate an alert when a file is changed.

- Log monitoring and log management: installs third-party log

---

67 Nathan Cooper, "Network Diagrams: Key to Compliance and Security," Security-Metrics.com, accessed October 5, 2020, https://www.securitymetrics.com/blog/network-diagrams-key-compliance-and-security.

monitoring and management software if needed.

- Intrusion detection/intrusion prevention systems: IDS and IPS tools help identify suspected attacks and find the associated gaps in security.

- Vulnerability scanning: automated internal and external scans that perform a high-level search for vulnerabilities.

- Penetration testing: in-person attempt by professionals to ethically "hack" into your environment.

- Security audits: may be required by PCI DSS or other security standards. Third-party audits help confirm your security posture and find resolvable problems before criminals do.

It's important to educate yourself and avoid buying products blindly, without understanding the different types of security tools, what they do, or if they are even necessary for your environment.

4. PREPARE YOUR EMPLOYEES TO RESPOND TO A DATA BREACH

Data breach attacks are inevitable. If these attacks are successful and your data is compromised, you will be glad you have a response plan in place. Depending on the security mandate(s) you comply with, you could face significant fines. Some severe data breach fines have already put companies out of business.

Different compliance mandates may require different breach procedures, especially regarding how you notify, whom you notify, and when you decide to notify. To help implement security awareness, begin your data breach response and start getting the word out.

Include updates on your efforts in internal newsletters, emails, meetings, trainings, announcements, and dashboards.

A data breach response plan has six phases: prepare, identify, contain, eradicate, recover, and review.

The success of your data breach response plan hinges on communication. If you have the plan on file but no one knows about it, your employees will waste a lot of time scrambling to organize a response to the breach right after it happens.

A proper data breach response plan will include things like a prewritten PR response, a contact list for emergency communications, and a forensic analysis list to begin your in-house forensic process. Training should include topics like roles, possible scenarios, and a heavy emphasis on what not to do (e.g., don't automatically wipe all your data if a breach occurs). Trainings should also include testing your data breach response plan. Testing with discussion-based exercises, tabletop exercises, and parallel testing can be used to ensure full understanding of this topic, so critical in all organizations.

5. KNOW YOUR COMPLIANCE MANDATES

It's your responsibility to train, educate, and bring all employees on board regarding the many different kinds of compliance that require data security controls.

Strong adhesions exist between PCI DSS (Payment Card Industry Data Security Standard) and GDPR (General Data Protection Regulation); it is important to know how to identify them and combine them in the user training program. The end user should not feel like they are asked to master too many abstract concepts.

CONCLUSION

As we mentioned above, preventing data breaches takes time, resources, and planning, but if you follow a straightforward process before problems arise, you will be prepared when a response is needed.

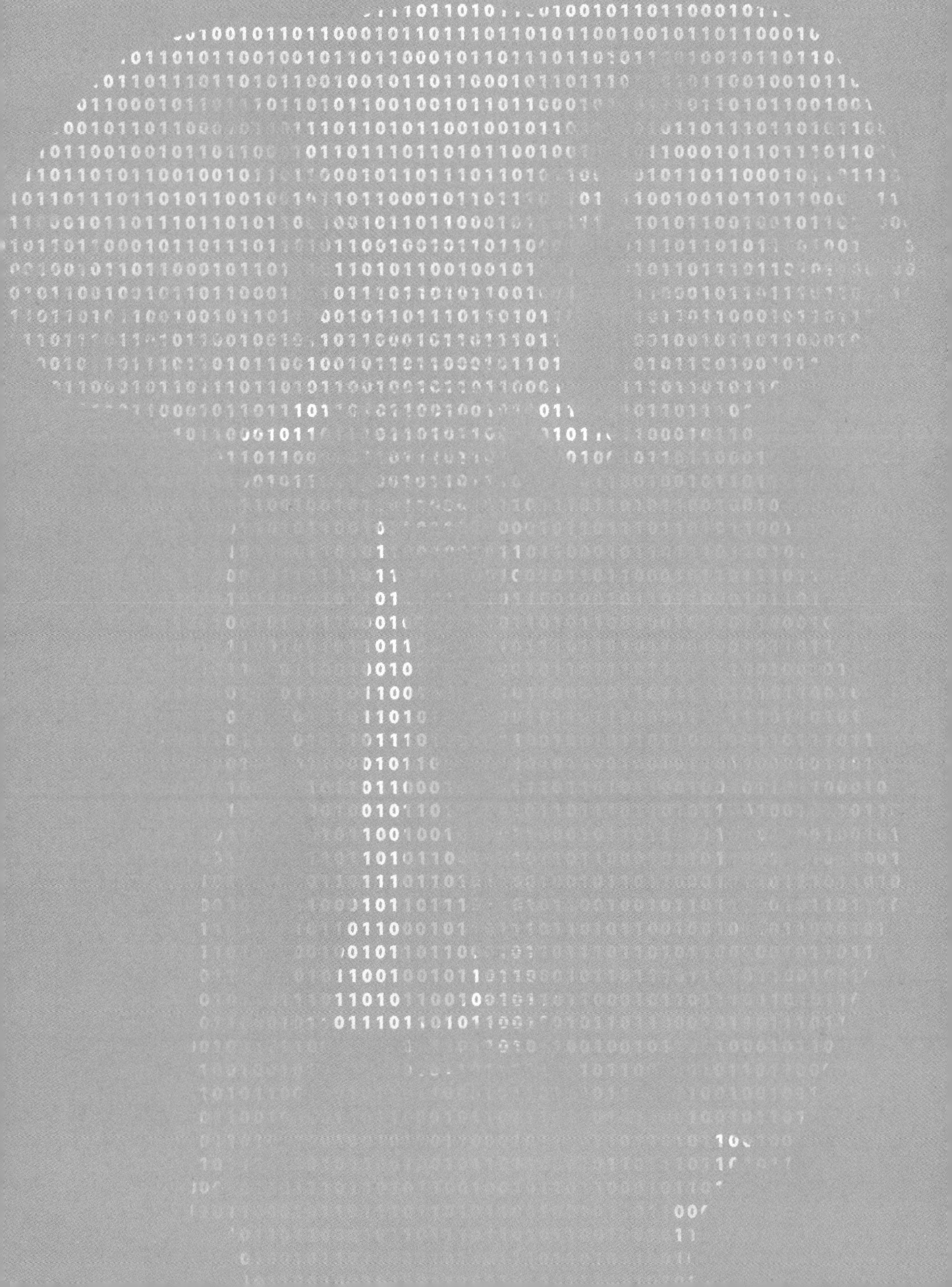

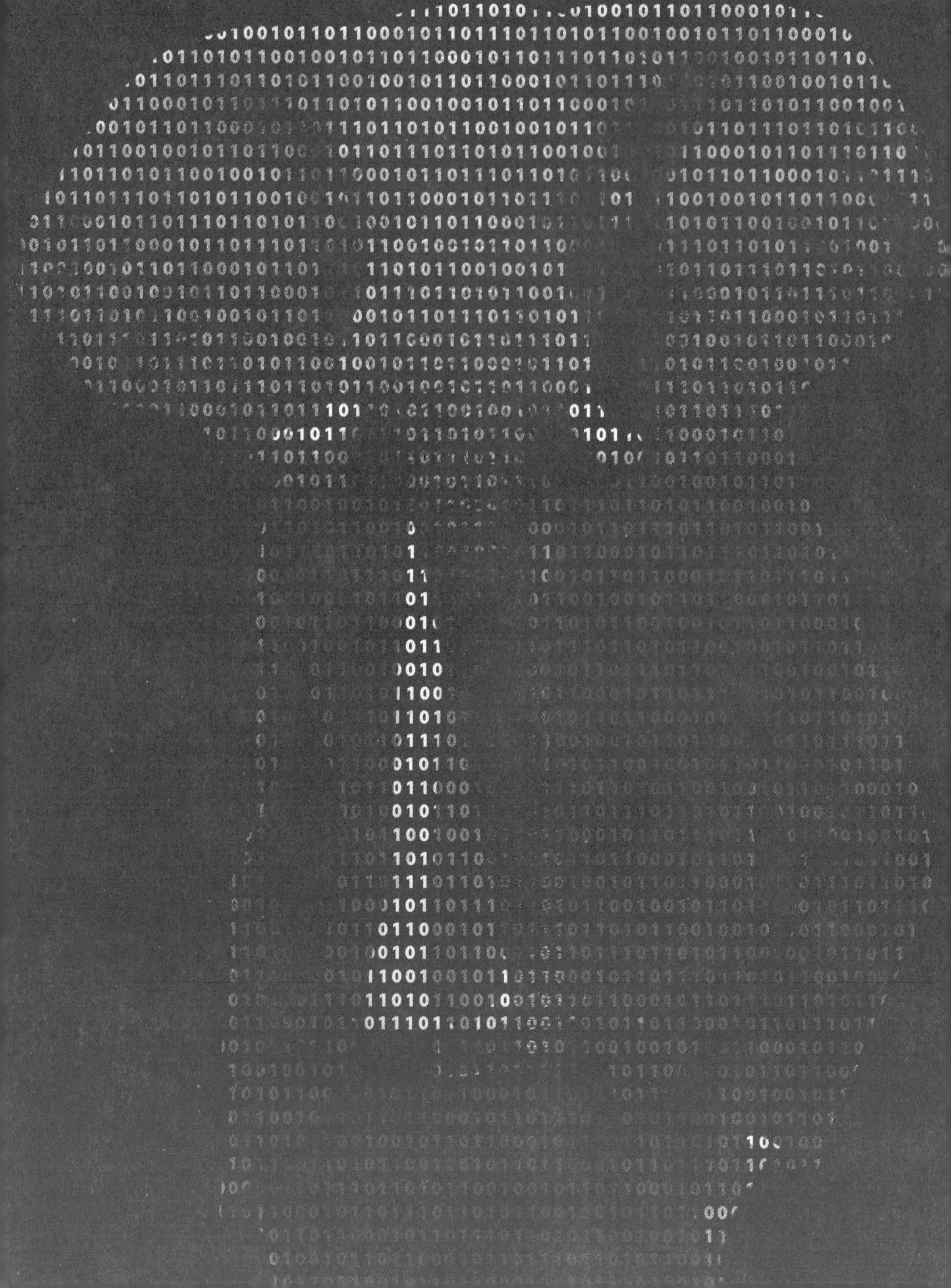

CHAPTER 14

CYBERSECURITY RISK IN HUMAN RESOURCES

BY CÉCILE MARTIN AND THIBAUD LAUXEROIS

Cécile and I met through an IAPP event in Paris a few years back. Her passion for data security and compliance was clear from day one, but it comes with a special flavor. She focuses on human aspects of data security from a legal perspective. In this chapter she teamed up with Thibaud, one of her colleagues and an expert in his own right. Together they cover key aspects of data security and compliance in the enterprise and focus on GDPR compliance implementation. Their focus also covers the impact of physical access to data, an often-forgotten part of the compliance challenge.

Cécile and Thibaud's chapter covers mostly data security, people security, infrastructure security, some physical security, and mentions crisis management. It also clearly showcases the value add of the 5 Pillars of Security Framework for GDPR compliance.

If hacking constitutes the most dramatic source of risk against the privacy of personal data collected by a data controller, members of staff may often unwittingly cause the unauthorized publication of personal data.

In 2017, data breaches cost companies an average of $3.6 million globally, according to a report from the Ponemon Institute. The French data protection supervisory authority estimates that human mistakes cause 15 percent of data breaches. Indeed, actions that may seem harmless can have devastating consequences.

Most data protection laws include obligations for organizing security measures to preserve and protect personal data. For example, Article 32 of the GDPR sets forth that the data controller and the processor implement appropriate technical and organizational measures to ensure a level of security appropriate to the risk. However, it is sometimes quite tricky to translate an appropriate technical and organizational measure for preserving and securing personal data into practice.

Tackling human risk is a complex, ongoing task. It requires a documented methodology allowing the company to determine the sources of risks using all available options, including legal ones, to protect the security of personal data.

ASSESSING THE SOURCES OF RISKS

The process must be mapped in a comprehensive and detailed way to organize the firm to better tackle its data-protection-related risks.

Mapping data properly is crucial to making a data controller compliant, be it to the GDPR, the CCPA, or any other data privacy legislation. Such data mapping is a useful tool to check for the legalities of data processing activity and is also necessary to assess the sources of the risks.

Data mapping involves listing the recipients of data, identifying third parties processing the data and, if applicable, countries where the data may be sent.

Thus, a data controller can assess thoroughly which persons actually require access to which data, exclude access from all other stakeholders, and focus security efforts on the staff that will handle personal data in need of protection.

To comprehensively identify appropriate members of staff, the data controller can document an in-depth identification policy, which will allow the supervisory authority to observe the attention paid to data security in case of a data breach. This documentation of how staff was identified may divide that staff into subgroups, each requiring their own specific actions by the company according to the seriousness of the risk for the concerned data subjects' rights and freedoms or the nature of the risk.

In this prospect, the mapping of the data processing activities and the risks incurred must be cross-referenced with each person's work environment to safeguard them from any unintended leak. These risks may concern the office layout, such as an open plan where unauthorized persons may more efficiently, even if unintentionally, view personal information on a computer screen or in a messy office. A remote employee may also put personal data at stake if they do not have a closed, dedicated office at home or if they can access personal data outside of the firm's secure network. Traveling sales representatives may let unauthorized people have access to personal data when working on a train or presenting to a client.

Not only must the appropriate people be listed, but the nature of their contractual relationship with the data controller also needs to be taken into consideration. Temporary workers, interns, consultants, and provisional staff of any kind constitute a severe source of risk and leakage. They may feel less bound by their obligation of loyalty and be tempted to store data on personal drives for reuse in positions in other jobs. Moreover, their short connection to the company may lead to a lack of concern over the specifics of the company's internal privacy policies.

Similarly, when the data controller resorts to data processors, he or she may request that the processor provide its own data mapping to oversee risk reduction in assessing staff.

ORGANIZING THE STRUCTURE TO LIMIT RISKS

The identification of appropriate staff is a prerequisite to organizing the structure by providing it with the most comprehensive yet proportionate security measures.

Otherwise, security measures, while necessary, may lead to monitoring of employees' activities, potentially risking employees' rights and freedoms.

The most basic, least intrusive measure is the creation of a specific accreditation policy and partitioning of personal data to only allow required staff to access each category of personal data. The process for extending one person's credentials must be very secure to avoid enabling anyone to continue without justifying their own or another person's credentials. Securing such a process may involve joint approval by several persons or a recurring and global check of each authorized person's credentials.

When required by specific risks, more intrusive measures may be set up—for example, tracking or monitoring access to files (both paper and computer files) or analyzing the data stored on external devices (flash or optical drives, hard disk, etc.) or sent by email. In that case, it would be necessary to analyze regularly the collected data to confirm any leak as quickly as possible and take action immediately to mitigate the risks. Moreover, this practice allows the quick deletion of the collected personal data, which is itself a measure mitigating the risk of any leak.

Sharing data with third-party recipients, which must be strictly limited to the specified instances, is also a risk factor. Sending data via email entails the risk of sending the data to a wrong recipient or of interception. Using specific communication channels or imposing a strict, systematic policy of password-encrypted emails are ways of tackling this risk.

Lastly, the protection of personal data privacy requires ensuring the security of hardware and software infrastructures. Hardware protection includes providing specific credentials to a limited number of employees whose position requires access to the facility. Software protection,

> *The protection of personal data privacy requires ensuring the security of hardware and software infrastructures.*

on the other hand, means both setting up a comprehensive system of firewalls and antivirus and removing administrator rights from users to prevent setting up any plug-in or software without authorization.

USING LEGAL TOOLS TO MINIMIZE THE HUMAN SOURCES OF RISKS

If staff must take specific actions to prevent risk to personal data, there may still be failures. If there is one, a precise corrective procedure needs to be carried out.

Prevention of Human Security Breaches

Though employment law varies from country to country, it still provides many tools employers can use to inform employees about data privacy concerns and implementation of data privacy policies on a day-to-day basis.

In a very general way, all employees must be informed, first as job candidates, then as employees, on the characteristics of the data processing activities. This prior information may, in itself, be a chance to remind data subjects that protecting data—including theirs—is only possible if all the members of staff comply with this policy and take care to prevent any breach. The internal regulations of the company may similarly highlight the necessity of compliance with the privacy policy and forewarn of disciplinary consequences proceeding from any intentional violation. They may even provide a nonexhaustive list of familiar yet prohibited actions, such as forwarding professional emails to a personal email address, taking files home without authorization, or leaving confidential documents on display on a desk while taking a coffee break. A number of employees admit leaving their computer unlocked and unattended when leaving their workplace.

More specifically, because data mapping allows a better knowledge of the personnel, action may be taken before, during, and upon termination of the contractual relationship.

At the start of the contract, specific clauses should be spelled out in the employment contract, such as a reinforced, detailed confidentiality clause for employees who access personal data, required security behaviors for working with personal data, and a reminder to hand over all business material (laptop, professional mobile phone, storage drives, written notes, or any document). The onboarding process may also feature a training session on personal data protection, specifically designed for the employee's position and work environment. This training must allow the trainee to understand how broad the notion of "personal data" can be (e.g., not all personal data is computerized) and the processes for sharing such data (e.g., how to verify the identity and credentials of a person requesting access, how to detect fraudulent requests such as phishing, how to react when in doubt, etc.). It is generally highly advisable to renew such training regularly during the contractual relationship and make sure employees understand the different notions, principles of security, and case studies described during the training by conducting regular tests at the end of the training.

Similarly, a reminder may be sent to the employee upon termination to remind them that loyalty and confidentiality obligations persist after the end of the contract. The outboarding process must also include standard security measures such as removal of access, verification of the handover of all business material, and specific monitoring of the activity of staff members during their notice period.

Correcting Security Hazards

Regardless of the security measures put in place, residual risks may persist and take place. A company needs to determine a policy on how to react to such an occurrence, taking into consideration the seriousness of the damage.

Companies need to ensure that their procedures are well documented in case of incidents and that employees

- know whom to inform in case of a stolen device or personal data leak,

- have implemented the appropriate emergency response plans and specific technical security measures to try to recover or block personal data, and

- and assure that the company's activity is not going to be disrupted.

One of the key steps of this policy may be to designate a data protection officer (DPO), whose role is to ensure data subjects' rights of data privacy and facilitate communication among all stakeholders—the company, its agents who operate on the data, its processors, the supervisory authority, and the data subjects.

Regulations that require companies to appoint a DPO are generally mandatory only for companies carrying out specific processing or handling a specific large amount of data subjects. This does not preclude other companies from appointing a DPO; dedicating a person specifically to the protection of personal data is efficient.

Where a DPO has been appointed, his or her identity and contact details must be widely disclosed to allow each stakeholder to quickly and easily report a data breach.

Moreover, data mapping must be used to determine who designs each data processing activity and who must be held accountable in case of a data breach. This accountability may be the basis both for disciplinary actions and for deferring criminal liability, if need be, on the people responsible for the processing.

An authority must formalize this accountability, which is an efficient way to remind the person in question of the importance of their task and of the risks they may incur. These members of staff may also be included in specific remuneration schemes, rewarding achievement in terms of data privacy based on carefully thought-out vital performance indicators. However, the company must be cautious to avoid using the mere number of detected violations as a key performance indicator to avoid a person concealing any data breach. But the speed of disclosure of an offense may be considered as a relevant indicator of a person's care for data privacy.

Lastly, the policy addressing data breaches must provide for reporting, where required, to the supervisory authority and to data subjects whose personal data has been exposed. This is done through finding and documenting all relevant information concerning the nature and scope of the breach, the identity of concerned data subjects, and the possible implications of the breach for said data subjects.

The policy must also provide measures for minimizing the risks associated with the data breach (such as freezing access to specific data where undue access has been noticed).

Finally, the policy must provide for corrective structural measures on the causes of the incident, such as reinforced training or disciplinary actions against negligent or malicious employees.

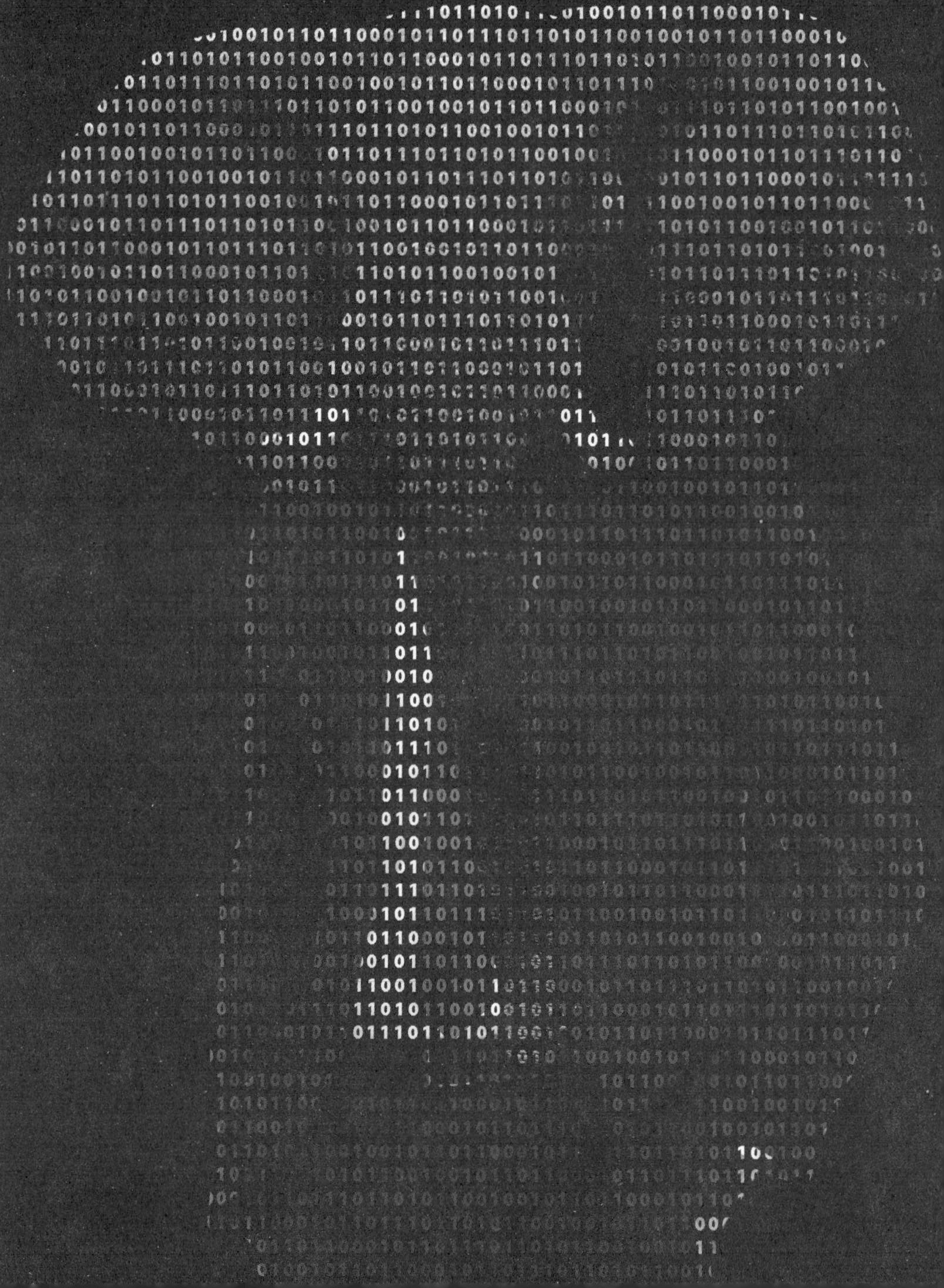

CHAPTER 15

EDUCATION FOR KEY DECISION MAKERS

BY ALEXANDER ABRAMOV

Alex and I had been in the same security circles for a while when I asked him if he could introduce me to some of his peers. He suggested gathering a few people for me if I could organize informal drinks in New York for us all to chat. This is how the advisory board idea came about. You can easily see that Alex believes in networking to foster security best practices by ensuring practitioners exchange ideas and collaborate. This is, in part, due to his longtime involvement in ISACA but also his passion for security education. His chapter is a mine of information on why and how security professionals need to skill up, what certifications they can get, and the value add for those individuals and the industry at large. A must-read to further your security career!

> Alex links his chapter to all 5 Pillars, with strong focus on people security, data security, infrastructure security, and crisis management.

The leading cause of cyber and data breaches invariably appears to be human error. According to Shred-it's 2018 State of the Industry Report, 84 percent of C-level executives believe that employee negligence is one of the biggest information security risks.[68]

In 2016, Bangladesh's central bank became a victim of hackers who had stolen $81 million from the bank's account at the Federal Reserve Bank of New York. According to Thomson Reuters, "deficiencies in training, lack of preventive controls and monitoring were the main contributors to this loss."[69]

> *The most effective antidote to mitigate the risk of human error and negligence is a comprehensive employee and stakeholder education program.*

The most effective antidote to mitigate the risk of human error and negligence is a comprehensive employee and stakeholder education program.

This reviews how professional associations, in partnership with governments, think tanks, and mentoring organizations, address the following:

- Cybersecurity workforce development

- Skill and talent gap

68 "Key Information Security Findings from the 2018 State of the Industry Report," Shred-it, accessed October 5, 2020, https://www.shredit.com/en-us/resource-center/original-research/security-tracker-2018.

69 Alexander Abramov, "The Evolution of the Cyber Risk Role Within the Three Lines of Defence," *Cyber Risk*, ed. Michael L. Woodson (London: Risk Books, 2016).

- Credentialing and continuing education needs

GOVERNMENT INITIATIVES IN CYBER WORKFORCE DEVELOPMENT AND PUBLIC-PRIVATE PARTNERSHIPS

The US government has recognized the importance of cyber workforce development and continues to increase budget allocations to support this critical initiative. President Obama signed several executive orders related to cybersecurity in 2016 and underlined that it is a bipartisan issue: "And that is something that we should all be able to agree on. This is not an ideological issue. It doesn't matter whether there's a Democratic President or a Republican President."[70]

The Obama administration's plan addressed cybersecurity both inside and outside the government: ordering more training and shared resources among government agencies, forty-eight dedicated teams to respond to attacks, and student loan forgiveness to help recruit top technical talent.

President Trump signed the Executive Order on America's Cybersecurity Workforce in May 2019 that followed the Executive Order on Strengthening the Cybersecurity of Federal Networks and Critical Infrastructure from May 2017.

The directives have stated the following:

The United States government must support the development of cybersecurity skills and encourage ever-greater excellence so that America can maintain its competitive edge in cybersecurity and required

- assessing the scope and sufficiency of efforts to educate and train the American cybersecurity workforce of the future,

---

70 Gregory Korte, "Obama Signs Two Executive Orders on Cybersecurity," *USA TODAY*, February 9, 2016, https://www.usatoday.com/story/news/politics/2016/02/09/obama-signs-two-executive-orders-cybersecurity/80037452/.

including cybersecurity-related education curricula, training, and apprenticeship programs, from primary through higher education;

- reviewing the workforce development efforts of potential foreign cyber peers in order to help identify foreign workforce development practices likely to affect long-term United States cybersecurity competitiveness;[71]

- establishing a cybersecurity rotational assignment program [for the federal workforce], which will serve as a mechanism for knowledge transfer and a development program for cybersecurity practitioners;

- using National Initiative for Cybersecurity Education (NICE) Cybersecurity Workforce Framework (NICE Framework) as the basis for cybersecurity skill requirements for program participants [for the federal workforce];

- encouraging the voluntary integration of the NICE Framework into existing education, training, and workforce development efforts undertaken by state, territorial, local, tribal, academic, nonprofit, and private-sector entities, consistent with applicable law.[72]

Several professional associations, such as ISACA and InfraGard, have recognized the importance of supporting these government initiatives and cooperating with the government in their implementation.

---

71 "Executive Order on Strengthening the Cybersecurity of Federal Networks and Critical Infrastructure," issued May 11, 2017, https://www.whitehouse.gov/presidential-actions/presidential-executive-order-strengthening-cybersecurity-federal-networks-critical-infrastructure/.

72 "Executive Order on America's Cybersecurity Workforce," issued on May 2, 2019, https://www.whitehouse.gov/presidential-actions/executive-order-americas-cybersecurity-workforce/.

ISACA, the global nonprofit membership association for information systems, audit, IT governance, risk management, and cybersecurity professionals, was established in 1969 and counts over 140,000 members organized in over 220 chapters across over 188 countries. Its members include internal and external auditors, CEOs, CFOs, CIOs, educators, information security and control professionals, business managers, students, and IT consultants.

In 2014, ISACA New York Metropolitan Chapter (ISACA NYM) hosted the White House director of critical infrastructure cybersecurity, Samara Moore, who presented President Obama's Cybersecurity Framework.

In 2017, ISACA NYM hosted Grant Schneider, the acting (confirmed in 2018) federal chief information security officer to present President Trump's Executive Order on Strengthening the Cybersecurity of Federal Networks and Critical Infrastructure.

These events, attended by several hundred executives and practitioners, helped to educate attendees about the federal government resources and strengthen public-private partnerships in cyber workforce development.

InfraGard is a nonprofit organization serving as a public-private partnership between US businesses and the Federal Bureau of Investigation (FBI). It was founded in 1996 with a motto of "Partnership For Protection" and has over fifty-four thousand members.

Tom Mustac, the president of InfraGard New York, believes that in today's fast-moving, internet-connected global culture, it is imperative that we keep our decision makers informed of not only the cyber threats that exist but also the capabilities of the most current technology and tool sets. Technology has no moral boundaries, and it can be used for evil as much as it can for good, as evidenced by the headlines we see every day. Cybersecurity is a team sport, and we need to keep all players updated on the rules of the game as they evolve. One of the best ways to ensure that we accomplish this is through the use of professional security associations such as InfraGard. InfraGard brings together subject matter experts, key decision makers, and policy makers from across industry and various government agencies to share best practices, the concerns that we are seeing "in the wild," and the vulnerabilities that are announced on a daily basis. The core mission of InfraGard is education and information sharing. InfraGard is dedicated to strengthening national security, community resilience, and the foundation of American life.[73]

> *Cybersecurity is a team sport, and we need to keep all players updated on the rules of the game as they evolve.*

InfraGard produces high-quality educational events that have impressive rosters of speakers, including members of the FBI and Department of Homeland Security (DHS) and industry leadership.

These events help to promote a wide range of services provided to the enterprises by the Cybersecurity and Infrastructure Security Agency (CISA) created by the US government in 2018.

CISA administers the Cybersecurity Advisor (CSA) program that maintains regional subject matter experts to cultivate partnerships with participating organizations and initiate information sharing. CSAs provide organizations with various no-cost DHS cybersecurity products and services, such as these:

- Cyber Preparedness: on-site meetings to answer questions, exchange ideas and information, and address concerns about cybersecurity—promoting best practices, resources, and

---

73   Tom Mustac, email to author, November 21, 2019.

partnership experiences

- Cyber Infrastructure Survey (CIS): survey focused on over eighty cybersecurity controls in five domains, resulting in an interactive decision support resource

- Cyber Resilience Review (CRR): strategic evaluation that assesses cybersecurity management capabilities and maturity as applied to protect critical information technology (IT) services

- External Dependency Management (EDM): assessment of the management activities and practices utilized to identify, analyze, and reduce risks arising from third parties

- Incident Coordination and Support: activities to facilitate cyber incident response and to coordinate information requests in times of increased threat, disruption, and attack[74]

In addition to ISACA and InfraGard, insurance and fraud- and crime-focused organizations help in building public-private partnerships and stakeholder education. These organizations include the Association for Cooperative Operations Research and Development (ACORD), the National Association of Insurance Commissioners (NAIC), the Federal Insurance Office of the US Department of Treasury (FIO), the Association of Certified Fraud Examiners (ACFE), and the High Technology Crime Investigation Association (HTCIA).

These organizations provide statistical, actuarial, underwriting, and claims information; policy language; information about specific locations; fraud-identification tools; and technical services.

---

74 "Stakeholder Risk Assessment and Mitigation," Cybersecurity and Infrastructure Security Agency, DHS, CISA, accessed October 5, 2020, https://www.cisa.gov/stakeholder-risk-assessment-and-mitigation.

They are also involved in implementation of regulations and standards that explicitly target cyber insurers. For example, ACORD, the global standards-setting body for the insurance industry, introduced the insurance industry's first-ever standard for cyber data breaches, called the ACORD Cyber Data Breach Standard (2018). Additionally, the NAIC implements a suite of cybersecurity regulations for the insurance industry, which is governed by the chief insurance regulators from the fifty states, the District of Columbia, and five US territories. Implementing a cyber program is no longer optional. Regulations are mandatory. ACFE looks to educate professionals through antifraud training, education, and certification. The expectation of these regulations, standards, and certifications is to establish a baseline for compliance and audit-related activities, enable solution providers to leverage standards for increased support, and increase the operational efficiency and effectiveness for cyber risk stakeholders.[75]

ISACA has also become an influential force in governance and frameworks. FINRA and NFA (the US self-regulatory organizations for financial firms) have identified ISACA's 7 Control Objectives for Information and Related Technology (COBIT) 5 as one of the leading frameworks used in the industry.[76]

The European Union has several important cyber initiatives that help in developing a cyber workforce.

In September 2017 the European Commission adopted the Cybersecurity Act that reformed the European Union Agency for Network and Information Security (ENISA) as the EU cybersecurity agency.

---

75 Thomas Yohannan, *Cyberinsurance: Market-Based Solutions and Legal Dynamics*, Cybercrime and Security, ed. Pauline C. Reich (Eagan, MN: Thomson Reuters/ West, 2020).

76 Sarah Swammy and Michael McMaster, *Governance, Compliance and Supervision in the Capital Markets*, (Hoboken: Wiley, 2018).

ENISA was put in charge of contributing training and training materials—"train the trainers," building on the Digital Competence Framework for Citizens; and supporting Member States in the field of cybersecurity awareness raising and education by facilitating closer coordination and the exchange of best practices between Member States. Such support could consist of the development of a network of national education points of contact and the development of a cybersecurity training platform.[77]

ISACA, as a global organization, is engaged via its European chapters with EU agencies as well as with country governments in helping to shape approaches to cyber workforce development.

In 2019 ISACA NYM established a partnership with Americas Institute for Cybersecurity Leadership (AICL), a nonpartisan think tank focused on promoting cybersecurity discourse based on rigorous research. AICL's mission is to impact global cybersecurity challenges, provide strategic insights, and foster cybersecurity leadership for a safer digital society. One of the important activities of AICL is the annual mission to the EU, designed to build understanding of approaches to cybersecurity by EU agencies and of the role of professional associations in cyber education (the author is the AICL Executive Fellow and has represented ISACA NYM on the EU Mission in the past).

In addition to the missions, AICL publishes contributions and intellectual output of AICL Fellows. These are made available in *Cybersecurity Perspectives* and *Journal of Cybersecurity Awareness &*

---

77 "Regulation (EU) 2019/881 of the European Parliament and of the Council of 17 April 2019 on ENISA and on Information and Communications Technology Cybersecurity Certification and Repealing Regulation (EU) No 526/2013 (Cybersecurity Act)," EUR-Lex, https://eur-lex.europa.eu/legal-content/EN/TXT/?qid=1574645091909&uri=CELEX:32019R0881.

Education.[78]

The VigiTrust Global Advisory Board, mentioned earlier in the book, is another prestigious think tank; it leverages its engagement with several ISACA chapters worldwide.

PROFESSIONAL CERTIFICATIONS AS ENABLERS FOR PROFESSIONAL DEVELOPMENT AND RECOGNITION

The importance of professional certifications has grown by leaps and bounds since the early 2000s.

From public accounting firms requiring IT audit managers to be certified as CISA (Certified Information Security Auditor) to country governments mandating technology-related certifications, the number of jobs requiring accreditation and credentials has expanded every year.

The way recruiters and hiring managers view certifications on candidates' CVs has evolved as well. The certifications are not only a sign of having technical knowledge, but more importantly are a sign of commitment to the learning, self-improvement, and drive to succeed in an increasingly competitive talent marketplace.

The difference in compensation between a person with a certification and without is significant. According to a report from Georgetown University's Center on Education and the Workforce and information from the US Bureau of Labor Statistics, men with certificates in computer/information services receive higher pay than 72 percent of men with an associate's degree and 54 percent of men with bachelor's degrees. For women, the numbers are 75 percent for an associate's degree and 64 percent for a bachelor's degree, an even larger margin of advantage.[79]

---

78   AICL: https://americascybersecurity.org/.

79   Anthony P. Carnevale, et. al., "Certificates: Gateway to Gainful Employ-

The certification landscape has changed over the last fifteen years with new certifications by the vendors, most notably Amazon and Google. In 2004, the top-paying credentials were CPA and CISA, and most of the current popular certifications had not been established. Amazon Web Services certification program launched in 2013 and now holds two spots in the top five categories for pay in 2019 for IT certifications, according to Global Knowledge, an IT and professional training provider:

- Google Certified Professional Cloud Architect—$139,529

- PMP®—Project Management Professional—$135,798

- Certified ScrumMaster®—$135,441

- AWS Certified Solutions Architect, Associate—$132,840

- AWS Certified Developer, Associate—$130,369

- Microsoft Certified Solutions Expert (MCSE) Server Infrastructure—$121,288

- ITIL® Foundation—$120,566

- CISM®—Certified Information Security Manager—$118,412

- CRISC®—Certified in Risk and Information Systems Control—$117,395

- CISSP—Certified Information Systems Security Professional—$116,900

- CEH—Certified Ethical Hacker—$116,306

- Citrix Certified Associate—Virtualization (CCA-V)

ment and College Degrees," Georgetown University's Center on Education and the Workforce, June 2012, https://cew.georgetown.edu/wp-content/uploads/2014/11/Certificates.ExecutiveSummary.071712.pdf.

—$113,442

- CompTIA Security+—$110,321

- CompTIA Network+—$107,143

- Cisco Certified Networking Professional (CCNP) Routing and Switching—$106,957

We should note that Certified in the Governance of Enterprise IT (CGEIT), the top-paying US certification of 2018, did not make the 2019 list, as it missed the respondent threshold. IT professionals with CGEIT had an average salary of $141,703 in 2019, which would have made it number one on this list.[80]

For comparison, according to a survey conducted by the Association of International Certified Professional Accountants (AICPA) in 2019, the average salary for a CPA based in the United States was $119,000. That would land CPA at number eight on this list.

The ranking by Global Knowledge is also generally confirmed by CIO.com and has CISA moved from number two in 2004 to thirteen on the 2018 survey.[81]

All the credentials on the list have elements of cybersecurity; however, if we were to extract pure-play cyber credentials, these would be the top four: CISM (ISACA); CRISC (ISACA); CISSP (ISC)2; and CEH (EC-Council).

ISACA manages several major global certification programs, including these:

- CISA credential, which has been earned by more than

---

80   "These Certifications Pave the Way for a Higher Salary," Global Knowledge, February 9, 2020, https://www.globalknowledge.com/us-en/resources/resource-library/articles/top-paying-certifications/.

81   Sarah K. White, "The 15 Most Valuable IT Certifications Today," CIO.com, October 10, 2018, https://www.cio.com/article/2392856/careers-staffing-12-it-certifications-that-deliver-career-advancement.html.

118,000 professionals since its inception in 1978. This certification is aimed at information systems professionals who monitor, control, and assess a company's IT or business systems. It requires five years of professional experience in the field.

- CISM, which is for professionals who design, build, and manage information security programs. It has been earned by more than twenty-eight thousand professionals. Qualifications include at least five years of IS experience and three years as a security manager.

- CRISC, which covers risk identification, risk assessment, risk response and mitigation, and risk control monitoring and reporting. It is held by more than eighteen thousand professionals. Requirements include three years or more experience in at least two of the four topics covered in the certification.

- CGEIT, which demonstrates knowledge of enterprise IT governance principles and practices. Requirements include five or more years of experience managing, serving in an advisory or oversight role, or otherwise supporting IT governance initiatives in an enterprise setting.

- The International Council of E-Commerce Consultants (EC-Council) created and manages the CEH certification, which is aimed at security officers and auditors, site administrators, and others responsible for network and data security.

- CEH credential holders specialize in penetration testing, cyber-forensics, cybersecurity engineering, and applications security. Requirements include two years of experience in information security.

- The CISSP certification is offered by the (ISC)2, accredited under ANSI, approved by the US Department of Defense, and is adopted as a standard for the US National Security Agency's ISEEP program.

- CISSP is a certification designed to help IT security professionals establish best practices across eight areas in computer security, including security and risk management, communications and network security, software development security, asset security, security architecture and engineering, identity and access management, security assessment and testing, and security operations. Requirements include at least five years of experience in information security and at least three years of experience as a security manager.

- GIAC was founded in 1999 to validate the skills of information security professionals. It offers over thirty cybersecurity certifications in cyber defense, penetration testing, incident response and digital forensics, cybersecurity management and audit, web application security, and industrial control systems/critical infrastructure. All credentials are mapped to Introductory, Intermediate, or Advanced levels, and the highest level is the GIAC Security Expert (GSE.)[82]

As the president of ISACA NYM and a board member for twelve years, I have had many conversations with members, colleagues, and sometimes even strangers on the New York City subway about the merits of the certifications, comparisons between different credentials, and how they could be helpful in the future career paths.

One notable coffee break was with a platform engineer working

---

82   "Get Certified: Roadmap," GIAC website, accessed October 5, 2020, https://www.giac.org/certifications/get-certified/roadmap.

for a major bank. He enjoyed his role and wanted to expand his horizons in cybersecurity. After a good conversation about the merits and strengths of CISSP, CISM, and CRISC, he'd mostly made up his mind to pursue CISA—a surprising choice, considering that he did not see himself becoming an auditor. He wanted to find out how auditors operate and to build successful relationships with the audit department. Besides, CISA is the most recognized ISACA credential, requiring a solid knowledge in many domains.

Overall, from my interactions with ISACA members, CRISC remains one of the top choices for a wide range of professionals. This could be attributed to continued demand growth for risk assessors, managers, and IT governance and regulatory support teams. Enrollment in ISACA NYM certification preparation classes reflects this trend as well.

When the decision is made as to what certification to pursue, the next question is how best to prepare for the exam.

Many candidates turn to self-study, and others prefer to take classes. Local ISACA chapters offer web-based and on-site classes and usually provide a good value for the attendees.

After a certification is attained, one must typically obtain continuing education credits to maintain a credential.

Professional associations can fulfill the continuing education needs of the members via a variety of activities: membership meetings, education classes, certification preparation classes, public speaking, writing books on relevant subjects, and mentoring.

In 2014, ISACA, InfraGard, (ISC)2, ACFE, and HTCIA New York–area chapters produced the first annual New York Metro Joint Cybersecurity Conference. The success of this collaborative event, attended by several hundred practitioners, put it on the list of the most important events during National Cybersecurity Month in the

New York City area. The key to the success was a rigorous selection of speakers and outreach to all associations' members (the author cochaired the program committee together with Cindy Cullen, then president of (ISC)2 New Jersey chapter).

According to M. Gorge: "ISACA always organizes amazing venues, and their attendees are seasoned professionals who are eager to learn and stay abreast of the latest security and compliance issues. This makes for extremely proactive training sessions."[83]

MENTORING AS A MAJOR DRIVER OF WORKFORCE DEVELOPMENT

In 2011, Dr. Charles Camarda, former NASA astronaut and a member of the NYU Poly Board of Emerging Technology, proposed a problem-solving methodology called Innovative Conceptual Engineering Design (ICED).[84] ICED methodology teaches students to use the analytical and logical left side of their brain as well as the artistic and innovative right side when solving problems as a team. The idea for teaching and utilizing ICED methodology was born from the work to identify the cause of the Space Shuttle Columbia accident in 2003 and develop technologies to prevent such catastrophes from occurring in the future.

Frank Cicio, founder and CEO of iQ4, recalls, "Charlie believed we should focus on why the skills gap exists between industry and students and that the solution would be to engage students on projects mentored by subject matter experts. This was not a new concept,

---

83   Mathieu Gorge, interview with the author, November 26, 2019.

84   Charles Camarda, Olivier De Weck, and Sydney Do, "Innovative Conceptual Engineering Design (ICED): Creativity and Innovation in CDIO-Like Curriculum," *Proceedings of the 9th International CDIO Conference*, Massachusetts Institute of Technology and Harvard University School of Engineering and Applied Sciences, Cambridge Massachusetts, June 9–13, 2013, https://pdfs.semanticscholar. org/7abd/a05381ff05a7006eae078518b3f5c1e61bb5.pdf.

with the exception that there was no scale and structure to existing programs such as co-ops, internships, apprenticeships, and capstones in terms of highly integrated industry engagement. ICED became a framework to launch the Epic Challenge for designing space suits for Mars and to build a software solution (iQ4) for students and schools."[85]

In 2015, iQ4 expanded the Epic Challenge to address a shortfall of 150,000 cybersecurity jobs, now projected to be in the millions. The Cybersecurity Workforce Alliance (CWA) was created to partner with industry subject matter experts to recruit mentors, develop content, and create models to engage the market. Frank Cicio continues: "We've started with Wall Street leaders, like Dennis Paige (FRB NYC), Allan Mace (BNY Mellon), Teresa Durocher (Citizens Bank), Robert Francis (FRB NYC), and Phil Venables (Goldman Sachs) and now have over 2,000 mentors engaged with 4,000 students."[86]

The next phase of iQ4 development is to expand the model with the Virtual Apprenticeship Challenge, engaging ten thousand cyber students worldwide.

iQ4 also partners with the National Student Clearinghouse (NSC) to maintain students' learning history and offer planning tools to accelerate over twenty million students' careers.

iQ4 has found a natural ally and partner in ISACA chapters. The organizations are aligned in their mission to unlock human potential in their members, mentees, and mentors. Both organizations are actively involved in outreach to students, via ISACA student chapters and via the iQ4 mentoring process.

Both organizations are developing corporate relations to recruit

---

85   Frank Cicio, email to the author, November 24, 2019.

86   Ibid.

mentors and offer educational, certification, and networking opportunities to foster professional development of organization members.

ISACA NYM was one of the first chapters to join forces with iQ4; several other chapters are now part of this expanding partnership.

"The partnership [with ISACA NYM] provides broad industry-driven certification programs for students and mentors, and levels the playing field for diversification and inclusion, while reducing the cost to find, develop, and retain talent by an order of magnitude."[87]

Professional associations serve an important role in developing leadership skills. Members who volunteer have access to a wide range of opportunities to contribute by serving as a committee chair, treasurer, secretary, or president. The role of president frequently includes both running the association as a CEO and serving as the chair of the board. Serving on a board can be truly a school of leadership, training, and preparing members to succeed in the corporate world.

Professional security associations play a major role in fostering cybersecurity education for executives and the workforce, from facilitating public-private partnerships with governments to providing education, networking, leadership, and mentoring opportunities to members to offering credentialing and recognition to professionals.

---

87 "ISACA New York Metropolitan Chapter, the Cybersecurity Workforce Alliance and iQ4 Corp. Partner to Massively Scale the Talent Pipeline in Cyber," Cision PRWeb, February 25, 2019, https://www.prweb.com/releases/isaca_new_york_metropolitan_chapter_the_cybersecurity_workforce_alliance_and_iq4_corp_partner_to_massively_scale_the_talent_pipeline_in_cyber/prweb16125389.htm.

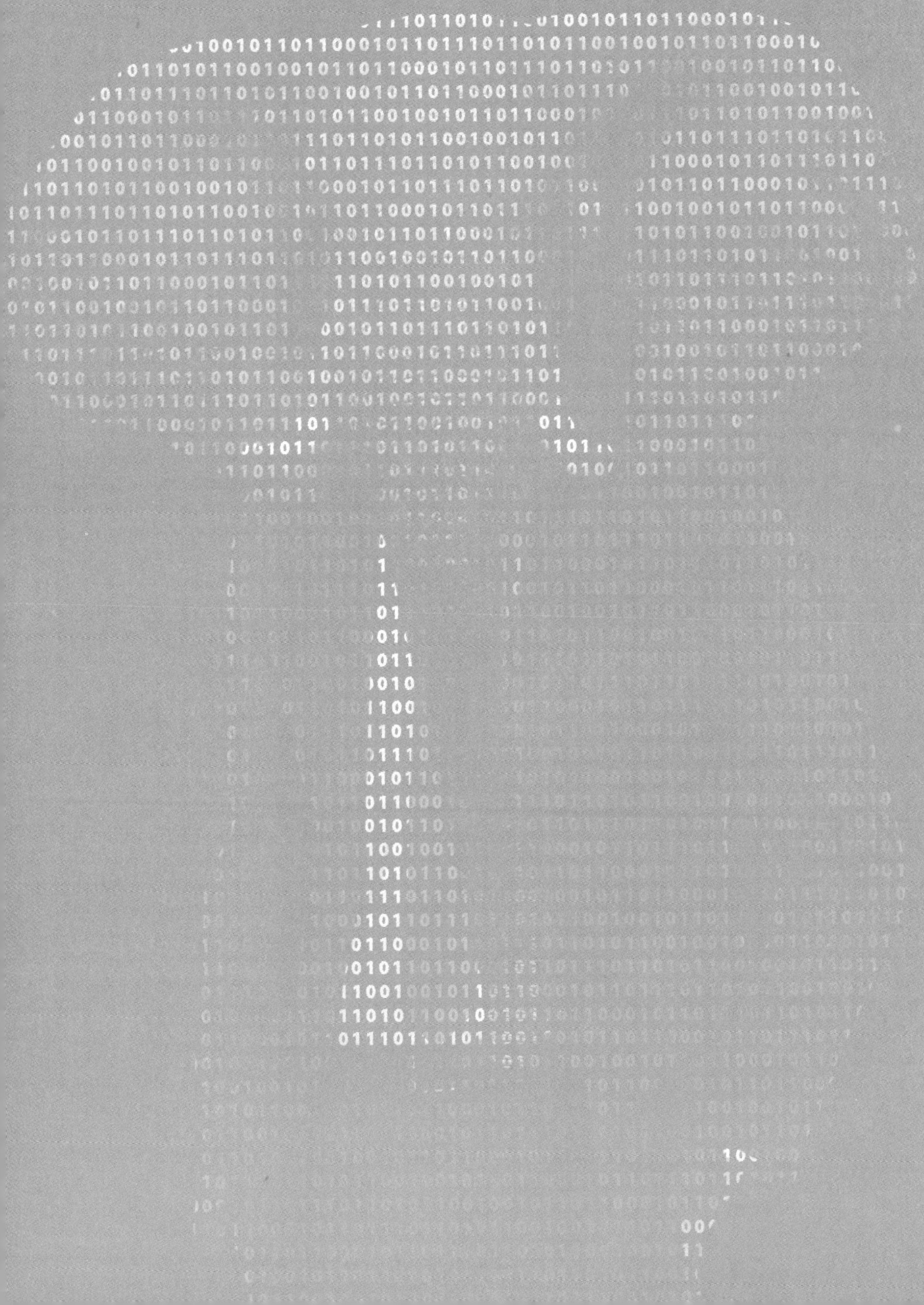

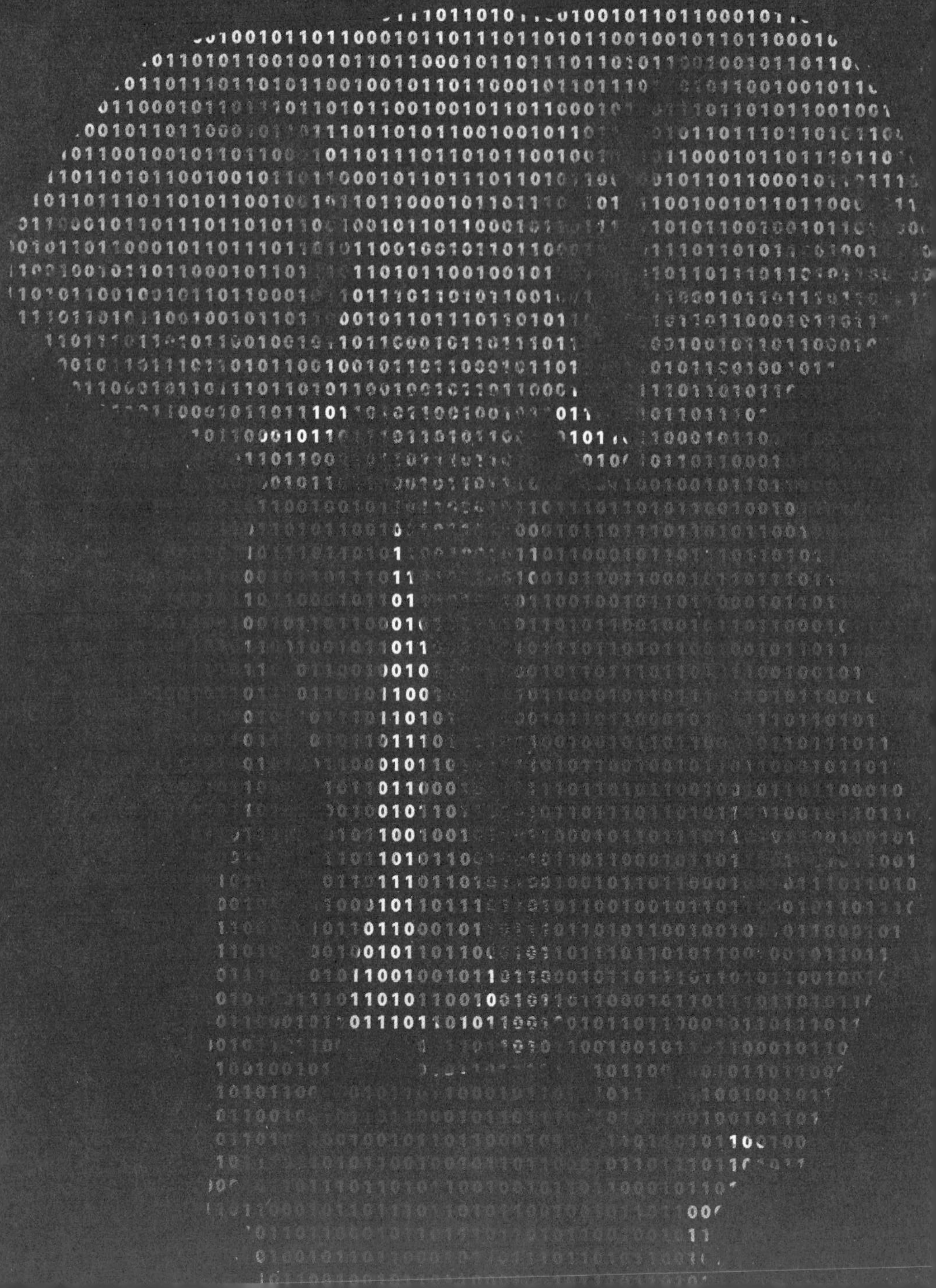

SUPER-STRATEGIC AND STRATEGIC QUESTIONNAIRES

PILLAR 1: PHYSICAL SECURITY

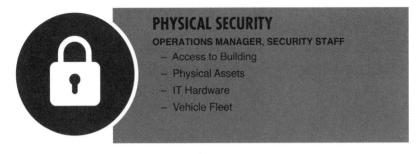

PHYSICAL SECURITY
OPERATIONS MANAGER, SECURITY STAFF
— Access to Building
— Physical Assets
— IT Hardware
— Vehicle Fleet

SUPER-STRATEGIC QUESTIONNAIRE

As a CEO/C-level exec/board member, am I confident/sure/happy that:

1.   Physical access to my firm is secured the right way?

2.   All physical assets in my firm, including, but not limited to, buildings, vehicles, computers, servers, printers, other physical IT equipment, tablets, iPads, phones, and iPhones are secured in a way that does not put the company's physical or data security at risk?

3.   All paper-based information or other physical media is secured at all times in a way that does not put the company at risk?

4.   Physical access to any area within the firm is granted on a need basis in a way that is secure and fully traceable?

5.   I can lawfully and effectively track at any time physical access to the firms critical and noncritical areas in real time and in retrospect, both for internal and remote staff as well as visitors who have been granted access to the firm?

STRATEGIC QUESTIONNAIRE

As a CEO/C-level exec/board member, am I confident/sure/happy that:

1. Access control to my building/site/facility via ID cards/near field communications (NFC)/RFID/biometrics is secure?

2. All access points such as doors/gates/barriers are access controlled, tracked, and audited?

3. Any passwords needed for building access are changed every ninety days?

4. Any access to the building and its different sections is revoked immediately for an employee who leaves the organization?

5. The building/site/facility is comprehensively monitored by alarms and CCTV systems?

6. Sensitive areas like the server rooms are monitored and audited as stringently as these areas need to be?

7. Swipes/spot checks of the building/site/facility are conducted to look for physical hacking devices such as keyloggers and unauthorized Wi-Fi access points?

8. Paper data is secured and that access and audit procedures are in place?

9. A clean desk policy is in place and adhered to?

10. Shredders are in place and are used in accordance with policy, and content is disposed of via a suitably certified company?

11. Physical penetration testing on the building/site/facility takes place at suitable time intervals?

12. The organization has put in place policies and technical measures to efficiently and legally monitor third-party physical access to my ecosystem?

PILLAR 2: PEOPLE SECURITY

PEOPLE SECURITY
HR, SECURITY STAFF
— Permanent & Contract Staff
— Partners
— 3rd Party Employees
— Visitors
— Special Events Security

SUPER-STRATEGIC QUESTIONNAIRE

As a CEO/C-level exec/board member, am I confident/sure/happy that:

1. The security team has mapped the organization's full staff, whether full time or part time, as well as their respective access to company data?

2. The organization is able to appropriately track all staff activity within the full company ecosystem including networks, application, and cloud systems?

3. The organization has put in place appropriate technical security solutions and/or security measures to legally and demonstrably track staff activity?

4. If the regulator(s) or enforcement bodies perform an audit, I can demonstrate my organization's compliance (or demonstrable road map to compliance) toward protecting staff while ensuring they do not willingly or unwillingly have access to data or systems that are on a "need to" access?

5. The organization has developed and demonstrably deployed security policies and procedures to protect itself when it has third parties onsite (visitors/suppliers) either on an ongoing basis or during special events?

STRATEGIC QUESTIONNAIRE

As a CEO/C-level exec/board member, am I confident/sure/happy that:

1. All staff have been vetted properly according to applicable screening regulations?

2. All staff are trained appropriately and have an understanding of the organizations security policies and procedures and understand the different levels of privacy

3. All staff have access to the latest security policies and procedures either online or in hard copy?

4. All staff who leave the employment of the organization will have all access to the organization disabled?

5. All staff are trained and aware of social engineering techniques?

6. The organization has security policies and procedures regarding third parties onsite?

7. The organization has policies and procedures regarding visitors onsite?

8. All staff are aware of emergency procedures in the event of fire or any other dangerous happening and their responsibilities in such events?

9. All staff who use either organization or personal devices (if allowed) to access data externally are aware of the policy and procedures regarding external access?

10. All staff are audited coming in and leaving the building/site/facility?

11. All staff interactions with sensitive data are audited?

12. If the regulator(s) or enforcement bodies perform an audit, I can demonstrate my organization's compliance regarding the staff's security awareness?

PILLAR 3: DATA SECURITY

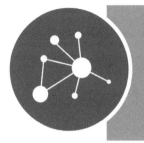

DATA SECURITY
HR, IT TEAM & MANAGER
– Trade Secrets
– Employee Data
– Database
– Customer Data

SUPER-STRATEGIC QUESTIONNAIRE

As a CEO/C-level exec/board member, am I confident/sure/happy that:

1. All data, including employee data, client data, and third-party data, is protected appropriately and in compliance with applicable laws and mandatory standards?

2. The organization is able to and does classify data according to its privacy level?

3. The organization has put in place appropriate technical security solutions and/or security measures to protect data we create, acquire, store, transmit, and also dispose of?

4. If the regulator(s) or enforcement bodies perform an audit I can demonstrate my organization's compliance (or demonstrable road map to compliance)?

5. The organization has developed and demonstrably deployed security policies and procedures to all staff across the organization, regardless of ranking level, location, business unit, or function?

STRATEGIC QUESTIONNAIRE

As a CEO/C-level exec/board member, am I confident/sure/happy that:

1. An up-to-date ecosystem diagram has been drawn up that shows the rest and flow of all data within the organization, including

all incoming and outgoing data?

2. Data is classified according to privacy level and in accordance with applicable laws and mandatory standards?

3. All data that flows out of the organization via electronic means is encrypted appropriately?

4. Any data that is deemed sensitive is encrypted while at rest in the organization?

5. Access to the various levels of classification of data is performed on a need-to-know basis and that appropriate audit software can log who accessed what and also alert to unauthorized access?

6. Appropriate applications are used to audit the downloading of sensitive data to devices such as USB keys and also that email and other messaging systems are monitored for the unauthorized transfer of any data?

7. The disposal of any data, be it hard copy or held on an electronic device, is dealt with appropriately or by a compliant third party?

8. Any penetration testing done on the internal network will test the security of all data held by the organization?

9. Sensitive data is not kept over any given legal limit it may come under?

10. All hard-copy sensitive data is kept locked and access is only given to those on a need-to-know basis?

11. The organization has deployed policies and procedures to all staff on how to handle data in a secure and confidential manner?

12. If the regulator(s) or enforcement bodies perform an audit, I can demonstrate my organization's compliance?

PILLAR 4: INFRASTRUCTURE SECURITY

INFRASTRUCTURE SECURITY
IT TEAM & MANAGER
- Networks
- Remote Sites
- Remote Users
- Application Security
- Website
- Intranet

SUPER-STRATEGIC QUESTIONNAIRE

As a CEO/C-level exec/board member, am I confident/sure/happy that:

1. The security team has mapped the organization's full ecosystem, including, but not limited to, internal networks, websites, ecommerce sites, third-party networks linked to our system, all cloud providers, all third-party providers, subsidiary networks and, if applicable, franchisees' networks, and any system that may have company data?

2. The organization is able to appropriately protect its full ecosystem's infrastructure?

3. The organization has put in place appropriate technical security solutions and/or security measures to protect systems, applications (whether built in-house or purchased) and data within its ecosystem?

4. If the regulator(s) or enforcement bodies perform an audit, I can demonstrate my organization's compliance (or demonstrable road map to compliance) toward protecting the overall company infrastructure?

5. The organization has developed and demonstrably deployed security policies and procedures to protect its infrastructure?

STRATEGIC QUESTIONNAIRE

As a CEO/C-level exec/board member, am I confident/sure/happy that:

1. The IT team has thoroughly mapped out the internal network(s), external-facing sites and applications, and connections to third parties, and that I have up-to-date schematics?

2. All public-facing IP addresses are protected by a firewall?

3. Appropriate IDS (intrusion detection systems) / IPS (intrusion protection systems) are in place to alert the IT team of any unusual activity on the internal network?

4. All workstations, servers, and laptops have anti-malware software installed and that all security patches/updates are added as soon as possible?

5. All access to the internal network(s) and devices on it is securely managed via passwords or multifactor authentication?

6. Appropriate permissions are managed to ensure that people only access what they need to in order to perform their work duties?

7. Auditing of access is in place and able—either automatically or manually—to alert to any unauthorized access to the different sections and devices of the internal network?

8. External access to the internal network and its devices is by secure and encrypted channels and only to authorized parties?

9. Policies and procedures are in place to oversee the secure use of personal mobile devices on internal network(s), whether those devices are company owned or, where allowed, personal devices?

10. WiFi connection to the internal network is secure and encrypted?

11. Penetration testing is performed on the internal network at suitable time intervals?

12. If regulator(s) or enforcement bodies perform an audit, I can demonstrate my organization's compliance toward protecting the internal network?

PILLAR 5: CRISIS MANAGEMENT

CRISIS MANAGEMENT
OPERATIONS MANAGER, IT TEAM, HR
– Documentation & Work Procedures
– Emergency Response Plans
– Business Continuity Plans
– Disaster Recovery Plans

SUPER-STRATEGIC QUESTIONNAIRE

As a CEO/C-level exec/board member, am I confident/sure/happy that:

1. The organization is generally able and ready to deal with a security crisis?

2. The organization has a written crisis management/incident response plan?

3. The organization has an incident response plan that has been communicated to all relevant stakeholders?

4. Staff have been trained on their duties and how to react should a security incident happen?

5. The organization has mapped out the type of security incidents that could happen, their likelihood, and the potential impact on the business?

STRATEGIC QUESTIONNAIRE

As a CEO/C-level exec/board member, am I confident/sure/happy that:

1. The organization has a crisis management and incident response plan in place?

2. The plan has been mapped out by the crisis management team in a fashion that truly represents the organization's infrastructure?

3. In the event of a disaster/crisis/incident there is a back-up site that can sufficiently continue the organization's operations?

4. The organization's staff are trained to carry out the instructions of the plan?

5. The crisis management team is proactive in monitoring for a crisis/disaster/incident and will, as early as possible, instigate its incident response?

6. The reaction to the crisis/disaster/incident on social media, news media, and television media will be handled in a proper and truthful manner so that the organization is seen to be handling the crisis/disaster/incident swiftly and honestly?

7. All clients affected are kept aware of the crisis/disaster/incident and regularly given updates on the situation?

8. Crisis management and incident response simulations are run at appropriate intervals by the crisis management team?

9. Organization data is backed up frequently and securely enough that any loss of data will be kept to an absolute minimum in the event of a crisis/disaster/incident?

10. Auditing and logging is of a sufficient degree to allow rigorous examination of the causes of the crisis/disaster/incident?

11. The organization's crisis management team has plans to rebuild client confidence in the organization after a major crisis/disaster/incident?

12. In the event of a major crisis/disaster/incident, the organization can go back to where it was before the disaster?

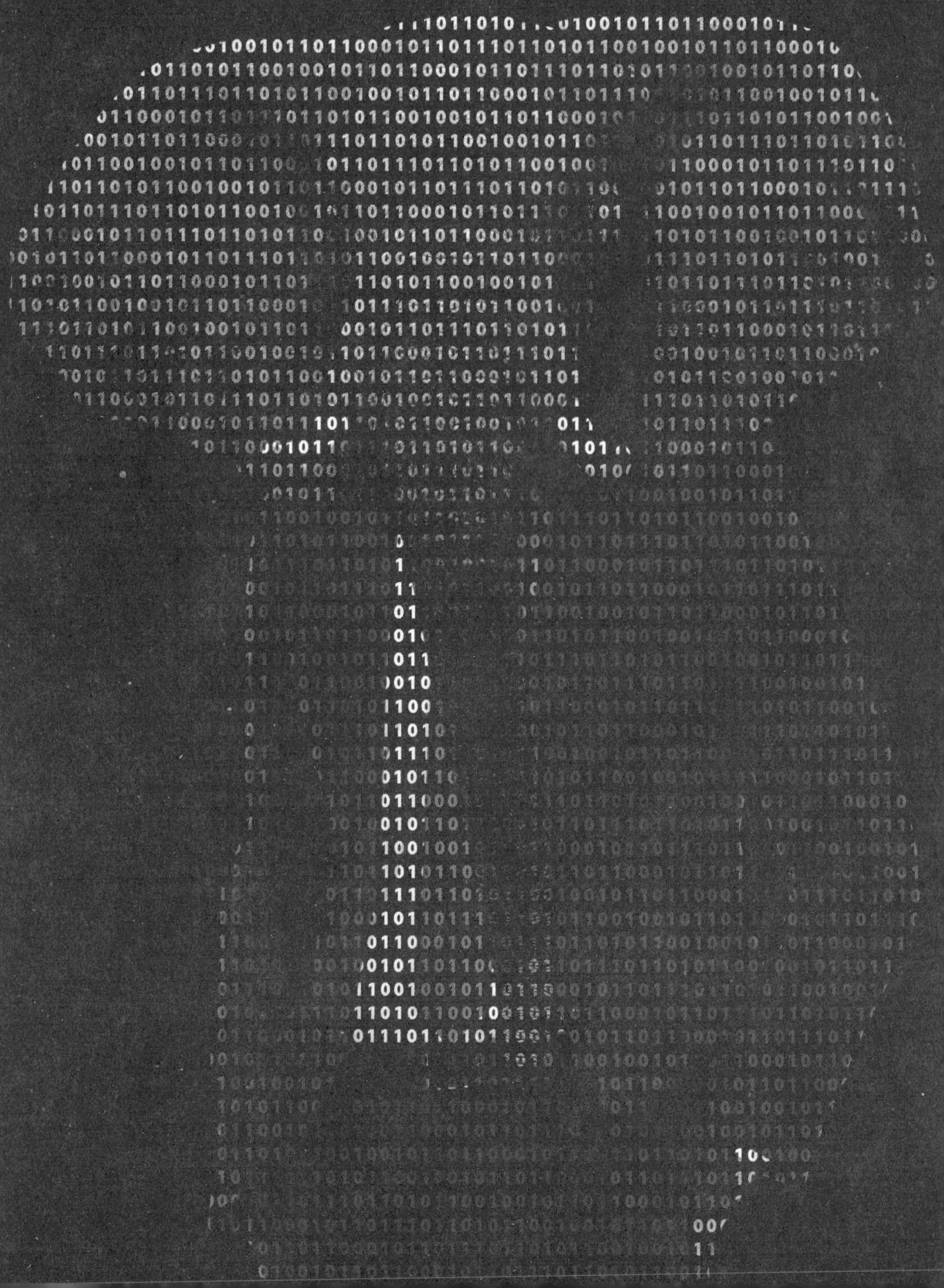

ABOUT THE AUTHOR

Mathieu Gorge, a global data security, information governance, and compliance subject matter expert with over twenty years of experience, is the creator of the 5 Pillars of Security Framework. Mathieu is the CEO and founder of VigiTrust, providing integrated risk management (IRM) SaaS solutions to clients in 120 countries in the hospitality, retail, transportation, higher education, government, healthcare, and e-commerce industries. An award-winning CEO for innovation, excellence, and security and compliance expertise, Mathieu has dedicated himself to helping CEOs, CXOs, and boards of directors manage cyber-accountability challenges and focus on opportunities that good cyber-hygiene and proactive cybersecurity compliance programs can bring to firms. Together with the help of the Global Advisory Board, a noncommercial think tank gathering compliance and security experts, researchers, regulators, academics, end users, CEOs, CXOs, and boards of directors, Mathieu continually updates the 5 Pillars of Security Framework to ensure it addresses the latest security and compliance regulations and newest security threats.

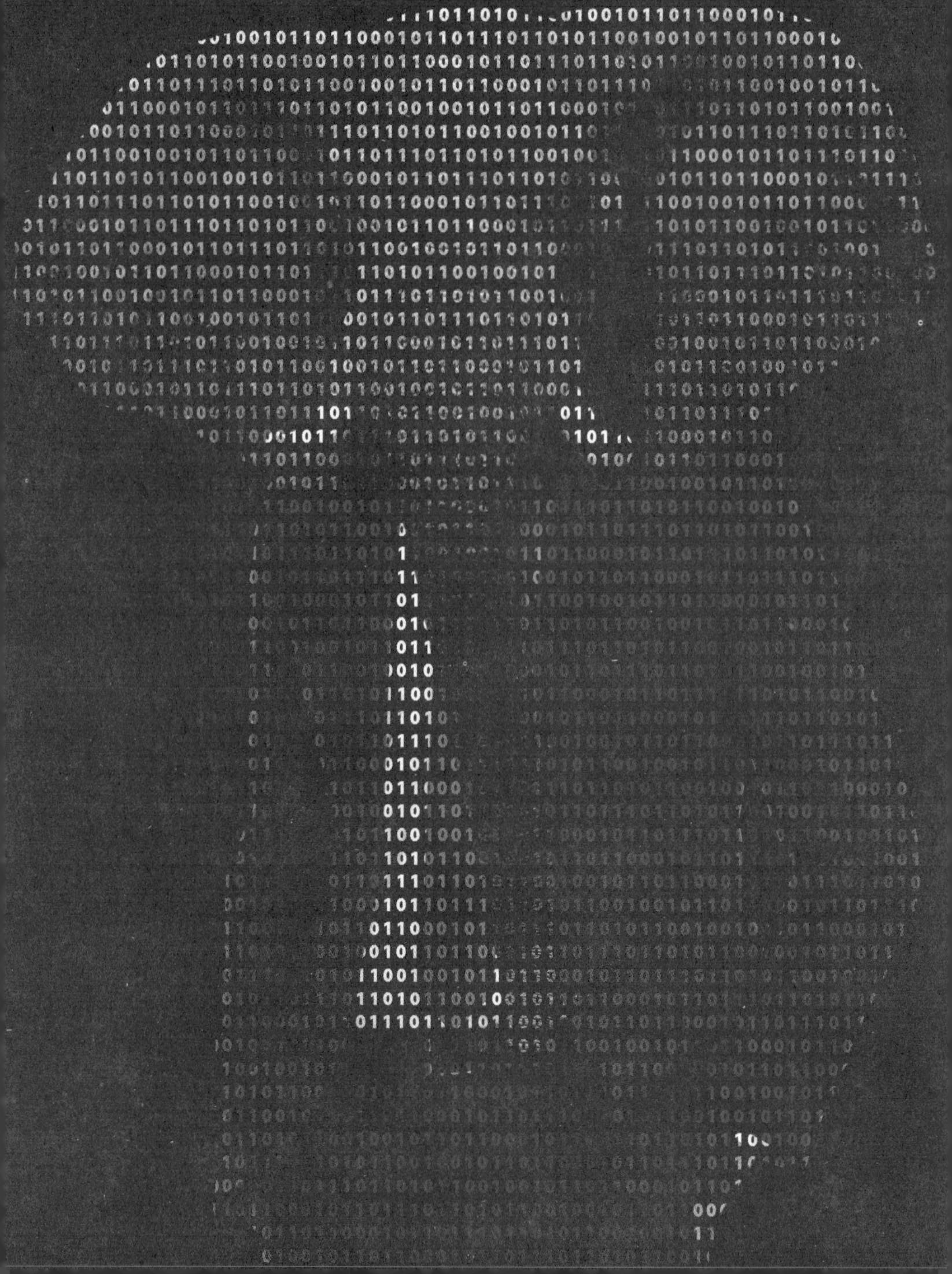

INDUSTRY RECOGNITION

In addition to being widely used by CEOs, CXOs, and boards of directors worldwide, the 5 Pillars of Security Framework has been recognized as a leading methodology to help key decision makers demonstrate cyber-accountability.

The methodology was also made available on VigiOne, VigiTrust's IRM solution, and the industry was quick to award it, as well as VigiTrust and Mathieu, a number of amazing accolades, including the following:

- Visionary Leaders at Forefront of Entrepreneurship 2020, Insight Success: Mathieu Gorge

- Corporate Vision Awards 2020, *CV Magazine*: Mathieu Gorge

- Cyber Security Awards 2020—Best Information Security Compliance Platform 2020, Acquisition International: VigiTrust

- Innovation & Excellence Awards 2019, *Corporate LiveWire*: VigiTrust

- Global Awards 2019, *CEO Today* magazine: Mathieu Gorge Corporate Excellence Awards 2019, IT CEO of the Year, *CV*

Magazine: Mathieu Gorge

- Global Excellence Awards 2019, Acquisition International: VigiTrust

- Game Changers Awards 2019, Finance *Monthly Magazine*: VigiTrust

- Innovation & Excellence Awards 2019—Most Innovative in Data Compliance Solutions, *Corporate LiveWire*: VigiTrust

- Cyber Security Awards 2019, Acquisition International: VigiTrust

- IT Security CEO 2019, *CV Magazine*: Mathieu Gorge

- Gamechanger of the Year (Information Security) 2019, ACQ5: Mathieu Gorge

- Leading Advisor 2019—Fundamental Package, Acquisition International: Mathieu Gorge

- Global 100 2019, Global 100: VigiTrust

- Information Security Company of the Year for Security Education (France) 2019, ACQ5: VigiTrust

- Best Information Security and Data Compliance Solutions Provider 2019, Acquisition International: VigiTrust

- Wealth & Finance Awards 2018—Best Data Security SaaS Solution: 5 Pillars of Security Framework

- Irish Enterprise Awards 2018—Best GRC SaaS Provider: 5 Pillars of Security Framework

- Corporate Excellence Awards 2018—Most Influential CEO of the Year 2018, *Corporate LiveWire*: Mathieu Gorge

- Most Advanced Information Security Services Company 2018 & Best Data Security SaaS Solution: 5 Pillars of Security Framework, *Fintech Awards*: VigiTrust

- CEO Awards 2017—Most Innovative CEO of the Year, *Business World*: Mathieu Gorge

- Certificate of Excellence 2017 Awardee—10 Fastest Growing Security Companies, *The Silicon Review*: VigiTrust

The framework has also been mentioned in the following articles:

- "Cybersecurity—2016–2018 outlook: Legal, Technical and Human perspectives," University of Oxford Department of Computer Science, November 6, 2019, https://www.cs.ox. ac.uk/seminars/1441.html.

- Alex Scroxton, "GDPR Compliance: Whose Job Is It and Is It Really Possible?" *Computer Weekly*, September 27, 2019, https://www.computerweekly.com/news/252471418/ GDPR-compliance-Whose-job-is-it-and-is-it-really-possible.

- "Improve Disaster Recovery with Data Classification," StorageCraft.com, June 28, 2019, https://blog.storagecraft.com/ improve-disaster-recovery-with-data-classification/.

- Mathieu Gorge, "Cybersecurity Trends for 2019," Medium, February 26, 2019, https://medium.com/@Mathieu.Gorge/ cybersecurity-trends-for-2019-e278d36d9377.

- "Most Advanced Information Security Services Company 2018," Wealth and Finance International, January 1, 2019, https://www.wealthandfinance-news.com/issues/fintech-awards-2018/16/.

- Antony Adshead, "GDPR Compliance and Storage in Digital Transformation Projects," *Computer Weekly*, September 20, 2018, https://www.computerweekly.com/podcast/GDPR-compliance-and-storage-in-digital-transformation-projects.

- Antony Adshead, Printing, Document Capture and Compliance Risk in the GDPR Era," *Computer Weekly*, September 14, 2018.

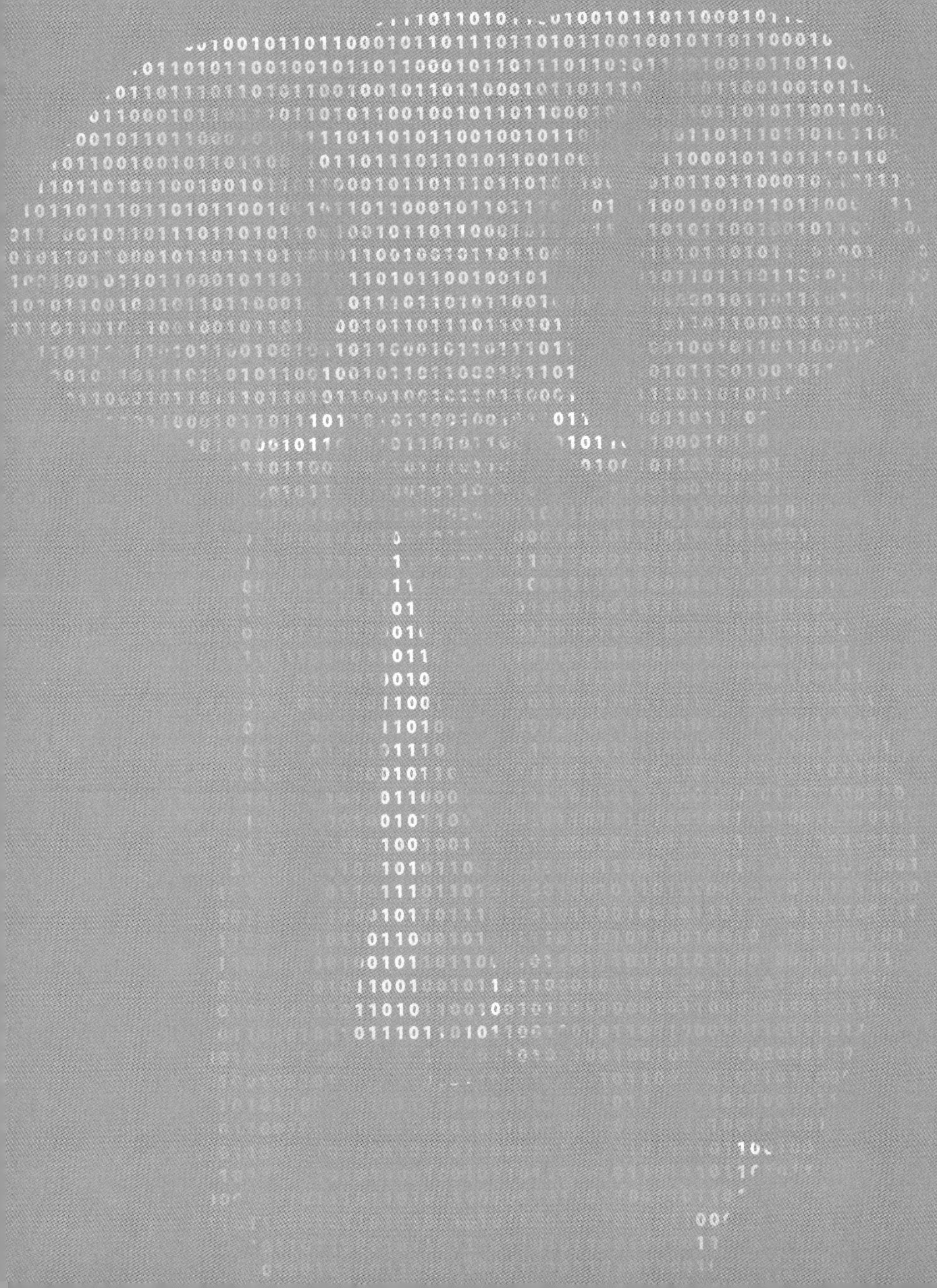

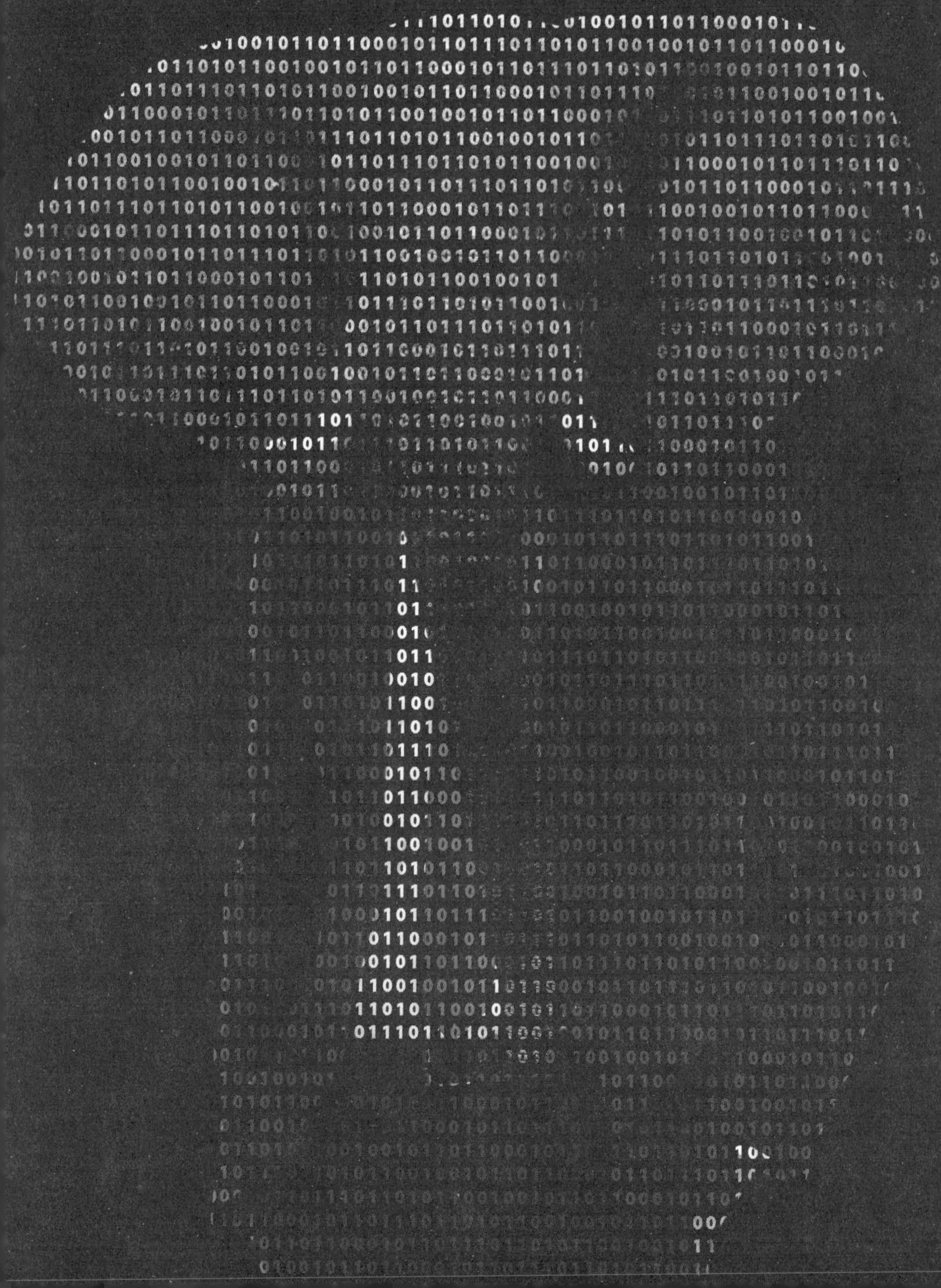

ABOUT VIGIONE

VigiOne is an award-winning IRM platform used in over 120 countries by thousands of organizations to prepare for, validate, and maintain compliance with legal and industry security standards such as PCI DSS, GDPR, HIPAA, ISO 27001, NIST, and many others. VigiOne also provides a full version of the 5 Pillars of Security Framework.

VigiOne is a true collaborative IRM platform that also allows you to work in partnership with third-party consulting firms to prepare for and maintain compliance and strategically work with assessor firms to conduct official certifying assessments, all from one single SaaS-based platform.

It is particularly well positioned for organizations that are multi-regional, multiregulation, and widely distributed that wish to prepare for, validate, and maintain compliance. It also uniquely includes the following:

- A full learning management system (LMS) with a portfolio of over twenty-five prepackaged role-based modules. Each module has sections ranging from one to five minutes in duration, which can be mixed and matched. It can also host third-party SCORM-compliant training.

- A full collaboration platform to allow for upstream and downstream workflows between all stakeholders: internal users, consultants, and assessors.

- Key IRM features within VigiOne include the following:

  ◦ Multiple data compliance and information security standards:

  ◦ Web-based platform allowing organizations to quickly and simply validate compliance with multiple standards, including PCI DSS, GDPR, and other information security standards such as ISO27001 and NIST.

- Internal and external online collaboration:

  ◦ Enables and encourages online collaboration between end users (IT functions, legal and compliance management, subsidiaries and franchisees) internally and externally.

  ◦ Enables online collaboration with external consultants and assessors, including a review and approval role-based system.

- Self-assessment functionality:

  ◦ Distribute, customize and create integrated off-the-shelf and bespoke assessments for multiple standards. Review, comment, and approve self-assessments with a full audit trail of the review process. Enable customers and partners to download, upload, print and/or mail assessment reports to the relevant parties.

- Evidence library and management tool:

  ◦ Upload, classify, and link evidence documents directly

from a questionnaire or control matrix. Manage the life cycle of evidence. Share evidence with third-party assessors on VigiOne.

▫ Enjoy a multidimensional view of documents linked to multiple controls, multiple users, scopes, entities, and users, including internal and/or external assessors.

- Policy and procedure management:

  ▫ A tool that allows large distributed organizations and service providers to track the alignment and standardization of policy and procedures to multiple target audiences with local, regional, and functional variation where required.

  ▫ Ability to preload VigiOne with standard policy templates that are easy for end users to download and assign a status to generic security polices (i.e., in place/ not in place).

- Project and task management:

  ▫ Task assignment and management tool with calendar allowing users to set up one-off and recurring tasks that can be assigned to individual users and business units with priorities and deadlines. These can be used to manage and track compliance and remediation activity and also to ensure that recurring tasks such as training, testing, vulnerability scanning, and assessment completion are scheduled and managed.

- Reports and dashboards:

  ▫ Full reporting, configured by user type, with dynamic

features for customization and drill down. Full data export functionality for more detailed analysis. Multi-level dashboards with statistics, trends, and charts, again with drill-down and export functionality. Dynamic reporting and preconfigured role-based reporting.

- Platform and user management:

  □ Multilevel organizational and user management with features such as self-service user management, multifactor authentication, and single sign-on where required.

- Modular, configurable, and role based:

  □ VigiOne is modular and configurable, designed to enable organizations to manage compliance to multiple data standards and information security regulations with one single program/platform.

- Integrated LMS for security awareness training:

  □ Option for service providers to resell online integrated learning management system (LMS) that links awareness and understanding with policy implementation. Interactive, multilingual eLearning courses with testing and certification. eLearning tailored for multiple user types, technical and payment staff, program managers, senior executives, merchants, and franchisees.

VigiOne is based on a number of submodules linking all the functionality mentioned above. Those modules are as follows:

VigiCheck

- Audit

- Self-Assessment

- Survey

- Checklists

VigiFile
- Risk Register

- IT Asset Register

- Evidence Library

- Policies & Procedures

- Regulations & Standards

VigiPlan
- Accreditation Plan

- Breach/Incident Plan

- Task Allocation

- Continuity Plan

- Milestone Tracking

VigiScan
- Vulnerability Scan

- Web App Scan

- Data Classification & Discovery

- Continuous Monitoring

VigiTrack

- Dashboard

- Alerts

- Reports

- Objectives/Targets

VigiClass

- eLearning

- Multimedia

- Awareness

- Blended Learning

Try the Super-Strategic and Strategic 5 Pillars Security Framework on VigiOne.

Many users incorporate the questions in the 5 Pillars for Security Framework into their existing IRM tools or project tools, as does the team at VigiTrust, the makers of VigiOne.

The 5 Pillars for Security Framework is available to you at no cost for a year. It can be found on the VigiStore, which is VigiTrust's e-commerce platform. Simply use the code 5PBOOK to get your access. Soon you and your firm can start benefiting from using the 5 Pillars of Security Framework on VigiOne!

You can try the 5 Pillars of Security Framework on VigiOne for free for three months by registering at http://vigione.com/vigitrust/self-registration/ and using the password **Ceibr2020**.

The registration process is very simple:

- Click the link to self-register.

- Type in the password.

- Access the self-registration form (Firstname, Lastname, Email).

- Receive credentials by email in order to access a customized version of VigiOne.

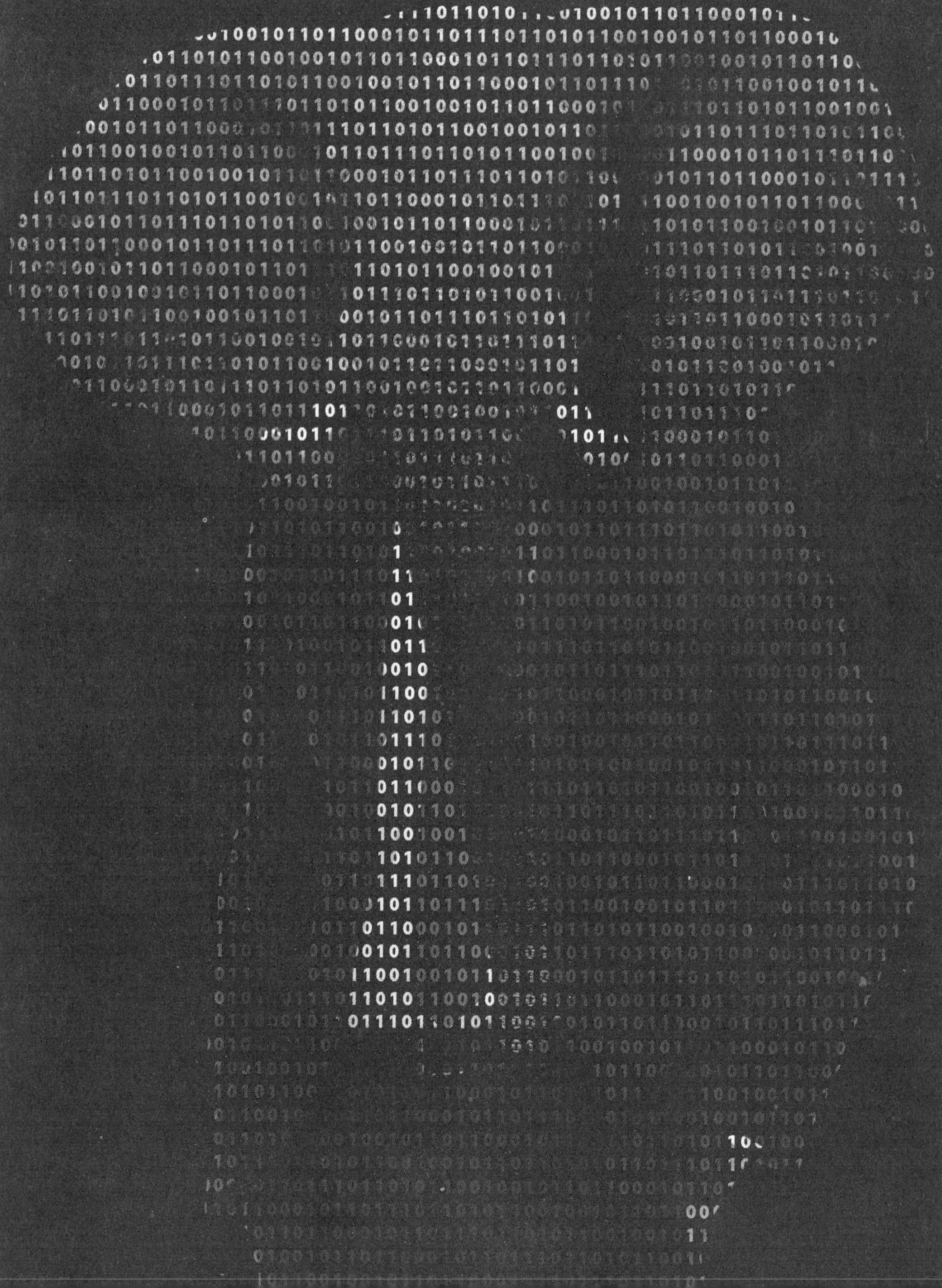